Language and Literacy
in Workplace Education

Language and Literacy in Workplace Education: Learning at Work

Giselle Mawer

with contributions from

Lee Fletcher
Julia McCall
Catherine O'Grady
&
Bee Jong Ong

LONGMAN
London and New York

Addison Wesley Longman Limited,
Edinburgh Gate,
Harlow,
Essex CM20 2JE,
United Kingdom
and Associated Companies throughout the world.

Published in the United States of America
by Addison Wesley Longman Inc. New York

First published 1999

ISBN 0–582–25764–6 CSD
ISBN 0–582–25765–4 PPR

Visit Addison Wesley Longman on the world wide web at
http://www.awl-he.com

British Library Cataloguing-in-Publication Data

A catalogue record for this book is available from the British Library

Library of Congress Cataloging-in-Publication Data

Mawer, Giselle, 1954–   .
    Language and literacy in workplace education / Giselle Mawer ;
    with contributions from Lee Fletcher . . . [et al.].
        p.   cm. — (Language in social life series)
    Includes bibliographical references and index.
    ISBN 0–582–25765–4 (pbk.). — ISBN 0–582–25764–6 (case)
    1. Employees—Training of.   2. Occupational training.
3. Workplace literacy.   4. Employees—Training of—Australia.
5. Occupational training—Australia.   6. Workplace literacy—
Australia.   I. Fletcher, Lee.   II. Title.   III. Series.
HF5549.5.T7M368   1999
658.3'124—dc21   98–35999
                                                             CIP

Set by 35 in 9.5/12 Palatino
Produced by Addison Wesley Longman Singapore (Pte) Ltd.,
Printed in Singapore

Contents

Acknowledgements

The publishers are indebted to the following for permission to reproduce copyright material:

Laurie Field for our Figure 3.1 'The organisational propeller: aspects of organisational functioning that affect learning' from *Managing organisational learning: from rhetoric to reality* (1995) by L. Field and B. Ford. Melbourne: Longman © Laurie Field; Merck, Sharpe & Dohme for extracts from Mawer, G. (1994) *Language, Literacy and Numeracy at Merck, Sharpe & Dohme (Australia) Pty Ltd: Evaluation Report of an Integrated Approach*. TAFE NSW / MSD.

General Editor's Preface

This latest contribution to the *Language in Social Life Series* by Giselle Mawer highlights and reasserts the objectives of all the books within the Series, dealing as they do with the intersections between the exploration of professional and organizational practices, the analysis of their associated discourses, and the grounding of both in the social theoretical study of communication in social life. Her book does so because it is originated from the following premises:

- that work is constructed in large measure through and by processes of communication,
- that its practices are reflective of social and cultural processes,
- that, accordingly, any analysis of these workplace practices ought to involve a parallel analysis of their associated and situated discourses.

Such analyses may then, as in the illustrative case studies described here, be drawn upon both to motivate and provide the grounding for whatever programmes of workplace change, necessarily involving communication, that organisations and their members have in mind to initiate.

What follows from this as a necessary preliminary to understanding the roles and practices of the people at work or to defining the tasks facing workplace consultants and trainers in the field of language, communication and literacy, is to begin by theorising talk (and writing) at work. To do this involves understanding that workplaces are key sites where all participants, (in the contexts of this book, workers, managers and teachers/trainers), are involved as members of overlapping communities of practice in the exploration and explanation of what the significance of communication is to their workplace practices. The connection being made between practices and discourses is not merely realised in the participant interactions themselves, it is also the object of evaluation and review by these same workplace participants. Indeed, some roles within the workplace are expressly directed at monitoring communication, and evaluating it in relation to workplace performance. Similarly, but more indirectly, workplace literacy and communication training is itself a way of documenting and evaluating both workplace practices and workplace communication.

Workplaces, then, are crucial sites where these participants, workers and trainers, through their language and literacy practices, regularly claim identities, signal memberships, manage relationships, address and solve problems. They do so essentially by the processes of 'talking and writing it through', as Ken Willing describes them in his 1992 book on intercultural communication in the white collar workplace. In short, they define by their communications what is meant by the *workplace* or the *organisation*, and indeed how they understand *work*, *workers* and *trainers*, in terms of purposes, roles and the exercise of authority.

In this context, acts of communication in the workplace and the way they reflect the underlying communicative competence of participants, become the key data from which to explore a range of ideological positions and beliefs. In particular, such data tell us about what views participants in any workplace hold about themselves, their roles and relationships, and what limits and extends that they are allowed to do and say/write in the sites in which they work. Analysing these data offers teachers and trainers, and the participants themselves, insights into how such positions and relationships are negotiated. This, in turn, tells us about how they value the nature and purposes of what they do.

In his 1992 book on *Discourse and Social Change*, Norman Fairclough captures exactly this view of communication when he writes:

> ... the analysis of discourse practice involves attention to processes of text production, distribution and consumption ... the analysis of texts should not be artificially isolated from the analysis of the institutional and discoursal practices within which texts are embedded ... there is also a need to bring together critical discourse analysis of discursive events with ethnographic analysis of social structures and settings, in the search for what some have called a critical ethnography.

It is to this critical ethnographic approach to the understanding of the discourses of the workplace, and the place of the worker-as-learner and the trainer-as-worker involved in training in such sites, that this remarkable book is dedicated, and it is this which accords it a central place in the *Language in Social Life Series*.

Why is such an approach appropriate? Principally, as Fairclough argues, because it is only a critical ethnographic analysis which:

- makes explicit the link between practices and discourses;
- involves the *voices* of the participants in the analysis through their own narrative accounts;
- locates the communicative and work events of the participants within the broader social, historical and structural framework of organizational and societal conditions.

Following Mawer's argument, any framework for training which draws on such a composite mode of analysis of workplace conditions and actions will need also to display such characteristics, since such training is equally a site of engagement open to critical ethnographic analysis. Thus, the actions and activities of teachers and trainers take on a doubly reflective perspective. In the one case, they are directed at the workplaces whose conditions they must analyse and explain so as to authenticate their own practice as reflective teachers and trainers, and in the other, more self-directed, they are aimed at a critical evaluation of these professional educational practices themselves. Explaining the *ecology* of this reflexive and interconnected research and practice is one of the triumphs of this book.

Although we may readily see how workplace sites, activities, purposes and conditions stand in some interdependent relationship, we may not sufficiently recognize their diversity, nor appreciate the constraining conditions they impose on the roles and actions of the participants. In part, this is a consequence of the participants' own professional, organizational and institutional place and affiliation. Workers as well as workplaces have their histories, after all, and if we are to hear and interpret their *voices*, and understand their practices, we need to take these personal histories into account.

For this reason, the writings theorising such topics by social theorists such as Bourdieu, Cicourel and others as far back as Weber, have a deep significance for the practicalities of workplace language and literacy training. It is also the reason why discourse analysts, ethnographers and educators need to draw on this theory to offer a coherent account of their practices. They need to do this if they are to offer explanatory accounts, for example, of how managers link their practices to their perceptions of the functions and agendas of their organizations, how managers characterise and relate to workers they manage, and how these activities are likely to be informed by ideologically invested positions, say in relation to the status of women in the workplace, the nature of workplace tasks, or in relation terms of one of several competing metaphors of management. Above all, this theory-based stance is necessary if we are to appraise how all these positions are *voiced* through acts of communication arising from, and interpreted in, particular contexts of interaction.

Such a picture is fraught with particular difficulties and problems for any potential agent of innovation and change, such as training and human resource development managers, or communication and literacy teachers. On the one hand, any activity they undertake needs to reflect closely the discourses of work if they are to be seen as authentic and credible by their constituents and clients: managers, workers, union representatives, supervisors. Yet in doing so, they risk reinforcing these modes of discourse, and the workplace practices that give rise to them. Such discourses and such practices may very easily be partisan, biased, and rooted in tradition and history, and often in direct contrast with new and alternative views of workplace learning, consultation and change. Indeed, it is often the promotion of such alternative views that attracts particular workplace factions, teachers and trainers to become involved in the first place. Communication is *never* only about issues of language.

It is no wonder, then, that Giselle Mawer centres a great deal of the heart of her book, especially in Part Three, on accounting for the partnerships struck between workplaces and teachers/trainers. That such a partnership in course design, delivery and evaluation is itself very largely defined communicatively, through processes of presentation, negotiation, instruction and evaluation, will not be lost on the reader. Nor will readers fail to recognize the inherent partisanship invested in the models and methodologies advocated in such courses. Training and teaching is after all just another workplace, albeit, as here, sometimes uncomfortably embedded in the matrix of the organization to which it has become contracted. Exploring the dysfluencies and communication breakdowns which inevitably occur in the processes of forging such partnerships. Seeing their significance, depends here, as elsewhere, on an explanatory analysis of those critical moments in the key encounters among the participants in these crucial sites of training and working. The data collected in the case studies offered here provide ample evidence for such analyses, as they do for any evaluation by the critical reader of the cases themselves.

What makes the training and teaching site so important is that it is here that such ideologically-motivated struggles among participants within the workplace often surface. This is especially the case where they are encouraged to do so by the self-revelatory and narrational quality of learner-centered instruction. This need not be accidental.

Consciously raising such struggles to the status of curriculum content has been a commitment by many literacy teachers and, less frequently by second language teachers, especially those working within a Freireian tradition. It is, however, still largely alien to another workplace world, that of corporate communications training, where the concern is with harmonising working and learning within the organisation. Much less well documented and understood in this context have been the pressures such potentially critical consciousness-raising events exert on the teacher/trainer herself. Although these pressures have been long recognised among literacy teachers, especially when pursuing their most missionary goals, it has been slow a-coming in the communications training and the second language teaching industries, with some notable exceptions. At issue here is a struggle of role, between pedagogy and advocacy, one not at all unfamiliar in many other professions concerned with communication, for example among interpreters, as Cecilia Wadensjo's recent contribution to the *Language in Social Life Series* illustrates. Grasping the existence of that struggle, documenting and explaining its nature by reference to case studies and accounts, forms the central argument of Part Four of this book, which addresses the *restructuring of the teacher/trainer* within educational institutions which are themselves workplaces characterised by change.

The articulations that this process makes necessary among teachers/trainers and between them and the representatives of their teaching/training workplaces, and between and among workers and their workplaces, could not be more powerful nor more convoluted. Each person and each place is geared to the practices of the other through interlocking and interwoven discourses. To have stripped down and revealed the gearings of this engine, as it were, is a major achievement, and a reason why this book is more than an exercise in applied linguistics. It will stand also as a contribution to the literature on workplace innovation and change and the study of organizations. And yet, it still remains as much a study of the struggles over the professional identity of trainers and teachers as it does about workplaces and their practices.

It is against the background of this theorising, then, that Giselle Mawer's book is to be located. In macro terms, its place is in the context of an Australian workplace in the throes of organizational change. From a micro perspective, the theoretical issues it explores are warranted in the key cases of workplace communication and workplace literacy programmes she and her colleagues explore in different workplace sites. At issue is how changes in industrial production processes and industrial structures have been clearly marked by associated changes in communication practices. Although located in the particular world of practice of herself and her colleagues, the relevance of what she writes is by no means limited to Australia. Such interdependent changes are generally characteristic of the post-industrial world in a range of countries, and bear out the theoretical positions outlined earlier. At their heart lies an acknowledgement of the changes in production processes that are taking place from traditional Fordist (or Taylorist) mass production, assembly-line modes of working to ones where there is greater devolution of responsibility at plant and team levels and where, in consequence, there is a new requirement on workers to take part in the communicative processes of workplace decision-making. This development, in turn, has led indirectly to an elevating of effective communication and language use to the position of becoming an arbiter of workplace performance. This is true both for managers and for workers. For *managers* in the newly restructured workplace, motivating workers and enhancing their communication skills and competencies is increasingly being linked to the achievement of increased productivity, and achieving that enhancement in turn poses demands on the communication skills of management, as does the ongoing reporting on that enhancement itself. Achieving more flexible work practices through job redesign, involving workers in multi-tasking in workteams, undertaking enterprise bargaining at the plant level, accommodating to and becoming involved in the increasing technologisation of the workplace, harnessing the cultural and linguistic diversity of what is in many contemporary societies an increasingly multilingual and multi-ethnic workforce, are all *new* communicative tasks facing managers.

For *workers*, communicative ability is not only a prerequisite for the successful attainment of training, it is increasingly allied to the measurement of technical skill, and one's ability to contribute as a worker. As such, and from the perspective of the workforce, this is likely to be seen as yet another means of differentiating among workers and acting as a management means of enhanced social and organizational control. To say this is to go much further than merely to note that changes in industrial production processes and industrial structures have been marked by changes in workplace discourse practices. Whatever the linguistic and communicative changes, what is clear is that such moves towards democratisation in the workplace and a concomitant growth of service, client and customer-focused enterprises imply a considerable shift in workplace power. More especially, they link worker job improvement, and workplace relations, to the enhancement of worker skills, both technical and communicative. As Fairclough (1992), again points out, the quality of language and the quality of service in the new economic framework become synonymous.

From the perspective of discourse, we may link the focus on changed workplace practices towards new technologies, flatter structures, multi-skilling and role-shifting, with a parallel communicative emphasis on variable modes of interaction. This in turn implies considerable *inter-textual* mixing of genres and text-types, and leads overall to much less predictability and much greater variability in discourses. A novel premium is consequently placed on the mastery by workers of effective communication strategies, and what we might call their *interdiscursive* competence.

From the cases and their discussion, it would, however, be quite wrong to assume some unanimity of purpose, some uncontested progress of development, either in terms of workplace practices or discourses. In fact, there is some considerable inconsistency in both, if still incipient and largely unreflected upon. On the one hand, the workplace reform argument appears to be focused on the development of productive diversity, innovation and responsiveness, while at the same time acknowledging a marked shift and narrowing in the focus of industrial training towards a graded progression of competency-based standards, with each stage firmly linked to employment conditions. There is thus, on the one hand, an emphasis on diversity and *divergence*, and, on the other, a focus on some unitary *convergence*. This contestation has its reflection in language and learning / teaching. Particularly, when one contrasts the emphasis on the capacity to use language variably and responsively that *divergence* calls for, with its associated pedagogic orientation towards developing of socially and culturally contextualised communication strategies, against a reductive and competency-focused emphasis on discourse as a product to be learned accumulatively and incrementally, in the light of standardised benchmarking, which is essentially *convergent* in nature. To identify the challenges posed to workers by this disjunction, both for host-language native speakers and for immigrants, is yet another of the major contributions of the book.

Finally, what of the teachers and trainers themselves? One of the major achievements of this book is to position these key participants in relation both to the workplace changes of their worksites and to the workplace changes of their own professional contexts. All workplace communication practice rests on two key supports:

- how the discourses of the workplace are to be described, interpreted and explained;

and

- how the teachers and trainers of language and communication in the
  workplace define their roles, practices and curricula in the light of
  those discourses and the ideologies that underpin them

It is in the light of these two factors that the effectiveness of programmes
and the competence of teachers will be judged. Addressing these issues
requires a pedagogic response which focuses on the role of the teacher
not just as articulator of some bought-in curriculum, but as an active
ethnographer of the workplace, one whose professional investigations
and tasks are always to be set in the context of an appreciation of the
structures and relationships of power in the workplace in question, in
particular in respect of its channels, modes and practices of decision-
making. Such considerations are not merely reflected in the diversity of
teacher competencies that are now demanded, but, as with workplace
communication demands themselves, serve to ilustrate how such competencies are themselves full of inherent conflicts and contestations. As
Giselle Mawer points out, just as with workers confronting the practices
of the restructured workplace, teachers are themselves being restructured, not only in terms of demands for greater multiskilling, but more
problematically ideologically and philosophically, in terms of how teaching is itself to be defined, and how they are being positioned as particular
types of teacher in relation to how the workplace sees itself and, especially, how it sees the demands of its agendas for training, learning and
change. The picture resonates well with what Douglas Barnes so many
years ago in the context of the primary and secondary classroom referred
to as the struggle between a *transmissive* pedagogy going hand-in-glove
with a reductionist view of language, and the *negotiative* teacher seeking
a way to encourage an expansive and more divergent communicative
competence. This factory may run on talk, in Bill Cope's classic phrase,
but it ought not to have to run only on some predetermined script.

Coping with these complex and critical demands, in particular how
to navigate the discourses of the curriculum and the classroom so that
teaching is not divorced from a critique of workplace conditions and
practices, and where learners are not prevented from seeing the global
context in which they are engaged, and where playing the 'workplace
game' does not require representing workplaces as unambiguous
social spaces where roles and practices are unproblematically designed,
clearly places considerable stress on workplace teachers. Such stress is
heightened in a climate where they are increasingly accountable to
their own educational institutions, where they have to accommodate

to national training and funding policies, and where their own profession is increasingly casualised and made subordinate to 'education as a business'.

Coping with the challenge of how teachers are to be professionally developed to sustain these stresses is where the arguments and illustrations of Giselle Mawer's book unerringly lead. What should be the professional development objectives and processes of the workplace teacher and trainer? What critical and reflexive stance should they be encouraged to take towards their practice? Too often in the recent literature, reflective teaching has come to mean little more than keeping some mental or actual diary of events linked to some loose interpretive accounting of learners' practices; a kind of teaching counterpart to the largely asocial precepts of much research into second language learning. What is needed is what we might call the development of *critical* or *praxis-based* teaching, where, as in action research, teachers are engaged in a cycle of critically reflective activity, but one which never departs from an understanding of the historical, structural and above all social conditions of the institutions and their memberships, within which, or in the light of which, it is carried on. To have provided the justification for such a shift towards the critical ethnography of workplace teaching and training practices will be a major outcome of the impact of this remarkable book.

REFERENCES

N.L. Fairclough (1992) *Discourse and social change.* Cambridge: Polity Press

C. Wadensjo (1998) *Interpreting as interaction.* London: Longman

K. Willing (1992) *Talking it through: clarification and problem-solving in the professional workplace.* Sydney, Macquarie University: National Centre for English Language Teaching & Research

Professor Christopher N. Candlin
Centre for English Language Education & Communication Research
City University of Hong Kong

PART ONE

ONE

The changing world of work

The last ten years have seen unprecedented changes in the way work is done in almost every industry sector. Financial deregulation, the removal of tariffs, restructuring, have all meant that world economies must become more internationally competitive if they are to survive. These developments have led to profound and fundamental changes to work practices, employment and recruitment patterns, as well as the need to develop new vocational skills.

This chapter will provide a brief overview of these developments as they are being experienced at the local workplace and on the broader social and economic levels. We will then briefly explore the implications of these changes for the skill development needs of the workforce, specifically in skill domains that have not traditionally been perceived as central vocational concerns – such as language, literacy, communication and learning to learn skills.

While many of the illustrations used refer specifically to the Australian context, these changes broadly reflect developments in many other developed economies, particularly with the increasing trends towards the globalisation of industries and marketplaces.

CHANGES IN THE LOCAL ENTERPRISE CONTEXT

The pressures experienced at the local workplace level have resulted from a combination of local and international factors. To remain viable, workplaces have had to deal with conflicting and interrelated pressures at a number of levels: economic, industrial and technological. The main ones include:

- stronger competition from local and overseas markets;
- reductions in numbers of employees;

- an increasing focus on quality standards;
- the introduction of new technologies;
- restructuring of industrial awards, and negotiation of enterprise-based agreements;
- more participatory management structures;
- a greater focus on skills development.

Competition from local and overseas markets

This increased competition has been mainly due to the creation of new markets such as the European Community and the rapid economic development of less developed countries in South-East Asia and South America. Removing protective tariffs has opened local industries to fierce competition from these emerging economies, where infrastructure and labour costs are often lower. In Australia – for example, the removal of tariffs has had a devastating effect on labour intensive industries such as textile, clothing and footwear industry – with a 40 per cent reduction in the number of people employed in the industry since 1988.[1]

Surviving workplaces have had to radically review their operations to contain costs – 'become lean and mean' – and concentrate on profitable aspects of work while also diversifying their services or seeking to capture niche markets. To sustain long-term viability, many have re-structured themselves so they can respond quickly to shorter timelines and new opportunities. In countries with small populations such as Australia, developing the export potential of products and services is increasingly necessary to ensure survival and profitability.

Doing more with less people

Becoming 'lean and mean' requires workplaces to manage strategically both their physical and human resources. As workplaces rationalise their operations, significant reductions have resulted for both lower 'unskilled' classification levels, and middle-level supervisors of such work. Labour intensive industries with highly multicultural workforces such as the metals, construction, textile, clothing and footwear and the motor vehicle industries have been particularly affected. An Australian study of immigrant workers in the steel industry, for example, noted that structural industry changes have led to 'devastating rates of long-term unemployment for this acutely vulnerable segment of the work-force' (Morrissey, Dibden and Mitchell, 1992: xi).

These retrenched workers are not likely to regain full, permanent employment, should economic conditions improve. Traditional sources of employment such as manufacturing are in decline, and restructured workplaces are requiring less employees because of investments made in technologies, structural efficiencies and, even more importantly, skills development for their 'core' workforce. A 1994 Australian study,[2] for example, surveyed fourteen large firms, 50 per cent of which employed more than 1,000 employees. It found that they had on average reduced their workforces by one-sixth in the last few years. The firms surveyed clearly indicated they were unlikely to increase their 'core' workforces as business picked up again:

> Companies had strong views about employment prospects . . . they had devoted considerable time and effort to restructuring and obtaining substantial productivity increases, and they were not going to jeopardise them by rushing back to the labour market as soon as sales picked up . . .
>
> A key component of the restructuring programs was the development of optimum, highly skilled, highly trained 'core' workforces. These 'smarter' workforces are able to more easily cope with fluctuations in demand – they can work the technologies to higher levels of efficiency and their flexibility helps prevent bottle-necks arising. If they needed more labour, they would firstly work their existing one more intensively, then hire temporary, casual labour. (p. 41)

For those 'core workforces' then, adaptability – in terms of being able to develop new skills and work flexibly – is a key factor to their continued survival. Similarly, for the increasing number of individuals working at the periphery, employability is contingent on proven skills and the capacity to adapt to new situations.

Focus on quality

A strong pressure has developed for enterprises to apply international quality standards such as ISO 9000 systems in design, manufacture and service across all sectors of industry. Apart from needing such standards to penetrate overseas markets, increasingly, local customers are insisting on quality standard accreditation as a means of ensuring satisfactory minimum standards. This focus on quality has meant that strict controls have to be built into all operations to ensure consistency. Documentation of these standard operating procedures requires workers to be able to develop and use procedural manuals, keep work records, undertake quality checks and report on variations and problems. As well as following procedural texts, employees are also expected to interpret statistical information presented in tables or paretographs.

Team-based approaches to work are usually an integral part of such quality management strategies, with teams often 'self-managing' or at least being actively involved in discussing and improving aspects of their work. Particular quality methodologies advocate the use of specific analytical tools – such as 'fish-bone' analysis – as ways of diagnosing problems and arriving at solutions.

As part of the increasing focus on quality, there is greater attention to customer needs, responsiveness and continual improvement to what is being provided. Customers are being defined not only as those purchasing the ultimate product or service, but also 'internal customers' such as fellow employees and suppliers.

Applying new technologies

Using different technologies – such as computer-aided design, planning and automated production – has increased productivity while also enabling workplaces to reduce the number of personnel needed for specific functions. Communication technologies – from computers to mobile phones – have also meant that more information has become immediately available for use by a wider audience. Production schedules and efficiency measures, for example, are now commonly available for employees at different levels to access.

This increased reliance on technologies has meant that at all levels, employees are expected to have the necessary skills to provide and use the information required. Calculators, faxes, computer screens and their generated graphs, tables and texts are no longer found just in managers' offices, but also on construction sites, in hospital kitchens and on factory shop floors. Making full use of the available technology requires more than just basic literacy and analysis skills to make sense of the information. It also requires contextual knowledge and complex interrelated skills in negotiation, decision-making, trouble-shooting and teamwork.

Restructuring industrial agreements and conditions

Through the restructuring of industrial awards narrow, discrete jobs are being replaced by more flexible structures which allow for multi-skilling, teamwork and integrated career paths. Instead of time or seniority based reward-systems, new agreements are tying rewards to skills – thus forging close links between employment and job advancement on the one hand, and the ability to demonstrate competence through training on the other. Yearly performance appraisals are becoming common mechanisms for reviewing employees' pay, conditions and career options.

Centralised wage-fixation and industrial relations systems in countries such as Australia, for example, are being increasingly replaced by local enterprise-specific agreements negotiated between employers and employees. The Australian Workplace Relations Act of 1996 further reduced the role of centralised negotiations by introducing individual workplace agreements which had already been in place for a number of years in countries such as the USA and New Zealand. Productivity-based increases and profit-sharing arrangements are used in a number of large and small companies to increase employees' commitment to their work.

These developments have put a high premium not only on technical skills, but also on broader contextual and communicative skills. They include identifying one's skills and training needs to bargaining and negotiating working conditions with one's employer.

As a result of these changes to the industrial environment, unions have also attempted to rationalise their structures and functions. A number of unions have amalgamated as a result of award restructuring and diversified their functions, to include, for example, vocational education and training in an attempt to retain broad membership support.

New organisational cultures

The flattening of organisational hierarchies has been accompanied by corresponding changes in management styles and organisational cultures. These new cultures tend to be more collaborative, recognising the expertise of employees and their contributions. New participative goals are often reflected in mission statements, organisational statements of objectives and enterprise agreements. The enterprise's 'core business', its goals and sometimes its basic values and philosophy are often crystallised in such documents, as illustrated in the following example:

> Our vision is to be the leading (manufacturer or supplier of x product or service) measured by sustainable profit and achievement, through the excellence of our people, product, quality and customer service.

Other organisations, such as the following Australian meat product manufacturer, explicitly set out their corporate priorities:

Major priorities:
- enhance and maintain market share
- focus on teamwork and employee involvement as key to achieving competitive edge
- achieve profitable sustainable growth
- increase financial return to shareholders

Corporate Values:
- We will strive to provide a healthy and safe working environment. We will aim to provide competitive remuneration and secure long-term employment to our employees in an atmosphere of mutual trust, courtesy, respect and open communication.
- We will provide training to all employees to improve skills, enhance performance and promote career advancement.
- We are accountable individually and in teams for our actions and results.
- We will not compromise in meeting and exceeding customer expectations.

More responsibilities are now being given to operators while supervisors are becoming trainers and team coaches. Increased employee involvement through consultative committees and task forces aims to create an environment where hierarchical and sectional boundaries are blurred, and replaced by cooperative, almost communal relationships. As well as making full use of available resources, such practices aim to increase job satisfaction and employee commitment to organisational goals.

These practices also presuppose a complex set of interrelated skills that were not in high demand previously. Negotiation, coaching and delegating are often new skills for managers who may have previously directed from a safe distance. In the same way, teamwork and innovation require employees to have well-developed communication and negotiation skills as well as a clear understanding of organisational priorities and directions. As Fairclough (1992: 4) points out, the 'conversationalisation of language practices' that goes along with democratisation can actually provide a strategy for exercising power in more subtle and implicit ways. Changing cultural norms as organisations become flatter and more participative often lead to misunderstandings and tensions – if not conflicts – as roles and responsibilities are redefined, and the rhetoric of empowerment and participation is tested on a daily basis.

Focus on skills

Each of these developments has increased the pressure for skills – whether simply to deal with significantly reduced workforces or the need to keep up with higher quality standards and technological advancements.

As a result, there is now wide recognition of the critical role of skills to the survival of enterprises and economies. Extensive national and international enquiries have come to remarkably similar conclusions. For example, a 1993 study by the Organisation for Economic Co-operation and Development examining industry training in the United States, Sweden and Australia concluded that further education and training is becoming critical for sustained economic growth and transforming that growth into social progress:

> The increased importance of skills and competences – and the higher cost of inadequate skills and in competences – have raised the stakes in further education and training for firms (as a way of staying competitive), for individuals (as a way of staying employable and providing an opportunity for wage growth), and for society at large (as a way of ensuring that national economies stay competitive internationally, and that the benefits of that competitiveness are widely accessible to all in society). (OECD, 1993: 8)

Similarly, the 1995 EUROTECNET study in Europe found that new technologies and work organisation structures meant more qualified, 'knowledge workers' were needed:

> Learning is increasingly being seen today by the successful companies as a major strategic weapon . . . Importantly, to be successful, the rate of learning must be equal to, or greater than, the rate of change in the community. European companies and the people working in them are recognising the need to develop the ability to be competent life-long learners who can cope with change. They must be able to continuously learn to efficiently manage new technologies and apply them in an effective way to meet their particular business objectives. This means they must be able to anticipate change and cope with change in a creative way. They must be able to shape technology as well as respond to it. (Nyhan, 1995: 4)

Some countries have introduced financial incentives as a way of encouraging workplaces to invest in skills development. In Australia, for example, a Training Guarantee Levy was introduced in 1990 to ensure that employers spent at least 1 per cent of their payroll on structured training activities. However, this levy was unpopular and was suspended in 1994.

In contrast, an increasing number of 'best practice' workplaces have linked their ability to remain competitive directly to the capacity of their personnel to acquire new skills, and continually adapt their products and services in order to remain market leaders. Employees that have survived successive retrenchment waves are often regarded as valuable assets, because of the skills and experiences they possess. At a pragmatic level, the costs of skill shortages are becoming more evident as enterprises begin to implement radical changes to the way work is done. A Canadian survey of 600 senior managers, for example, found that 'about one third of businesses reported serious difficulties in areas such as the introduction of new technologies, product quality and productivity because of basic skills deficiencies in the labor force'.[3]

As part of applying a continuous improvement model to all aspects of their work, 'best practice workplaces' often critically review their communication, management and skill development practices to ensure they are consistent with the new priorities and directions. This model of organisational learning goes beyond the digestion of nationally accredited training packages by attempting to integrate formal and informal learning into daily work.

RATE AND SCOPE OF ORGANISATIONAL CHANGE

While there may be evident trends of change in the way work is now being done, the rate and scope of these changes varies markedly across industries, workplaces and even different sections within the one workplace. Business viability remains the major priority in most workplaces, and significantly affects the possibility of forward, long-term planning. A 1994 survey of some 3,000 Australian and 1,000 New Zealand manufacturers, for example, noted the existence in Australia of a significant group of sites that appeared to have recognised neither incentive, nor an imperative to change.[4] The rate and scope of change is also greatly dependent on the abilities and motivation of those in positions of influence in workplaces.[5] In Australia, for example, the 1990 Training Guarantee Levy, requiring employers to spend at least 1 per cent of their payroll on structured training activities was strongly resented by employers, and was eventually removed in 1994. Recent studies in Australia for instance have highlighted the weaknesses in managers' skills to lead changes in work practices and management, and meaningfully involve their employees.[6]

More progressive workplaces, for example, attempt to promote a stronger sense of corporate identity and common goals through mission statements and concepts such as *the learning organisation, synergy, partnering* and *re-engineering*. In many restructured, best practice workplaces, employees may become known as 'business associates', and supervisors who have not been replaced by rotating team members are referred to as 'coaches' and team leaders. Powerful status symbols such as blue collar uniforms and control mechanisms such as time clocks are replaced by more egalitarian structures and symbols.

However, even in these workplaces, tensions and contradictions still abound. Employees may well be encouraged to multiskill, collaborate and work in teams, but at the same time, it is common knowledge that further staged redundancies are planned, and more must be produced with less. The enterprise agreement may have been negotiated to allow for favourable pay and working conditions, even training time, but plans may also be in place to relocate offshore in Asia, where infrastructure costs are much lower. Some decisions may have been devolved 'down the line', but key issues are still made by senior management, with little consultation with employees or unions.

In one workplace, for example, a newly established 'self-managing team' had decided to oust their externally appointed team leader in favour of a rotating leadership position. After considerable 'counselling' and negotiation, the powers of the 'self-managing team' were significantly redefined to narrow the scope of their influence. On a wider scale, Australia's largest steel manufacturer, BHP Ltd announced early in 1997 its intention to scale down steel production, and other less profitable sectors in Australia, in preference to similar establishments in Asia. For regional 'steel-cities' such as Newcastle and Port Kembla, the impact of such decisions is far-reaching in economic and social terms.

In the same way, workplace rhetoric about innovation and life-long learning is usually not matched by resources to allow such learning to take place. A major Australian construction company's experience is a case in point. In a newsletter to its employees on ways of 'improving the future' senior managers invite them to participate and support principles such as continuous improvement, life-long learning, openness to new ideas, client responsiveness and a commitment to quality. The message recognises that 'the key to implementing the above principles is the ongoing education of our greatest resource – our people'. It accordingly announces that 'the education process will now spread, with all employees receiving between nine and 20 hours training, depending on each person's role in the organisation'. While such training may represent a significant investment in a company where little previous formal training was offered to employees, it is unlikely to be sufficient to bring about the desired cultural and structural changes.

Increasingly, those in employment are needing to accommodate uncertainty, ambiguities and change as a constant factor at work. Part of this accommodation involves interpreting a new set of discoursal practices which is often multilayered in its meanings and implications. Applying and helping to shape the discourse of human resource management and empowerment in daily work requires contextual and cultural knowledge as well as sophisticated levels of competence in interpersonal communication and negotiation.

A CHANGING LABOUR MARKET

There are major labour market changes occurring in most advanced industrial economies, due to a number of key, interrelated factors. The first centres on the systematic decline of manufacturing, particularly the more labour-intensive forms of manufacturing, and its replacement by services and more technologically mediated industries. The second relates to the greater flexibility and casualisation of the labour market, with changing patterns of employment and workforce participation. Along with an acceptance of relatively high percentages of long-term unemployed, these changes have also increased vocational skills requirements and expectations. The average rate of unemployment in OECD countries, for example, has risen from 6.2 per cent in 1990, to 7.6 per cent in 1996 – with European countries rating an average of 10.4 per cent and Australia 8.7 per cent.[7]

Changes in recruitment practices

The increasing emphasis on skills and qualifications has led to a considerable change in recruitment practices in recent years. While employers may be prepared to make some investment in the skill development needs of their present employees, they are also recruiting 'smarter' to minimise their training costs.[8]

General selection procedures for new employees in many countries now require not only screening in terms of technical skills (e.g. mechanical skills, dexterity), but also English language, literacy and computer skills, interpersonal skills such as teamwork and general aptitude and reasoning tests. Increasingly, the previously common practice of recruiting through kinship or word of mouth has now been replaced by a much more formal and systematic screening, often undertaken by employment agencies. This targetted recruitment focuses on the skills that employers feel will fit their present, and, more importantly, future workplace needs.

Because of the large pool of job seekers, employers are often able to set recruitment criteria that are well above those required for the actual work. Such practices tend to favour those employees with formal qualifications and who are proficient in English language and literacy skills. A test currently used by a large Australian manufacturer, for example, asks applicants for an operator's position to provide the appropriate synonym for words such as pernicious, avarice and erudite.

A frequent and sobering comment made in recent research was that many of the current employees would not be re-employed under the present recruitment criteria if they left.[9] In one particular situation, for example, an Australian worker with several years' experience, who was deemed competent by his supervisor, resigned to return to his Asian country of origin for a family visit. He was unsuccessful in gaining his job with the firm on his return because of the new selection guidelines.

The trend towards more participative, team-based work can also indirectly discriminate against those who do not meet the perceived new role and cultural expectations. More than just technical and communicative skills, employers are also seeking to attract individuals with a particular stance to their job and workplace. The following extract from an application for employment in a supermarket chain, for example, clearly illustrates the shift of emphasis in the skills sought in the retail and service industry. The form contains five pages of detailed questions about applicants' personal, education and employment record, health and safety and general information such as the following:

- Why do you want to join the X team?
- What do you think makes a job more satisfying?
- Can you give an example of a challenging experience you have encountered and what you did?
- What has been your single greatest personal achievement?
- What skills would you bring to the business?
- What do you see as your personal strengths?
- What self-development have you undertaken in the last three years?

Changing patterns of employment

Over the last ten years, different patterns of employment have emerged, in great part due to the rapidly changing demands of the restructured, efficient, technological workplace, and the globalisation of industry. As we move towards the next century, the skill mix profile needed for the restructured workplace favours younger, highly skilled, technically proficient individuals. Increasingly, permanent, secure employment is being replaced by part-time, casual or contract work – 'off the hook' workers – who require relatively little training and can be easily shed when no longer needed.

Workforce 2000: Work and Workers for the 21st Century,[10] a national US report, indicates, for example, that by the year 2000, for the first time in the history of the US, the majority of new jobs will require some education beyond high school and 30 per cent will require a college degree. New jobs in the low skill categories, will represent only 27 per cent of all new jobs – an all-time low.

Recent developments in Australia highlight the implications of these trends for people in vulnerable positions. Two characteristic features of Australia's workforce have been its cultural diversity and its gender segregation. From the early 1970s to about 1990 the migrant proportion of the Australian workforce has remained around 30 per cent, with non-English background workers (NESB) often having greater participation rates in the workforce in comparison with the Australian-born.[11] However, this participation was mainly due to their concentration at the lower occupational classification levels, in categories such as labourers, plant and machine operators and trade persons and under-represented in the clerical, professional and para-professional categories.

Since 1990, the labour force participation of NESB people has declined substantially, relative to their Australian-born counterparts, and current statistics indicate that this difference is becoming greater rather than smaller. The differences in workforce participation are particularly marked for those without post-school qualifications.[12] A recent *Business Review Weekly* article put it rather bluntly:

> Unskilled workers once added value to processed goods. Now technology has made the knowledge gap so wide, that the unskilled are unwanted.
> (James, 1997: 68)

Statistics indicate that growth in the Australian workforce in recent years is due largely to women entering the workforce and the growth in part-time and casual jobs. Women now comprise over 43 per cent of the Australian labour force and constitute the majority of part-time and casual employees, yet remain significantly behind in terms of pay parity. Part-time employment in Australia is now 27 per cent – with women outnumbering men three to one – , casual employment currently accounts for 20 per cent of the total workforce and both are predicted to increase.[13]

These Australian figures reflect trends in many other industrialised countries, where there are clear indications of the increasing diversity and casualisation of the labour force at the same time as greater skills are required.[14] The *Workforce 2000* report, for example, predicts that the majority of new entrants into the American workforce will be women, minorities and immigrants. In the UK, women are expected to make up 45 per cent of the workforce by the year 2000.[15] There are clear trends in countries such as the UK of a core, secure workforce, with a periphery of insecure and casualised jobs.[16]

Increasing job mobility is already evident as a feature of a more turbulent workforce, changing technologies and skill requirements. It is estimated, for example, that individuals currently entering the workforce are likely to have seven to ten different jobs across different areas in a working life. More significantly, experts predict that nearly 70 per cent of current ten-year-olds will enter the workforce to occupy jobs that do not exist in their current form, using technology that has not yet been invented.[17]

These developments are already being reflected in workplace structures. Traditional career structures are being replaced by a precarious combination of casual, contract, consulting work. With the increasing popularity of computers and modems, tele-working is becoming a viable replacement for workplace or office-based work. Joint ventures and the formation of 'virtual corporations' to undertake project-specific work are beginning to challenge the concept of a physical workplace or company.

SKILLS FOR EMPLOYABILITY

If permanent, secure employment is increasingly being replaced by part-time, casual or contract work, then for the individual job seeker, developing transferable skills is, in many ways, becoming more crucial than securing actual employment. These developments have major implications for workers and job seekers who score low on any aspect of employability.

Until recently, in many developed economies, the basic skills required for work were understood to refer to the three r's: reading, writing and arithmetic. However, in recent times, these have been greatly expanded to include such skills as: analysing information, oral communication, problem solving, creative thinking, goal setting, interpersonal skills, teamwork, negotiation, self-learning, using technology, organisational effectiveness and leadership. Similar lists of these 'key' or 'core' competencies have been adopted in the US, Europe, Australia and New Zealand as the new 'basics' required for today's work.[18]

As these 'basic skills' are redefined upwards, communicative competence and literacy emerge as critical issues, both for individuals and workplaces. As the 1992 OECD study observed:

> Many employers who formerly regarded illiteracy as a minor worry
> have now begun to view the issue as critically linked to competitiveness
> . . . The problem appears to lie in the alarmingly high incidence of what
> many observers call 'functional illiteracy', where individuals are unable to
> participate fully in the economic and civic life of today's advanced nations
> rather than simply the inability to decipher printed words. (1993: 9, 10)

Similarly, an extensive survey of employers in the UK in 1993 found that basic skills, particularly oral communication, have become more important for work.[19] As workplaces move from a culture of control to one of commitment and collaboration, communicative competence becomes more central to doing the job and maintaining the relationships upon which the job depends. Yet large-scale surveys regularly reveal that the workforce is ill-prepared in terms of these 'foundational' or 'basic' skills across all occupational classification levels. Studies of management skills in Australia, for example, have highlighted the weaknesses in the skills of Australian managers in modelling and communicating new ways of working collaboratively.[20]

Depending on how literacy is defined and measured, the annual costs of limited language and literacy skills to the economy in lost production and efficiencies have been estimated to vary from several billion dollars in small countries such as Australia, to £5 billion in the UK or $40 billion in more populated countries such as the USA.[21] In the USA for example, an estimated quarter of the labour force (20–27 million adults) are deemed to be lacking in the basic reading, writing and math skills necessary to perform in today's increasingly complex job market. In Australia, a national survey undertaken in 1989 found that one in seven adults is functionally illiterate, whereas in France, a similar survey estimated that 9 per cent of the adult population was affected by illiteracy.[22]

For the individual employee, it is clear that skill recognition and development are becoming major determining factors in their ability to retain their redesigned jobs and access skill-based advancements. Even

in work where communicative requirements have not as yet dramatically altered, the increasing emphasis on credentialism and greater availability of skills in the employment market mean that communicative
competence has become highly valued and expected. Analysis of labour
market statistics, for example, show with monotonous consistency a
strong association between proficiency in English and labour market
success, in terms of being able to firstly obtain a job, and then keep it.[23]

As unskilled jobs disappear, there is an increasing number of experienced, older workers, often unemployed for the first time in their working lives, with little prospect of re-entering the workforce. Fluency in
English has a marked impact on these prospects. In 1996 for example,
the unemployment rate for people born in a non-English speaking country was 12.1 per cent compared with 8.9 per cent for those born in
Australia. Those reporting 'language difficulties' experienced an average
duration of unemployment of eighty-one weeks for males and ninety-
two weeks for females.[24] The precarious nature of casual employment
likewise puts a high premium on technical skills, communicative competence and the ability to continually learn and adapt to change.

NOTES

1. Australian Textile, Clothing and Footwear Industry Training Plan, 1994.
2. Bureau of Industry Economics, 1994.
3. Quoted in Centre for Educational Research and Innovation, 1992: 46.
4. Australian Manufacturing Council Manufacturing Advisory Group (NZ)
   Leading the Way: A Study of Best Manufacturing Practice in Australia and
   New Zealand. Interim Report June 1994, p. 5.
5. See, for example, Australian Manufacturing Council Manufacturing Advisory
   Group (NZ) Leading the Way: A Study of Best Manufacturing Practice in
   Australia and New Zealand. Interim Report June 1994; studies commis-
   sioned by the Karpin Task Force on Leadership and Management Skills.
6. For example, comprehensive studies of Australian managers show that
   although more managers are using the rhetoric of human resource management, there is very little consultative decision making on key issues (Callus,
   1993). Similarly, in a comparative study of Australian, Japanese, Taiwanese,
   German, US and British managers, Australian managers were ranked last
   overall on their ability to 'look well into the future' and to 'convert their
   firm's mission into well-defined objectives'. (Institute of International Competitiveness, 1994. Customers' Views of Australian Management: Asia-Pacific
   Viewpoints: Canberra Karpin Task Force on Leadership and Management
   Skills, p. 29.)

7. Organisation For Economic Cooperation and Development, 1996. *Employment Outlook*. OECD: Paris.

8. See for example, Centre for Educational Research and Innovation, 1992, Hull, 1993, Taylor, C., Lewe, G. and Draper, J. (eds), 1991, Mawer and Field, 1995.

9. Mawer and Field, 1995.

10. Hudson Institute, 1987. *Workforce 2000: Work and Workers for the 21st Century*. Washington, p. 2.

11. See, for example, Collins, 1988, Wooden 1990.

12. February 1997ABS 6203.0 Statistics.

13. See, for example, Australian National Training Authority, May 1996. *Participation and Attainment of Individual Client Groups within Vocational Education and Training;* and *Stocktake of Equity Reports and Literature in Vocational Education and Training,* June 1997a, Australian National Training Authority: Brisbane.

14. See for example, Centre for Educational Research and Innovation, 1992.

15. Central Statistical Office 1992 *Social Trends* 22, London: HMSO.

16. Hutton, W. 1994.

17. Train locally – Work globally, Burrow S., *The Australian TAFE Teacher* Vol. 28: No. 3 Sept. 94, Melbourne.

18. Mayer, E. 1992 *Key Competencies: Report of the Committee to Advise AEC and MOVEET on Employment Related Key Competencies for Post-Compulsory Education and Training*. Canberra: AGPS, Nyhan, 1995.

19. Atkinson J. and Spilsbury M. 1993. *Basic Skills and Jobs*. Institute of Manpower Studies ALBSU, London.

20. The Boston Consulting Group (Karpin Report) Industry Task Force on Leadership and Management Skills, 1994.

21. Wickert, R., 1989. *No Single Measure*: A Survey of Australian Adult Literacy. DEET, Canberra. DEET, Training for Productivity 1994, Centre for Educational Research and Innovation, 1992. ALBSU, 1993. *The Cost to Industry* London. Hull, G. 1993, 'Hearing other voices: a critical assessment of popular views on literacy and work', *Harvard Educational Review*, Vol. 63, No. 1, pp. 20–49.

22. Gorman 1988, quoted in Hull 1993: 22, Centre for Educational Research and Innovation, 1992: 28.

23. See, for example, Ackland, R. and Williams, L. 1992, Wooden, M. 1993. Australian National Training Authority, May 1996. *Participation and Attainment of Individual Client Groups within Vocational Education and Training*. Brisbane.

24. ANTA 1996, op. cit., p. 46.

TWO

The changing world of education and training

For those involved in adult education, the changes over the last few years have to a great extent parallelled those in industry, as the skill demands of new ways of working increasingly impact on education systems, in particular, 'general' and 'basic' education fields, such as language and literacy. In this chapter, we examine briefly some of the main trends emerging from national government policies, the pressures on educators, and changing education and training practices in workplaces.

THE NATIONAL POLICY CONTEXT

In many industrialised countries, different reviews of traditional vocational education and training systems have found them to be 'expensive, inefficient, partial, narrow and locally constrained.'[1] As a result of these criticisms and the increasing importance of skill development, reforms to education and training systems have occurred at both structural and pedagogical levels. In the UK for example, the National Council for Vocational Qualifications was established in 1986 to develop a cohesive system of vocational qualifications, which provides clear, progressive, skill-based pathways.

Reforms to vocational education and training have also extended to curriculum and methodologies. In many countries such as the UK, USA and Australia, competency-based approaches have been adopted with the aim of improving the processes and outcomes of education and training. Competency-based approaches place primary emphasis on what a person can actually do in the workplace as a result of the training (the outcome) rather than the processes involved in training (the inputs). They are concerned with training to industry specific standards rather than with an individual's achievement relative to others in a group. Thus they represent a major shift in focusing on the outcomes of learning as opposed to time-served notions of formal training. Competency-based approaches have been the subject of much debate and controversy among educators in both vocational and general skill areas – with points of contention centring on the definition of competence and the appropriateness of methods used to develop and assess the skills in question.[2]

In Australia, the reforms to education and training have been more ambitious than in many other countries. For the first time in the country's history, federal, state and territory governments as well as employer and employee groups worked together to develop a set of reforms, initially known as the national training reform agenda. Their main aim was identified as 'to lift the skills of the Australian workforce (and of those intending to work), whatever their industry, occupations or employment status'.[3] by providing:

- nationally-consistent competency-based standards and training;
- nationally recognised and portable qualifications;
- an integrated entry-level training system;
- an open national training market with more flexible pathways and delivery;
- increased participation for groups of people who have missed out on training opportunities in the past.

Much has been invested in these training reforms. Total expenditure on vocational education and training in 1994 for example was estimated at $2.6 billion (ANTA, 1994: 20).

However, despite claims that the national training reform agenda is 'industry-driven', reviews of its implementation revealed it to be overly bureaucratic and unresponsive to industry needs. At the local workplace level, employers often felt little ownership, and many employees were unaware of its component structures and processes. More significantly for educators, industry parties have been strongly critical of the responsiveness of public education systems to the changing requirements of the working environment.[4]

Studies indicated, for example, no significant increase in employees undertaking formal training between 1989 and 1993. This problem was more marked for low-skilled, operative jobs. While these make up 48 per cent of Australia's labour force, they accounted for only 7 per cent of total training activity in 1993.[5] Although there has been a substantial increase in public funding for vocational education and training, much of this expenditure was aimed at unemployed and entry-level training rather than those in employment.

In part, the difficulties were due to the need to accommodate the various priorities of national and state governments, employers, unions, industry groups and vocational education bodies – and their respective factions. The overriding concerns have focused on national recognition, consistency, and clear interrelations for this revolutionary change in education and training, rather than outcomes and clients.[6] Reform strategies adopted in 1994 to address these issues were followed by further major changes with the election of a new Conservative government in 1996. The aim of these changes has been to reduce costs, streamline regulatory requirements and increase flexibility. In the place of a detailed 'agenda', a more flexible 'National Training Framework' has been adopted, with two major components:

- new recognition arrangements based on streamlined registration of education and training providers and services;
- training packages consisting of nationally endorsed competency standards, linked to national qualifications and assessment guidelines.

A new Australian Apprenticeship and Traineeship system has also been introduced to increase flexible, workplace-based training options and user-choice. Rather than 'industry-driven', the emerging vocational education and training system aims to be 'business-led' and 'enterprise-focused', with local workplaces being able to determine 'what training they receive, from who and when, where and how'.[7] The national strategy for vocational education and training for the years 1998–2003 has been redesigned to achieve four basic objectives:

- equipping Australians for the world of work;
- enhancing mobility in the labour market;
- achieving equitable outcomes in vocational education and training;
- maximising the value of public vocational education and training expenditure.[8]

Language, literacy and vocational education

Over recent years, there has been increasing recognition of the importance of language, literacy and numeracy competence in the workplace and in vocational education. However, as the international OECD study into adult literacy found, the translation of this recognition to action is often less straightforward. The obstacles to this process are often varied and complex:

> Despite signs of strong support for fighting illiteracy, we also find persisting barriers to effective alliance building among participants in the field. So far, employers often still fail to match rhetoric with significant investments. Many educators continue to resist recasting their programs to make them more effective, particularly if doing so might mean compromising institutional interests. Governments still devote insufficient resources and often prefer bureaucratic reshuffling to substantive changes in policy. In most cases, learners too remain marginalised from decision-making about curriculum and program goals and often fail to grasp their right to have a say in guiding policy. (1993: 9)

At policy levels in Australia, for example, there has been much debate regarding the need to explicitly identify language and literacy skills as part of industry standards and vocational training programmes. Apart from potential discriminatory effects, the resource implications of such a move have also been contentious – with employers and vocational education providers not wishing to shoulder the responsibility for the development of these skills.

As different implementations of vocational reforms have failed because of mismatches between curriculum, methodologies on the one hand, and learners' skills and workplace needs on the other, the need to address language and literacy issues has become more accepted. In 1991, for example, Australia released its national *Language and Literacy Policy* emphasising the need for all Australians to attain proficiency in spoken and written English. The 1993 *National Collaborative Adult English Language and Literacy Strategy* went further to recognise English language and literacy as 'fundamental to the whole of the education and training effort'. This strategy identified the diversification and expansion of the provision of adult English language and literacy programmes as one of its six areas for action, and specifically targetted the integration of English language and literacy in vocational training.[9] Similarly, the 1994 national strategies to improve the vocational education and training system have identified language and literacy issues as integral to the success of reform initiatives. Increasingly, training needs analyses undertaken by industry advisory training bodies, such as the national 1996 VET plan are identifying literacy and numeracy training as a 'corner stone activity'.[10]

As in many other countries, these policies are usually supported by rather modest government funding for workplace language and literacy programmes – with an expectation that employers will bear at least some of the costs of up-skilling their employees in these areas. In Australia, the main funding source for workplace education is the Workplace English Language and Literacy Program which is administered by the Department of Employment, Education and Training. For 1995–7 $A11.4 million dollars per annum have been allocated.[11] This amount is to be supplemented by a contribution of at least 25 per cent from the employer towards the cost of tuition, in addition to the provision of suitable accommodation and paid training leave for employees participating in the programme. The stated aims of the Programme are to:

> Provide assistance to enable workers to develop literacy and ESL skills that are sufficient to enable them to remain in their current employment and to meet their future employment and training needs. The program seeks to enable workplaces, through improved workplace communication, to support changes in industrial arrangements associated with award restructuring and industry and workplace reforms. (1994: 1)

Evaluations of the programme have pointed out that while a number of strategic and innovative projects have resulted, the programme is severely underresourced, and some of its funding guidelines are out of step with good practice. The way funding arrangements operate for example encourage a short-term focus on individuals' language and literacy deficiencies, rather than on systemic, integrated approaches to learning and links with accredited vocational certificates.[12]

CHANGES IN EDUCATORS' WORK

Both school and adult education sectors are undergoing fundamental changes to the purpose, form and content of provision. For language and literacy educators, part of the cost of gaining recognition has been the increasing infiltration of the world of work and vocational education into these previously relatively insulated, 'social justice' and general education programmes. Some of the main changes that educators have had to deal with include:

- privatisation of vocational education and training;
- a greater focus on measurable, recognised outcomes;
- increasing use of technologies and flexible learning arrangements;
- blurring of discipline and role boundaries.

Privatising vocational education and training

In Australia, for example, government policies have encouraged education and training providers to become more entrepreneurial by competing for a fee for service customers, and by entering joint ventures with industry. As a result, there is now greater competition between traditional large providers as collegiate relationships are replaced by a more market-oriented, competitive approach. A number of smaller private agencies have also emerged with large enterprises, unions and voluntary organisations, for example, diversifying into the provision of education and training services.

As many critics have pointed out, the privatisation of education and training poses major inherent equity issues.[13] The concept of a more open training market tends to be in conflict with that of more equitable education and training services. Lack of facility in English, limited formal educational experience or disability tend to involve special forms of provision which make learners with these characteristics more expensive to teach. Writers, such as Keat (1991) in Britain, for example, have noted how the use of market criteria in cultural activities (e.g. academic research, teaching and the arts) can work to undermine the values by which such activities have been previously judged. He argues, for example, that the integrity of such cultural and professional practices can be damaged by the pursuit of goods external to the practice, such as money, power and prestige. Standards of excellence are determined by the preferences of funding agencies and consumers rather than those intrinsic to the profession.

Part of the privatisation push has also been a trend towards short-term, project-based, funding arrangements. For educators in emerging fields such as adult language and literacy, this has led to increased casualisation of teaching positions and the erosion of traditional working conditions. At the same time, greater challenges to traditional teaching roles have developed with the adoption of new responsibilities, such as consultancy services, tendering and marketing.

Focusing on measurable, recognised outcomes

The rhetoric of skills may have led to additional resources in certain areas of education and training, but these resources have been accompanied by a strong focus on accountability and performance-based outcomes – particularly those meaningful to funding providers and industry. Consequently, there has been a large-scale shift towards a competency-based, nationally accredited curriculum, based on national industry standards.

The narrow, 'behavioural objectives' view of competency-based education has come under a good deal of criticism in countries such as the US, Canada, the UK and Australia – both from the vocational education and language and literacy areas.[14] In Australia, given national policy directions and funding guidelines, educators' efforts have been increasingly directed towards the refinement and adaptation of competency-based approaches to language and literacy. While there are – as yet – no national competency standards for language and literacy, a number of large providers have developed their own competency-based curricula, with moves to coordinate these through a national reporting system.

Accredited, competency-based curricula are intended to provide a quality assurance mechanism, as well as a recognised credential for the learner. However, these predetermined parameters can also severely limit the negotiation of more relevant learning content and format with learners. Given the rapid pace of change in workplaces, such curricula can also quickly become outdated. In workplace education, where relevance and responsiveness are primary considerations, these limitations have resulted in interesting tensions. Educators have, in a number of instances, been able to collaboratively negotiate courses based on learners' and enterprise needs, and by-pass accreditation issues, or address them indirectly.

Using technologies and flexible learning arrangements

Traditional teaching practices are increasingly giving way to more flexible, learning arrangements, utilising a wider range of methods, and technologies. 'Flexible delivery' for many types of adult education is promoted as a way of increasing participation by groups which have difficulty accessing traditional forms. In a workplace context, such flexibility might involve informal on-the-line support from a teacher, or peer tutoring from a work-mate. Contract or project-based learning is becoming more commonly used in vocational education as a way of integrating a number of different skills and providing an opportunity for learners to apply those skills to real-work situations. Self-paced learning materials and computer-based programs, for example, enable learners to participate despite constraints such as shift-work or distance – especially when combined with the use of interactive communication technologies. Fax machines, CD-Roms and access to the Internet has spawned an increasing number of creative ways of learning and teaching, with teachers adopting more indirect facilitation and management rather than direct instruction roles.

Blurring of discipline and role boundaries

Widening the traditional client base of vocational education and training has had a major impact on educators across a number of disciplines. Up until recently, there has been no structured training available for employees at lower skill classification levels, except perhaps for those undertaking apprenticeships. Clear distinctions existed between specific vocational 'training' and broader 'education'. As vocational educators and trainers address the skill development needs of these new groups, and the requirements of collaborative workplaces, language and literacy invariably emerge as priority areas. Conversely, there has been a greater focus on vocational skills in language and literacy courses, whether for those employed or for those seeking employment. These pressures to integrate language and literacy have led to greater interaction and cross-skilling between educators from different disciplines, with collaborative approaches to curriculum development and delivery emerging. One of the results has also been a blurring of boundaries and roles between previously distinct and separate disciplines – e.g. education and training, business and communication skills, language and literacy.

Even within the same discipline area, significant changes are occurring to the roles and functions of practitioners. A recent Australian project examining 'what is a competent adult literacy and basic education teacher?' for example, found that community consultation, communication and advocacy formed an integral part of teachers' roles. It proposed that the term 'teacher' was no longer an adequate descriptor for the roles of functions of educators in increasingly diverse and complex learning/teaching contexts (Scheeres, Gonczi, Hager and Morley-Warner, 1993).

With the increasing focus on the new skills needed for work, teaching venues have also changed to align themselves more closely with that context. Many vocational and literacy educators are now fully based in a workplace for the duration of a particular project. More than just a change in physical environment, this move has led to different approaches and methodologies emerging, as educators become immersed in the workplace culture, and seek to utilise the learning potential of that context. Direct teaching input is being replaced by approaches focusing much more on the facilitation of learning through a wide range of formal and informal strategies. Learning activities tend also to be much more closely related to daily work concerns and organisational priorities. The scope and effectiveness of such approaches are however, to a great extent, determined by the prevailing priorities and attitudes to skill development in the particular workplace concerned.

APPROACHES TO EDUCATION AND TRAINING IN THE WORKPLACE

Skill development – cost or investment?

While there may be increasing convergence between working and learning at work, the resulting approaches to learning are far from uniform. Field and Ford (1995) depict the range of approaches to skill development at the workplace as lying along a continuum. At one extreme, skills development receives little or no attention and learning is haphazard. Towards the mid-point of the continuum, enterprises begin to take quality seriously, and consequently, begin to formalise their operating procedures and become more explicit about process and product standards. Specific, goal-based learning is formalised through training for routine procedures and efforts to increase flexibility by multiskilling employees.

At the other end of the continuum, skill development may be regarded as the key to long-term survival, and a wide range of formal and informal learning opportunities may be recognised and valued. These 'learning organisations' value flexibility and employee involvement, and seek to integrate thinking, learning and doing into all aspects of organisational functions. As the comparative OECD study pointed out, such organisations recognise the need for a systematic effort to build short-term adaptability:

> 'The pipeline for curriculum updating and actual training is longer than the half-life of emerging skills and qualifications requirements . . . The way to deal with change and adaptability is by enhancing people's capacity to develop new skills and to apply those new skills quickly and effectively.' (1993: 36)

In terms of the learning continuum just described, most training activity at enterprise level clusters around the lower and mid-points of the continuum as workplaces make a transition from haphazard learning towards goal-based learning. In general, training activity in the workplace is only supported to the extent that it adds immediate value. It demands time for experienced workers away from the workplace, and is at odds with day-to-day work pressures and the strong emphasis on productivity, quality and profit. This is partly because direct links between increased investment in training and improvements in productivity are difficult to establish – although a small number of studies have indicated that higher skill levels translate into greater adaptability, higher individual earnings and higher firm productivity.[15]

In organisations where training is seen as peripheral to 'core business', there is often little infrastructure and no one to drive the skill development process. Many enterprises for example, do not have dedicated trainers or training managers. Planning for training tends therefore to be somewhat haphazard, with a considerable use of external expertise, either through employer organisations, private or public providers. Consequently, most training activity in such workplaces relates to a specific task area such as forklift driving or using a particular computer software. As a training manager from a metals manufacturing plant put it, such training is very much needs-driven:

> We have 'Just-in-time' training here, but more often than not, it's 'Just-too-late' training. The training department often only gets called in when a problem has occurred.

Many organisations, particularly larger ones, have, in general, had to develop some training infrastructure, and negotiated training plans as part of industrial agreements or the implementation of new goals and quality management strategies. In tangible terms, the establishment of such infrastructure is a lengthy and complicated process, involving the development of strategic plans, standard procedures, competencies and training objectives. The ratification of these by management, employee representatives and accreditation bodies adds to both the time and financial costs of the process.

For many workplaces, the value of such a process lies in its potential to achieve cultural change through collaboration, rather than simply by developing vocational skills. During the last few years, a considerable number of enterprises (for the first time ever) have involved experienced employees in the long and time-consuming process of documenting procedures, developing their own training programs, or customising accredited courses so they can more effectively meet their own needs. Aspects such as quality, communication, employee involvement and occupational health and safety are often integrated in the content and structure of such programmes. This process is sometimes undertaken in conjunction with the assistance of external vocational or literacy education providers.

To a great extent, skill development is closely synchronised with the pace of cultural change and senior management support in the organisation. While some workplaces may adopt training as the main vehicle for achieving change in employee relations and work organisation, others, such as the employee development manager quoted below, are aware of the need to 'go softly' and adopt a more incremental pace:

> We can't put the cart before the horse and at the moment we don't have a very visionary management. Once you get training happening, we'll have people organising their own tools or testing their chemicals in water. This challenges customs and practices and managerial prerogatives. It can be very difficult for management to handle.

Flexible learning at work

As workplaces develop more systematic approaches to skill development, they have had to develop a range of ways to maximise the value and effectiveness of training on the one hand, and minimise its 'disruptive' effect on 'core' business on the other. A wide range of non-classroom training arrangements is developing, partly because of practical difficulties in releasing employees to attend formal training due to factors such as production pressures, shift work, multisite work or lack of numbers. For many adults unaccustomed to formal learning situations, 'hands on' and informal approaches have definite advantages and are much preferred to more traditional ones.

Some of these alternate or complementary modes of training include one-to-one, peer tutoring or computer-based packages. Informal learning arrangements are often integrated with work practices, with the provision of learning resources at the work stations, or project-based, action learning models. Experiential, adventure learning approaches are sometimes used to achieve attitudinal change, such as in team building courses.

With the increasing focus on skill development, the role of in-house trainers has become more prominent. In Australia, this role has been formally recognised through the development of national standards and the inclusion of trainer roles and functions in most industrial classifications. In many organisations, workplace trainers are no longer just instructors, but are also becoming active change agents in terms of facilitating new ways of doing work. As well as helping other employees develop new technical skills, they also bring in a new emphasis on quality, consultation and teamwork. Trainers often become *de facto* mediators between senior management and employees, especially if they have themselves come from the lower skill classification ranks.

Dealing with diversity

Just as approaches to skill development vary markedly, so do the ways that workplaces deal with language, literacy and cultural diversity issues. Often, these issues are evident later rather than sooner – after failed attempts to implement training programmes, or changes to work practices. The following comments from two different industries illustrate the effect of mismatches between the form or content of the new initiatives and the intended target group:

> We had a walk out the first time we tried to run a course. The guys felt we were setting them up, because they couldn't see how all the reams of paper related to their jobs. (Section supervisor, construction industry)

> We spent all this money training them on the use of the new equipment, but it was only when they kept making mistakes that we realised most of them had not been able to follow either the consultant or the manuals. No-one felt confident enough to tell us there was a problem. (Plant manager, manufacturing)

Because of operational pressures and prevailing power relationships, employees with language or literacy difficulties are often not involved in the early stages of developing or planning training – or the delivery and piloting of such courses. It is not until a programme is fully operational that problems with language, literacy and cultural assumptions are usually discovered. This can lead to frustrating efforts to remedy workers' 'deficiencies' so that they can match the demands of the unchanged training modules. Similarly, failed attempts at self-managing teams can often be attributed to difficult personalities, rather than inappropriate methodologies and cultural expectations.

With government subsidies for workplace language and literacy programmes, a number of organisations have used such funding to 'kick off' training for their workforce by developing their employees' 'basic' skills. Others have used the funding to set up more systematic, collaborative approaches, with many educators being based in the workplace. These approaches go beyond the boundaries of a workplace classroom in their aim to address the communicative and skill development needs of the whole organisation. In the next two chapters, we look at some of the theoretical and practical parameters of these emerging approaches.

NOTES

1. Centre for Educational Research and Innovation. *Adult Illiteracy and Economic Performance* 1992: 82. Organisation for Economic Cooperation and Development, France. See also, *Dispatches* 1993: *All our Futures: Britain's Education Revolution,* Channel Four Television, London.
2. Collins, M. 1991. Dispatches 1993: *All our Futures: Britain's Education Revolution,* Channel Four Television, London. Deakin University 1994.
3. ANTA 1994: 1.
4. See, for example, National Board of Employment, Education and Training 1991, Allen Consulting Group 1994, Lundberg 1994.
5. Australian Bureau of Statistics study 1994(b): 1, ANTA, October 1993: 14.
6. See, for example, Lundberg 1994: 5.
7. Australian National Training Authority, Ministerial Decisions, 1996. August, p. 2.
8. Australian National Training Authority, 1997b *Australian Training, Special Edition* June, p. 11.
9. NCAELLS 1993, p. 1, 7.
10. Australian National Training Authority, 1996. *Report on National Industry Vocational Education and Training, Plans,* May: Brisbane, p. 11.
11. Of the $11.4 million, $7.8 was provided in the *White Paper on Employment on Growth* for the literacy component and $3.8 million for the English as a second language component.
12. See Baylis, 1995; Mawer and Field, 1995.
13. Lundberg, 1994; Mawer and Field, 1995.
14. See, for example, Auerbach, E.R. 1986. Tollefson, J. 1986. Collins, M. 1991. Deakin University 1994.
15. A comparative research study undertaken in the clothing manufacture industry in Britain and Germany, for example, indicates that substantial vocational training predisposes workers to adapt to change and work more flexibly – the higher levels of the German work force accounted for all the observable differences between the success of the firms in the two countries. (Steedman H. and Wagner K. 1989, Productivity, Machinery and Skills: Clothing Manufacture in Britain and Germany *National Institute of Economics Review,* May pp. 40–57). Similarly, the 1992 OECD study into Adult Illiteracy and Economic Performance cites US research by Denison, indicating that more than half the productivity increases in the US economy during 1929–69 can be associated with on the job training and learning. It was twice as important as technology in boosting productivity.

PART TWO

DEFINING THE PARAMETERS FOR WORKPLACE EDUCATION

THREE

Developing a theoretical framework

What does it mean to use language and literacy in today's work context? To what extent does competence in these areas limit individuals' ability to achieve their personal and vocational goals? What is the role of education in a workplace environment? If communicative competence is integral to effective work, then how best can educators enable its development?

The way educators respond to these questions will inevitably shape their approach to workplace education, their focus, role and expectations. Social theorists such as Layder (1993: 15) define theories as 'networks or integrated clusterings of concepts, propositions and world-views', which act as background assumptions to practice. It is important therefore for such theoretical understandings to be explicit and their relevant connections clear. This chapter will briefly explore different theoretical perspectives about language and learning that can inform a holistic approach to workplace education. It is an approach that attempts to hold in tension the conflicting pressures impacting on workplace educators and their clients.

CONCEPTIONS OF LANGUAGE AND LITERACY

Different traditions of linguistics all consider the primary function of language to be that of 'making meaning'. Beyond this core area of agreement, they differ on a number of important aspects. Where, for example, is this meaning situated: in the speaker/writer, hearer/reader, or the text itself ? What does it take to use language effectively in negotiating meaning? What roles do psychological, social or political factors play in shaping that meaning? What is the relationship between language and success, or power?

In the context of workplace education, a framework for explaining how language is used needs to be sufficiently broad to deal with the psychological, interpersonal, institutional, cultural and political dimensions of this meaning-making potential. Such a framework also needs to be sufficiently dynamic to respond to the fundamental changes occurring to language at work. Some of these changes are the result of more collaborative and interactive ways of working, whereas others are due to shifting power and functional relationships or the integration of new communication media and technologies into everyday activities.

Roberts, Davies and Jupp (1992), in explaining the particular framework informing their work in Industrial Language Training in England point out that theories of interaction can have three major functions for practitioners:

to describe: they provide descriptive accounts of what is involved in interaction and thus they can also help us to develop a critical awareness and analysis of interaction;

to interpret: they provide analytical tools for understanding how people make sense when they talk to each other;

to explain: allied to interpretation, they can help us to relate the specific and local in interaction to the social institutions through which things get done and which determine our social and economic well-being (1992: 30).

These three functions are stressed to varying extents by different theories of linguistics. In the following section, we will look briefly at some of the insights from the main traditions of linguistics that could be drawn on to inform a theoretical framework for workplace education.

Language, text and context

Socio-linguists such as Gumperz (1982) and Hymes (1974) see language as culturally relative, 'undivorceable from its social context'. They attempt to show systematic correlations between social variables – such as role, status, topic, setting and message – and resulting variations in the forms of language used.

The Systemic-Functional model of language, developed by Halliday (1978, 1985) has had a significant influence in shaping language and literacy education in recent years. In this model, Halliday attempts to show the systematic relationship between meaning, the wording, and its particular context through a functional system of grammar. Language is perceived as a system of meanings which are socially and culturally determined through the code or grammar used. Martin and Rothery (1980) developed these concepts further by introducing the notion of *genre* as a separate semiotic system underlying language:

> A genre is a staged, goal-oriented purposeful activity in which speakers and writers engage as members of our culture . . . for example making a dentist appointment, buying vegetables. Language functions as the phonology of register, and both register and language function as the phonology of genre. (Martin, 1984: 25)

By providing tools for analysing the grammar that lies behind the text, the Systemic-Functional model of language enables us to describe the way language is as it is. The sociological emphasis of the model, and particularly the notion of genre, is useful in pointing out the culturally specific and relative nature of texts.

However, there are also significant limitations to this model because of its perhaps natural linguistic emphasis on texts and genres. A major criticism of the model relates to the notion that one gains power, or control over discourse by understanding the rules that govern the text, and by being able to analyse and approximate powerful genres. Theorists such as Foucault, for example, point out that access to powerful forms of discourse involve more than knowing and using the rules:

> Neither texts nor genres themselves have power. Rather they are sites and capillaries where relations of power are constituted and waged, and these relations are contestable. (Foucault, 1972)

In a similar way, Fairclough (1992) asserts that while individuals may be shaped by discursive practices, yet they are also capable of reshaping and restructuring those practices (1992: 45).

Another criticism relates to the perception of spoken interactions as texts. Writers from a more pragmatic orientation, such as Levinson, for example, stress the dynamic and fluid nature of such discourse: conversation is not a structural product in the same way that a sentence is – it is rather the outcome of the interaction of two or more independent, goal-oriented individuals, with often divergent interests (1979: 294).

Such interaction may become a 'text' if transcribed for analysis purposes, but this scripting acts in the same way as a two-dimensional snapshot of a multidimensional event.

Discourse is also dynamic in the way it reflects and interacts with other discourses. Bakhtin (1986), for example, sees each utterance as a link in the chain of speech communication. 'Our speech is filled with others' words, varying degrees of otherness and varying degrees of "our-owness", varying degrees of awareness and detachment' (in Fairclough, 1992: 102). For Bakhtin, texts and utterances are shaped by prior texts that they are responding to and by subsequent texts that they anticipate. This notion of 'intertextuality' – a term coined by Kristeva (1986) sees texts as responding and reworking past texts, as well as anticipating and trying to shape subsequent texts.

In a pluralist, rapidly changing society, how valid then is it to assume that text types or genres can be clearly identified? Writers such as Kress (1993), for example, claim that generic form is never totally fixed, but is always in the process of change. The genre of a job interview in 1992 for instance, is very different from a job interview in 1932 (1993: 28). In a similar way, Fairclough (1992) points to the striking contemporary phenomenon of the rapid transformation and restructuring of textual traditions and orders of discourse. Rather than searching for discrete texts, he suggests instead that intertexuality ought to be a major focus in discourse analysis.

Work-related discourse – both spoken and written – reflects the multi-dimensional changes and pressures of the particular context of situation (the workplace) and culture (industry, unions, society). The generic features of new processes such as consultation are still in their formative stages, and tend to reflect mixed generic elements drawn from a variety of sources. Depending on the particular context and stage of consultation, these may, for example, include elements from formal meeting procedures, the discourse of conflict resolution, bargaining and advocacy, as well as the rhetoric of organisational learning and quality management.[1]

Writers such as Leech (1981) and Butler (1988) also question the ability of text analysis to capture the subtleties of meaning contained in much of human communications. Utterances, or 'texts' can, and often do, have more than one message and reflect more than one generic structure. Depending on the context, for example, a simple statement such as 'It's Friday!' in a work context, may be an effective way of avoiding an onerous task, a gambit for arranging a social outing as much as a factual reminder of the day in question, or a range of other mutually understood messages. Yet this dynamic, multifunctional use of language is not easily accommodated within the Systemic-Functional model. Nor does it satisfactorily account for the way people can decode the meaning of obscure utterances through inference or assumed shared knowledge.

While the strength of the Systemic-Functional model is in describing how a particular text is as it is, its potential for workplace education is limited by its reluctance to look critically at the text's underlying intentions, and the resources that people bring to their communicative interactions. Why, for example, would a speaker choose a particular form of expression rather than another in a particular setting? In fact, Halliday explicitly discourages such a search by asserting that 'There is no way of tracking the process whereby a speaker or writer has arrived at a particular mode of expression in the discourse' (1985: 345).

Language as interactive communication

While also perceiving language as meaning potential, the field of Pragmatics stresses the processual aspects of language as interactive communication. Meaning resides in people and their intentions rather than the product – or texts – of their interactions:

> The broadest interpretation of pragmatics is that it is the study
> of understanding intentional human action. Thus, it involves the
> interpretation of acts assumed to be undertaken in order to accomplish
> some purpose. The central notions in pragmatics must then include belief,
> intention (or goal), plan and act. (Green, 1989)

The Pragmatic understanding of meaning takes into account the lexico-grammar and the social context, as well as the more psychological aspects such as speaker's intentions and hearer's interpretation that may not be evident from the message itself.

> Meaning, in this sense, is something which is performed, rather than
> something that exists in a static way. It involves action (the speaker
> producing an effect on the hearer) and interaction (the meaning being
> 'negotiated' between speaker and hearer on the basis of their mutual
> knowledge). (Leech, 1981)

Meaning cannot be interpreted without reference to its particular context, but it is possible to negotiate meaning only because the processes of inferencing that are required. These processes in turn, are based on general maxims or principles. Grice (1975) identified the *Cooperative Principle* and its maxims of *quantity, quality, relation* and *manner*, which underlie interactions, while Brown and Levinson (1987) are concerned with the universal phenomenon of *politeness* or *preservation of face*.

Pragmatics offers a powerful framework for providing insights into understanding language as a complex, dynamic meaning making process, where there is not necessarily a direct relationship between the intentions and the words used. This framework is particularly relevant in interactions between different cultures or subcultures, where many misunderstandings occur because of mismatches in schemas, cues and interpretations, as much as, if not more than, mismatches in the actual grammar.[2]

However, the field of Pragmatics has limitations in its relevance to workplace education because of its tendency to focus on oral interaction, often in the form of individual speech acts, rather than a wider range of discourse. While providing insights into individual interactions, and cross-cultural communication, this is often at the expense of ignoring wider, structural and social factors of which the interaction is part. As with psychological models of reading, the focus on individual interactions and situations has been criticised for its 'tendency to privatise and individualise social and cultural knowledge' (Freebody and Luke, 1990).

Meaning across media

A viable theoretical framework also needs to accommodate the ways that communication media and technologies are fundamentally changing what and how language is used. Answer machines, mobile phones, computers, modems and faxes are now commonly used in a wide variety of traditionally 'non-office' working environments. The Internet is making it possible for individuals to communicate around the globe, across their geographic, linguistic and cultural boundaries.

As well as developing the technological competence to deal with these new technologies, new discoursal practices and protocols are emerging to deal with these new processes and products of interactions. E-mail and fax messages, for example, are a fluid mixture of spoken and written discourse, when contrasted with the more explicit generic features of memos and letters. Similarly, with the greater use of computers, graphs, illustrations and sophisticated layout have become an integral part of much written communication – which in turn is becoming integrated with more interactive media such as videos and sound-clips.

'Multi-literacies' is a term recently coined by an international group of educators – the New London Group – in an attempt to describe the emerging forms of literacy that are required in today's world:

> [Multi-literacies relate to] the increasing multiplicity and integration of significant modes of meaning making, where the textual is also related to the visual, the audio, the spatial, the behavioural, and so on . . .

When technologies of meaning are changing so rapidly, there cannot be one set of standards or skills that constitute the ends of literacy learning, however taught . . . Effective citizenship and productive work now require that we interact effectively using multiple languages, multiple Englishes and communication patterns which more and more frequently cross cultural, community and national boundaries. (Cope and Kalantzis, 1995: 24)

Discourse and power

Other traditions in language and literacy are particularly concerned with the relationship between discourse and power in society. Critical schools of linguistics and literacy have emerged as an alternative orientation which is based 'not only on theories of language and discourse, but more importantly a sociological vision of work, social institutions and social change in the next century' (Luke, 1992).

Critical Language Study asserts that language is social practice and not a phenomenon external to society and that language is seen as discourse rather than as accomplished text. This discourse shapes and is, in turn, shaped by society, in a two-way, dialectical relationship. (Candlin and McNamara, 1989, Fairclough, 1992). It is critical in the special sense of aiming to show up connections between language, power and ideology:

Access to and participation in the power forums of society is dependent on knowing the language of those forums and how using that language power enables personal and social goals to be achieved. (Ibid. *ix*)

Discourse then becomes a social and political act through which meanings and power relations are negotiated. Critical literacy writers such as Freebody and Luke (1990) point out that *controlling the text* is only one aspect of accessing power, as part of the complex strategies involved in interpreting and using social rules. To achieve proficient, critical literacy, they suggest that the following elements are needed:

- coding competence – learning to break the code: the relationship between spoken sounds and written symbols and the contents of that relationship;
- semantic competence – engaging the meaning systems of texts;
- pragmatic competence – developing social and sociolinguistic resources to participate in what this text is for, here and now;
- critical competence – analysing the text in terms of what it is trying to do to the reader.

Critical linguists also stress the crucial importance of some communicative interactions such as medical and legal encounters, where life chances may be at stake. As Candlin observes, in these encounters, 'participants may be placed at a social risk, suffering disadvantage in consequence of the inequalities of communication' (Fairclough 1989, viii–ix). Critical linguistics suggest that particular attention needs to be paid to such 'critical communicative sites'. In analysing such discourse, they adopt an eclectic approach, drawing on functionalist approaches of systemic linguistics, pragmatics or cross-disciplinary trends.

Roberts, Davies and Jupp adopt a similar approach and refer to an 'expanded view of language':

> Such a view of language goes a long way beyond a structural or functional view. It includes a critical view which engages with language as creating social identity, with the role of language in creating and maintaining social structures, and so with issues of language and power . . . It has to take account of the socio-political context in which language has to be learned, how learners perceive themselves in relation to that language and its speakers, and how they are perceived and received by that language culture. (1992: 10)

One of the major challenges in adopting such a seemingly all-encompassing framework is developing the necessary analytical skills and methodological tools to translate such perspectives into practice. How, for example, can critical linguists ensure that their own values and assumptions are not imposed on those whose discourse they analyse? To what extent are the explanations provided by critical linguists themselves socially and culturally bound? What are the appropriate research and teaching methods which allow for such a multiplicity of perspectives?

Educators' theoretical understandings about language are fundamental in shaping their practice – in terms of focus, role and methodology. If, for example, language is seen as primarily discrete genres and texts, then the focus of practice will be on the collection, analysis and approximation of these authentic texts. If, however, language is seen as continually evolving social practice, then the focus needs to include cultural, psychological and social perspectives.

Insights from different social disciplines are necessary, for example, to develop pragmatic and critical competence in dealing with multiple and interrelated ways of making meaning. Identifying 'gate-keeping' encounters or 'critical communicative sites' would have high priority for those emphasising the political dimensions of language. As well as assisting individuals to deal with linguistic aspects of discrimination in these interactions, they would see a legitimate role in pointing out the institutional dimensions and helping to shape more equitable discursive practices.

Each of the linguistic traditions briefly described offers significant contributions and insights to workplace education. However, as the British Industrial Language Training experience indicates, on its own, each has inherent limitations because of the particular perspective foregrounded: 'There is no single theoretical model which will encompass the very many ways in which language reflects, reinforces and structures social relationships.' (Roberts *et al.* 1992: 368).

Language, literacy and their relationship to achieving goals

As well as coming to terms with the different theoretical constructs for language and literacy, a framework for workplace education needs to examine the importance of these factors in individuals' working lives. Almost by definition, language and literacy educators place a high value on competence in these areas, but to what extent does this competence affect individuals' ability to achieve their personal and vocational goals?

Given the different theoretical understandings of the nature of language and literacy, it is not surprising that there is little agreement – both in research and practice – on a number of fundamental issues: what exactly constitutes communicative competence? How can it be measured? How much of it is necessary for individuals to perform satisfactorily in the workplace?[3] The criteria used, and their relative importance, can vary greatly depending on the people involved, contexts and purposes of the enquiry.

Accuracy, for example, may be a primary and general consideration for a classroom context, but not so important or restricted in its requirement in the workplace. Many immigrant workers have acquired basic interactional skills and learnt to use approximate grammar, vocabulary and pronunciation, and are therefore likely to be assessed by educators as having low language and literacy skills. They are, however, as Canale (1987) pointed out, 'spontaneous, fluent communicators who make full use of contextual clues and communicative strategies'. Similarly, in commenting on the experience of the Industrial Language Training Centre in Britain, Roberts *et al.* (1992: 38) note that

> Learners can sometimes develop a sophisticated communicative
> competence in inter-ethnic communication even when their grammatical
> competence is quite limited. Cultural assumptions enter into language

interactions and may affect their outcome. Interpersonal skills can be more significant than the accuracy with which meaning is conveyed at any point in a conversation.

Writers such as McNamara (1990) and Brindley (1994), for example, note significant discrepancies between the different criteria used by workplace personnel, communication theorists, and linguists in determining communicative competence. Workplace personnel typically tend to be outcome-focused – did the individual successfully complete the task or not? Communication theorists tend to emphasise criteria such as empathy, behavioural flexibility and interaction management and linguists, on the other hand, focus on aspects such as the staging of discourse, grammatical and linguistic accuracy.

A recent Australian study, for example, looked at different parties' perspectives on language proficiency in the workplace and found little agreement as to workers' perceived language strengths and difficulties:

> English as a second language teachers, workplace supervisors and learners did not share the same concepts, understanding and expectations of the language abilities of non-English speaking workers in the workplace. (Manidis, 1993: vii)

Attempts to draw direct links between individuals' general linguistic or literacy competence and their ability to perform in the workplace have been therefore highly problematic. There has been much controversy in recent years, for example, over the use of standardised tests or explicit language and literacy competencies as part of industry competency standards, or their alignment with occupational classification levels. These debates have extended beyond educational and academic forums to the industrial and legal arenas.[4]

Quite apart from problems over what these generalised assessment tools are aiming to measure and how biased they might be, they have had little success in predicting how individuals are likely to perform in real communicative tasks. Sticht (1980), for example, reports that studies of the most widely used standardised basic skills test in the United States, the *Armed Forces Qualifications Test*, have demonstrated poor predictive validity. Similarly, Mikulecky and Ehlinger (1987) also point out the low correlation between performance on traditional standardised literacy tests and the ability to deal effectively with the literacy demands of work. Even in academic contexts, where language and literacy requirements are more demanding than those of the workplace, researchers have found that:

Language level at the beginning of a period of study is not a good predictor of final success. Language plays a role but not a dominant role in academic success once the minimum threshold of adequate proficiency has been reached. Thereafter it is individual, non-linguistic characteristics both cognitive and affective that determine success. (Criper and Davies in McNamara, 1989)

Part of the difficulty is that communicative competence is more than just the acquisition of a discrete body of knowledge. It is basically a set of interactional skills, dependent on the particular context, and the different parties' ability and willingness to negotiate meaning. Its effectiveness can therefore be significantly improved if the parties involved are prepared to modify their communication, or use compensatory strategies (Ellis 1990, Roberts *et al.* 1992).

Different parties may not therefore perceive that a problem exists, let alone agree on its scope, whose problem it is or what should be done about it. A national study of literacy needs in the Australian Forest Industry, for example, reported some employers perceiving no connection between low literacy skills, inefficiency and loss of money. Employers valued skills such as manual dexterity and, where necessary, systems were developed to get around the fact that some people couldn't keep written records (Serle, 1994: 123–4).

Despite low general proficiency in spoken or written English, workers have often shown themselves able to successfully acquire the specialist registers of their technical field, or 'shopfloor language'. In summarising extensive research findings into literacy and basic skills in the American workplace, Mikulecky (1984: 254) for example concludes that 'Workers tend to read job material more proficiently than they do general material'. Similarly, Sticht, Armstrong, Hickey and Caylors' study of American military personnel (1987) found that adults in work-related literacy programmes made twice the gain in job-related reading than they did in general reading.

While limited proficiency in English may significantly restrict workers' ability to access formal training opportunities, they have often used compensatory strategies, such as relying on bilingual workmates, or taken 'short-cuts' in acquiring the necessary skills. In observations of employees in the metals industry, strategies such as the ones used by Anna were typical:[5] As part of her job, Anna had to accurately measure and record the 'aperture', 'chuckfit' and 'countersink' of products prior to packing. She had been doing the job quite satisfactorily for over five years but was unable to correctly pronounce the terms or give a correct technical definition. She followed the numerical ordering of the measurement checks provided on the form (1. aperture, 2. chuckfit, etc.) rather than referring to the terms and could explain in understandable, but broken, English the consequences of a defect on the final product. These strategies may be less than ideal, but were nevertheless considered effective by her and other workplace personnel in achieving the required work outcomes.

In more structured contexts, such as training programmes where much of the communication is through formal, print-based media, the English language and literacy demands of the training are often far more complex and abstract than the actual job demands. As a result, occupational competence becomes confused with competence in English and many employees who are already performing competently in the workplace find themselves unable to participate in training. Experiences such as the early implementation of the Vehicle Industry Certificate in Australian vehicle manufacturing plants are not unique:

> When nearly half the workforce were having problems with the training program that had been designed specifically for them, one has to question the program. This is especially so when it is apparent that employees who cope with complex work processes are being redefined as incompetent in the classroom. (Sefton, 1993: 41)

Yet a number of Australian literacy projects in the automotive and food industries have demonstrated that workers with limited proficiency in English can successfully achieve learning outcomes of vocational training programmes, provided that the content, methodologies and training are appropriately pitched.[6] Similarly, in the USA, Hull (1993) cites a number of work-based projects where workers with low levels of language and literacy were able to successfully complete training programmes and perform vocational tests because of factors such as motivation, familiarity with the subject matter and appropriate learning methodologies.

While correlations do exist between low language and literacy skill levels and overall job-performance, it is evident then that the relationship is not a simple, causal one. Scribner and Cole's wide-ranging investigation of the impact of literacy on society, for example, came to the modest conclusion that 'literacy makes some difference to some skills in some contexts'.[7]

Language and literacy skills are increasingly important for participation in the new workplace, but greater skills in these areas alone are not likely to be the panacea for all the difficulties faced by restructuring or be the only factor limiting workers' access to the benefits of the new opportunities.

Large-scale surveys of language and literacy skills regularly reveal that the workforce of many developed economies is ill-prepared in terms of the foundational or basic skills required. These surveys may be useful in drawing attention to the need for funds to address skill development in these areas. However, they have a tendency to 'blame the victim' in overemphasising the role of literacy at the expense of other systemic factors. As indicated in Chapter one, concerns with literacy are more commonly being addressed in the labour market by a growth industry in screening tests. In reviewing the US experience in workplace literacy, Hull, for example, points out:

> Popular discourse of workplace literacy tends to underestimate and devalue human potential and to mis-characterise literacy as a curative for problems that literacy alone cannot solve. Such tendencies obscure other social and economic problems and provide a questionable rationale and *modus operandi* for current efforts to make the US work force literate. They also provide a smokescreen, covering up key societal problems by drawing our attention to other issues that, while important, are only symptomatic of larger ills. (1993: 28)

There is substantial evidence pointing to the importance of factors other than just the English language in determining individuals' success both in formal learning situations and workplace communicative tasks. Many problems can be attributed to 'language or literacy skill deficiencies' when they may often have more to do with inappropriate methodologies, unrealistic requirements or discoursal practices that reinforce institutional power.

In terms of enabling employees to participate more effectively in the new workplace, communicative competence is necessary, but it is not the only factor, and often not even the main one. A complex set of other considerations influence work-related outcomes and organisational change. These include work practices, power relationships and management styles, learning opportunities, reward systems, the appropriateness of vocational training programmes, and a range of sociocultural factors such as gender, ethnicity and class. In the words of two workplace managers involved in workplace literacy programmes:[8]

> Sure, English is necessary, but it is not sufficient. There are a lot of other factors involved in bringing about change that are just as important: leadership, trust, commitment, support, respect. (Plant manager)

> English language and literacy is an important issue, it is not the only issue. We should be looking at a range of strategies to facilitate access to formal training, like making sure that structures and training delivery modes are accessible. (Training manager)

The tenuous link between the skill an individual has and their ability to perform successfully is not just limited to competence in language and literacy. In an extensive survey of Australian industry's experience with skills development, the researcher noted that

> Successful performance in the workplace demands more than just skill or competence. In the emphasis of the current debate on skill acquisition and assessment, factors such as responsibility, commitment and performance have tended to be overlooked. (NBEET, 1991: 46)

Studies of management skills have also highlighted the weaknesses in the skills of Australian managers in modelling and facilitating new ways of working.[9] Similarly, the lack of progress in vocational skills development has been identified as partly due to the difficulties of training providers to respond to the needs of industry and their new target groups.[10] Labelling problems as communication difficulties or skill deficiencies when often they may really be about power or inefficient management shifts the blame onto those already marginalised and vulnerable.

So, what is the role of language and literacy educators, if issues of language are so intertwined with wider skill development needs, motivational and institutional issues of power? As adult educators, what else should we be concerned with, besides language, literacy, and cross-cultural issues if we aim to enable our prospective learners to achieve their goals? Given the almost inevitably limited time and resources, what can be realistically achieved? What communicative sites should educators concentrate on? Whose communicative competence should they focus on? How can educators contribute to developing more responsive and equitable communication and training practices?

Some of the answers to these questions will be influenced by practitioners' views of their own role as educators, and the role that learning plays in a primarily non-educational context, where not only language, but learning is often perceived as peripheral to core business.

VIEWS OF ADULT EDUCATION, TRAINING AND LEARNING

The debates in the language and literacy fields have both influenced and reflected developments in adult education, with a number of different traditions of adult education, or androgogy, emerging. These give varying emphasis to the personal or social contexts of education and the roles of teacher and learner in these contexts. Common core features of such traditions include the recognition, for example, that adults are often voluntary participants in the learning process, and that perceived relevance is therefore crucial to their participation: learning needs to be seen by them to be directly related to their immediate priorities to cope with real-life tasks rather than some possible future application. It is also generally recognised that adult learners bring a wealth of life experience to the learning situation and that they attach more meaning to learning gained from experience than passive, theoretical learning.

In the following section we look briefly at some of the main traditions, and their relevance for language and literacy, and wider education activities in the workplace.

Different traditions of adult education

Behaviourist models of learning, such as those supported by Mager (1975), Tyler (1960) and Davies (1976) have influenced much vocational, 'outcome-focused' education and training. This approach values careful analysis of the knowledge and skills required to perform the required task, the breaking down of an entity into its constituent parts, as well as deliberate step-by-step planning, organisation and evaluation procedures. Programmes are structured to allow for stated learning objectives to be achieved as efficiently as possible, with teachers or trainers managing the learning process, and avoiding distractions or variations from the predetermined course. Being highly structured, such models can offer consistent, predictable learning processes and outcomes. They also reflect a highly efficient mode of traditional teaching methodology, where the teacher is the expert holder and transmitter of that knowledge.

For vocational or workplace contexts, the benefits of consistent outcomes and efficient processes offer many advantages, and a systematic, cost-effective way of addressing 'skill gaps' – often through 'off the shelf' professionally produced training modules. Being highly structured and content-focused, such approaches tend to be less demanding in terms of process-oriented teaching skills. With 'explain–demonstrate–imitate' techniques forming the basic repertoire of trainer skills required, workplace trainers can be easily drawn from different technical areas as skill gaps emerge.

Behaviourist approaches to workplace education have been strongly criticised for being narrow and reductionist.[11] Because of the emphasis on measurable, predetermined objectives, learning is focused on areas

which can be divided into self-contained, observable tasks rather than
the development of insightful capacities or reflective abilities. In terms
of facilitating more flexible work practices such as cross-skilling – where
employees are able to do a number of tasks of similar levels of complexity –, such approaches may be appropriate. They are not likely though
to develop the contextual understanding and adaptability required by
new forms of work organisation.

The other main criticism relates to 'mug and jug' approaches to teaching and learning, which often assume that learners are empty vessels
waiting to be filled and fail to actively engage the learner in the process.
As Brookfield, for example, points out:

> The most fundamental flaw with the predetermined objectives approach, is
> its tendency to equate one form of adult learning – instrumental learning
> (how to perform technical or psycho-motor operations effectively) with
> the sum total of adult learning. It neglects completely the domain of the
> most significant personal learning – the kind that results from reflecting
> on experiences and from trying to make sense of one's life by exploring
> the meanings others have assigned to similar experiences. (1986: 213)

Critics of narrow approaches to education often make a clear distinction between training and learning. Training is the transmission of
discrete skills for a specific purpose – as Ford (1991) asserts, dogs are
trained, people learn. Marsick and Watson for example, point out that
training and education are delivery systems, while learning, and learning-
centred approaches are much broader in scope:

> Learning is more broadly defined as the way in which individuals or
> groups acquire, interpret, reorganize, change or assimilate a related cluster
> of information, skills and feelings. It is also primary to the way in which
> people construct meaning in their personal and shared organizational lives.
> (1991: 4)

More holistic views of learning such as those advocated by Brookfield (1986) suggest that individual components cannot be meaningfully considered or taught in isolation from one another. The parts only
make sense in relation to one another. Such models are based on humanistic psychology and psychotherapy and tend to put the learner rather
than the training or performance objective at the centre of the learning.
These models are typified by a respect for participants in the teaching-
learning transaction, a commitment to collaborative modes of programme development, and an acknowledgment of the educational value
of life experiences.

Self-directed learning, as advocated by Knowles (1978), for example, stresses individual learner goals as central to the learning process. Rather than clearly analysed, predetermined learning objectives, Knowles stresses the importance of collaborative curriculum to the success of the learning. He asserts that people tend to feel committed to a decision or activity in direct proportion to their participation in influence on its planning and decision making. For educators such as Knowles and Tough (1971), the teacher is seen as a resource or facilitator whose role is to assist and support learners to achieve their self-defined tasks in a climate of mutual respect, trust, collaboration and supportiveness.

One of the significant limitations of this model, however, is its assumption that learners are able to independently identify and manage their own learning needs. With the many changes at work, how can adult employee/learners know what they don't know, and what they need to know? Given prevailing power relationships, to what extent can they 'negotiate' their learning? With busy working and private lives – and more often than not, anxieties about work and learning – how realistic is it to expect them to manage their own learning?

Theorists from learner-centred and humanistic models of adult education, such as Rogers (1951), for example, recognise that it is difficult for learners to acknowledge and express their needs, especially if their early experiences of learning have been negative. They emphasise the need to focus on internal barriers to learning that individuals may have, such as anxiety or fear of failure. For learners who are new to the learning situation, building confidence and a belief in their own potential is seen as a necessary first step. As well as the 'what' of learning, attention is needed to the 'how' so that learners are better able to reflect, organise and manage their learning independently and in the long term.

Similarly, Brookfield points out that programmes that are based on learners' characteristics and engage learners in a dialogue about content, aims, and methods are likely to be more effective than those where organisational and institutional needs are dominant. The 'why' and 'what for' of learning also need to be explicit if learners are to be actively involved:

> Prior to teaching new skills to adults, one must encourage them to become familiar with the new contexts in which they are to operate. Once employees reinterpret their function and redefine the context within which they are working, then the identification of the skills necessary to function in that context will follow. (1986: 248)

Real-life experience is more than just a source of data, it is the context for applying and reflecting on learning. In Kolb's (1984) experiential learning model, the learning cycle moves from experiencing to observing to conceptualizing to experimenting and back to experiencing, thus forming a dialectical interaction between action and reflection.

The evolving, dynamic nature of learning changes the role of the teacher from transmitter to 'facilitator' whose aim is to foster in learners a spirit of critical reflection and self-direction. According to Brookfield, 'praxis' is at the heart of effective facilitation:

> Facilitators and learners are engaged in a cooperative enterprise . . . this collaboration is seen in the diagnosis of needs, in the setting of objectives, in curriculum development, in methodological aspects, and in generating evaluative criteria. This collaboration is also constant so that the group process involves a continual renegotiation of activities and priorities in which competing claims are explored, discussed and negotiated. (1986: 10)

Educators such as Boud and Griffin (1987) see facilitators' roles as going beyond the conventional teaching role into the wide and varied contexts in which adult learning takes place. The flexibility of facilitators and their ability to draw on contextual factors are key elements in enabling successful learning interactions. Brookfield, for example, argues that the 'improvisational ability' of educators is critical to successful learning:

> Programmers should recognise that contextual distortion of neatly planned programs is likely to be a recurring feature of their professional practice. Without a realisation that context is crucial in affecting the possibilities and forms of practice, practitioners are likely to experience something close to despair each time a carefully planned program has to be altered because of some unforeseen eventuality. . . Altering program forms, methods, or content to take into account contextually specific features is not equivalent to an unprofessional deviation from plans for which practitioners should feel guilty. Instead, they should learn to value their capacity to make programs more meaningful and relevant in terms of contextually specific features. Hence improvisational ability should be recognised as crucial to successful practice. (1986: 25)

Inevitably though, in a work context, such 'customisation' and attention to process adds to the time involved in developing training programmes, and ultimate cost. It also places considerable demands on the skills and flexibility of the facilitator involved. Almost by definition, if continual negotiation and improvisational ability are crucial to successful practice, the outcomes of learning become less consistent. Under a centralised vocational education and training system, this flexibility can present real tensions. If predetermined competency-based courses provide the gateway to pay increases and job advancements, can workplaces and learners afford to trade relevance for accreditation? With the increasing focus on credentialism and cost-effectiveness, can educators afford to be so client-centred and negotiable? To what extent can these wider social, political and economic considerations be accommodated in a negotiated learner-centred approach?

Other models of adult education focus specifically on the wider context within which learning takes place, and issues of power. Critical pedagogy and social action models give a dominant role to the socio-political context and nature of learning rather than individual, psychological factors. Freire (1972), whose literacy work has been greatly influential, argues that learning is never value free, it must either work towards supporting the status quo or undermining it and replacing it with more equitable structures and practices. Learning therefore is not solely an individual intellectual process – it should lead to social and political change to transform society.

The teacher's role is primarily one of raising learners' consciousness and perspectives of their situations through enquiry-based, 'problem-posing' learning which promotes critical thinking, dialogue and reflection. Such learning can then empower individuals and lead to actions which improve their social and political position in society. More than a neutral facilitator, the workplace educator is an active social change agent, who aims for change at individual and organisational level.

In the context of workplace education, there is a great deal of rhetoric about employee participation and empowerment. However, research shows less evidence of significant power-sharing and devolution.[12] Beyond producing more with less and taking more responsibility for their work, how empowered a workforce is desirable from a management perspective? How likely are educators to be 'active social agents' on behalf of the 'oppressed' in a competitive, casualised, employer-driven education market? To what extent can or should educators intervene in workplaces' politically charged industrial relations?

Work and organisational learning

Despite their different perspectives, models of adult education give central place to work as a focus and context for learning. They recognise work as a primary activity for most adults, a significant element in their identity, and a determiner of self-esteem and social power.

With the greater convergence of learning and working, learning in the context of the workplace is increasingly seen as much more than acquiring a set of technical skills. Learning which occurs in a training room is only a small part, with informal and incidental learning playing a crucial role in applying and informing the need for new knowledge and skills. Rather than just individual skill development, learning is part of system-wide processes of change. For a significant number of enterprises, it is becoming evident that competitive effectiveness requires companies to invest in the development of their capacity to learn and translate this learning into action, not only as individuals, but in groups and as a whole organisation.

As a result of these developments, there is greater interest in organisational learning from a number of areas. Field and Ford (1995: 10), for example, point out that the literature on organisational learning encompasses a range of different disciplines, such as social psychology, sociology, information theory, adult learning, management theory, anthropology and employee relations.

The characteristics of learning organisations reflect many of those that apply to adult learners, such as critical thinking and reflection, self-directed learning and learning from experience. Contextual factors such as security, role models, reward systems and supportive networks are considered by most schools of thought as crucial in facilitating learning.[13] As with schools of language and education, approaches to organisational learning differ on the importance they place on personal, social or systemic factors. So that while some advocate the use of unifying inspirational visions and missions, others stress a sociotechnical, re-engineering approach to all aspects of work.

In 1991, for example, Peddler, Bourgoyne and Boydell defined the learning company as 'an organisation that facilitates the learning of all its members and continuously transforms itself'. More recently, Field and Ford have defined a learning organisation as having 'a well-developed capacity of double-loop learning, where there is ongoing attention to learning how to learn, and where key aspects of organisational functioning support learning. These key aspects relate to employee relations, work organisation, skill formation and technology/information systems' (1995: 11). At the centre of their model, they place organisational vision and concepts, and the managers whose leadership role is pivotal in the translation of these ideals to reality.

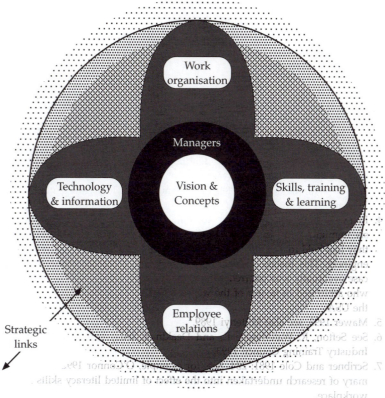

Figure 3.1: The organisational propeller: aspects of organisational functioning that affect learning

Source: Field and Ford (1995: 23)

The educators' role in this process is far from clear-cut. In facilitating learning at an individual, group and organisational level, the focus is on process as much as, if not more than, on content, and on making a real difference to daily work practices. The management and facilitation of change is a complex process, full of tensions and contradictions, as individuals learn new ways (and unlearn old ways) of doing and relating, as they challenge established norms and experiment with new ones. For educators who are external to the workplace, this poses questions as to who their learners are, and what the appropriate curriculum or methodologies might be. To what extent can critical reflection be encouraged when the nature and direction of change itself is zealously and unquestionably advocated? In using the learning potential of the workplace to improve communication, training and management practices, where is the line between teacher, manager and social change agent?

NOTES

1. See, for example, Candlin, Maley and Sutch 1995 for a study of workplace disourse relating to the negotiation of enterprise agreements.
2. Thomas 1983, for example, has identified these in terms of sociopragmatic and sociolinguistic failures.
3. See, for example, Nunan 1988, Criper and Davies 1988, McNamara 1989, Mawer, 1991, Hull 1993.
4. In a well-publicised instance in Australia, (Lewis, S.M.H. 30.6.92 and 4.7.92) six immigrant sewage plant workers were forcibly redeployed from jobs they had held for up to 15 years, after failing a literacy test designed by an engineer. This instance resulted in widespread industrial action and the case eventually was referred to the State Industrial Relations Commission who arbitrated in favour of the workers. Hull, (1993) cites similar cases in the USA.
5. Mawer 1993, see also Miltenyi 1989.
6. See Sefton, R. Waterhouse P., and Deakin R. (eds) 1994; National Food Industry Training Council 1993.
7. Scribner and Cole 1981: 234. See, for example, O'Connor 1992 for a summary of research undertaken into the effect of limited literacy skills in the workplace.
8. Mawer and Field 1995: 33.
9. Karpin Task Force on Leadership and Management Skills.
10. See, for example, Centre for Educational Research and Innovation. Adult Illiteracy and Economic Performance 1992 Organisation for Economic Co-operation and Development, France, National Board of Employment, Education and Training. 1991, Allen Consulting Group 1994, Lundberg 1994.
11. See, for example, Marsick 1988, Brookfield 1986.
12. For example, comprehensive studies of Australian managers show that although more managers are using the rhetoric of human resource management, there is very little consultative decision making on key issues (Callus 1993).
13. Brookfield 1989, Mezirow 1990, Boud, 1987, Kolb 1988.

FOUR

Exploring the scope and role of workplace education

Given the dramatic changes to both education and work, and the general position of disadvantage held by employees of different cultural background or limited competence in English, what is the role and scope of language and literacy educators in the workplace? What do they have to offer? Who to?

Just like our counterparts in industry we are also needing to critically reassess our aims and approaches and negotiate new ways of thinking and working. Increasingly, these negotiations are not only with traditional stakeholders such as educational institutions and government agencies, but also with workplace management, unions, individual employees and vocational educators and trainers. Inevitably, such negotiations are also influenced by the priorities set by government policies and funding sources.

In this chapter, we propose a multifaceted approach which aims to share the responsibility for effective communication among the whole context of the workplace, and reduce barriers to employees' participating and accessing skill development opportunities. It also aims to develop workplace practices that reflect the diverse characteristics and interests of its members.

POTENTIAL FOR COMMON GROUND

The last two chapters have outlined some of the main differences in perspectives often held by and within the different parties involved in workplace education. As well as different views on the place and value of communicative competence, there are significant differences in the priorities given to addressing skill development needs in this area. While particular values and issues, for example, are central concerns to some parties, they are only of peripheral interest to others.

Despite these marked differences, it is perhaps surprising to note the considerable common ground that is shared. At the levels of 'vision' and official rhetoric, for example, there are many mutual concerns and aspirations for both educators and workplace personnel to build on. Industry, for example, is increasingly stressing the need for skills, life-long learning and regarding the skills of their employees as being their most valuable asset. Participative work practices and learning organisation principles aim to involve workers in shaping their environment and taking pride in as well as responsibility for what they do. In terms of skill development, there is an acknowledgement of the need for thinking team members rather than human units of production, and on-going learning that goes beyond the digestion of pre-packaged training programmes. Successful management is seen more in terms of delegating, supporting and facilitating than directing. The globalisation of the marketplace, and the trend towards niche markets mean that workforce diversity is becoming valued as a competitive leading edge rather than a liability.

At the educational level, notions of empowerment and critical thinking have always been integral to language and literacy educators. So have adult learning principles, learner-centred approaches to curriculum, and the valuing of cultural diversity. The new and changing contexts of work, technologies and communication media require not only a broader repertoire of communication skills, but also the ability to deal with ambiguity and complexity. With the converging of notions of working and learning, reflection and critical thinking have become vital, every-day aspects of work.

At government levels, there is an abundance of policy statements recognising the increasingly diverse nature of the workforce and customer base. These policies usually express commitment to access and equity, to increasing the opportunities of disadvantaged groups and to developing responsive curriculum which addresses broad rather than narrow notions of competence. The importance of language, literacy and numeracy competence to the workplace and in vocational education and training is increasingly recognised in such statements.

These policies are usually supported by limited government funding to establish workplace language and literacy programmes. In the USA, for example, the National Workplace Literacy Program is designed to 'improve the productivity of the workforce through the improvement of literacy skills needed in the workplace'.

In Britain, funding for workplace projects is available through the government's Basic Skills Agency (formerly the Adult Literacy and Basic

Skills Unit). Similarly, in Australia, the main funding source for work-place education is the federal government's Workplace English Language and Literacy Program (WELL). In a number of countries, workplace education projects are also financed by employers – such as the Ford Employee Development Assistance Program in Britain, or employee groups – such as the Ontario Federation of Labour's BEST tutoring program.

Government subsidies are typically available for seeding purposes only, that is to assist the establishment of a programme, with the expectation that employers will continue programmes once their value has been proven. Experience in a number of countries indicates that these expectations are often not realised. Corrigan and Kelly (1993), in commenting on British workplace education experience point out:

> Projects which may have achieved good outcomes during the external funding period can often flounder or disappear completely when the funding ends. The interest of employers may evaporate into thin air once the basic skills training has to be paid for at the commercial rate.[1]

Similarly, in commenting on US workplace programmes, Zacharakis-Jutz and Dirkx (1993)[2] observe that 'it is not at all clear what happens when the money runs out. Corporate commitment appears anemic at best.' The same lack of clarity is reflected in Australia, where a recent survey of WELL programmes indicated that only one-fifth of companies would continue in the absence of government funding, and even those would be conducted at a reduced rate.[3]

TOWARDS AN INTEGRATED, MULTI-FACETED APPROACH

How then can educators use this commonality of purpose and limited resources strategically to maximum effect? Given the cultural and lin-guistic diversity of the workforce, and the dramatically increased work communication demands, a systemic approach is needed, rather than a remedial, Band-Aid solution. Yet with unreliable, short-term funding arrangements, a tension clearly exists between immediately reaching those with the greatest need and working towards changes in workplace systems, attitudes and practices for the long-term benefit of all employees.

How can educators work to develop individuals' communicative competence and at the same time try to equitably share the responsibil-ity for effective communication across the whole workplace? With our understanding of language and culture in reflecting and shaping social structures, how can we actively contribute to shaping more inclusive work practices? In what ways can we help workplaces translate the heart-warming intentions of mission statements into practical, tangible communicative, training and management practices?

Focusing on the development of individual workers' oral and written English alone will clearly be neither sufficient nor effective. The 'client' for workplace language and literacy programmes clearly needs to be both the individual worker/learner and the enterprise employing them. To a large extent, the workplace itself becomes the curriculum, with its particular explicit and implicit dynamics, purposes and methodologies. More than just a source of rich data for contextualising language learning, the communicative context of the workplace shapes what needs to be learnt. In turn, this communicative context and its discoursal practices can be collaboratively evaluated and modified to serve its users more effectively.

In critical linguistic terms, such an approach means focusing on 'critical sites' and points of intervention where those at a linguistic disadvantage suffer because of the inequalities of the communicative resources at their disposal. As educators, we can use our knowledge about language to enable individual workers access to these discourses of power, while avoiding

> a deficit model which focuses all responsibility of language and literacy improvement on the trainee/worker [and aims instead to] distribute the responsibility among the whole communicative context of the workplace. (Candlin, 1992: 112)

This approach is not about subsuming our differences, but rather acknowledging and valuing them while working collaboratively to negotiate common goals and priorities. It involves clearly articulating our priorities and our ethical and professional standards, rather than being passively subservient to whoever happens to be paying for the services provided. By extending and challenging narrow views of competence, and focusing on the person rather than just the task in question, educators can assist workplaces to value and use the rich diversity of skills and experiences of their employees, rather than seeing them as 'have nots'. As educators from the New London Group point out,

> In responding to the radical changes in working life that are currently underway, we need to tread a careful path in which students have the opportunity to develop skills for access to new forms of work through learning the new language of work. But at the same time, as teachers, our

role is not simply to be technocrats. Our job is not to produce docile, compliant workers. Students need to develop the skills to speak up, to negotiate, and to be able to engage critically with the conditions of their working lives. . . .

Rather ironically perhaps, democratic pluralism is possible in workplaces for the toughest of business reasons, and economic efficiency may be an ally of social justice, though not always a staunch or reliable one. (Cope and Kalantzis, 1995: 26)

Such a multidisciplinary approach to our work inevitably also involves give and take, where there is a willingness to learn as much as to teach. It can mean giving up some of the autonomy and intimacy of the language and literacy classroom and going beyond familiar knowledge and role boundaries. More often than not, the resulting changes in workplace attitudes and practices will not be directly attributable to any one particular person, because of the different parties' involvement and contributions.

In essence, an integrated, multifaceted approach aims to provide relevant learning arrangements for individual employees as well as support for workplaces in developing inclusive, user-friendly communication, training and management policies and practices. We will briefly look at what this might mean in tangible terms.

Providing learning arrangements for individuals

The main offerings of workplace language and literacy educators up to recently have consisted of courses negotiated with learners to meet their perceived needs. These courses often incorporated workplace communicative tasks or texts but their main focus was developing learners' general language and literacy skills. The workplace environment may have served as a rich source of authentic texts, or a site for the analysis of discoursal practices and the contextualisation of course content. But it was typically regarded as a convenient venue for the same sort of activities that would be undertaken in an educational institution. The central priorities and concerns of the workplace remained peripheral to those of educators, and learning was defined as that which happened in the classroom, with the teacher directing a range of suitable activities.

While focusing on the improvement of learners' oral and written communication skills, such courses were not usually directly linked to formal education and training qualifications. Their needs-based, customised focus meant that course outcomes may have been highly valued by the individuals concerned, but had limited recognised currency in the wider education and training context. Up until recently, there was little in the way of formal credentials for employees at lower classification levels, and no linkages between those credentials and pay rates.

This has now changed. Learning is becoming recognised as a legitimate part of work for a number of reasons: multiskilling, increased responsibilities, coming to terms with changing technologies and organisational directions. The formalisation of work-related skills is encouraged by an increased focus on credentials and the linking of skills to remuneration rates. At the same time, in an efficiency, productivity-driven workplace, time away from work is a precious, ill-afforded commodity.

To have a place in the new vocational agenda, and provide a vehicle for genuine access for employees, viable work-related education will increasingly need to:

- show direct, immediate relevance between course objectives and workplace outcomes;
- be closely aligned with organisational goals and strategies at the local enterprise level;
- aim to develop the new, 'enabling' workplace competencies such as problem solving and teamwork;
- be accredited as part of an employee's industry-based qualifications and provide for articulation to further training.

The use of training as a vehicle to effect changes in organisational culture has implications for both the modes and content of training programmes. Grouping learners into homogeneous skill levels is, for example, usually desirable from an educational perspective, but this may be outweighed by other considerations such as the benefits of closer teamwork resulting from a mixed ability work-team or a 'vertical' slice of the organisation undertaking training.

For a wide range of reasons, traditional classroom-based teaching is becoming less appropriate or feasible at work. Some of these reasons are pragmatic ones to do with the cost and practicalities of releasing employees from their normal duties to attend training. Others are to do with employees' lack of familiarity with abstract, theoretical learning and preference for more practical, 'hands on' modes. Action-learning or project-based methodologies, for example, where learners work on a current problem, are considered effective because they allow learners to tackle relevant workplace issues, reflect on their learning as well as develop a range of enabling skills such as teamwork or presentation skills.

Workplaces seeking to develop a 'learning culture', or become a 'learning organisation' are adopting a less formalised approach to skill development, and integrating learning more closely with everyday activities and organisational objectives. Rather than planning a lock-step series of training courses, skill development in such workplaces occurs through a wide range of activities – only some of which may take place in a training room or with a teacher. Some of these include the use of self-paced or computer-based materials, peer-tutoring, on-line support and distance learning modes. Others involve capitalising on 'shut-downs', or 'down-time' to develop new skills, or giving employees the responsibility for developing or reviewing work procedures and training manuals.

With the changes in the worlds of work and education in recent years, it is clear that while the aim of the 'teaching programme' may remain the same, its form and content will need to change if it is to remain meaningful and relevant. Modular and flexible formats are needed that allow for a wide range of needs, abilities and learning modes. The integration of language, literacy and cultural issues into vocational training, for example, is an effective way of ensuring that employees develop competence in these areas as they need them, in a way that does not marginalise or penalise them.

As well as vocational content, employees will also need to develop a broad repertoire of communication skills to deal with changing contexts, and actively participate in shaping their work environment. Useful methodologies then will be those that enable them to reflect and use their skills and experiences in dealing with the new ambiguities and complexities of work.

Within the constraints of time and resources available to workplace educators, the focus of learning needs to be on immediate, visible learning outcomes, as well as maximising the impact of learning in terms of longer-term results. Some of those include developing individuals' confidence, their ability to cope with the unexpected, and transfer skills to wider work and training contexts. It can be as simple as making explicit some of the gains that employees make from the development of their communicative repertoires in ways that make sense in terms of workplace priorities and directions: the 'bottom line' impact of more effective teamwork, reduction in communication breakdowns and greater flexibility.

The accreditation of such integrated provision presents real tensions to educators – how to account for such learning in the context of accredited training systems in ways that do not disadvantage either educator or learner? The moves to accredit language and literacy courses, for example, may be beneficial for language and literacy practitioners, however, for learners and their workplaces, vocational outcomes and credentials are usually much more meaningful. Increasingly, workplace education providers are including vocational qualifications through an integrated pathway as part of their offerings.

Supporting the development of inclusive workplace practices

Experience in workplace education in countries such as the United Kingdom, the USA and Australia indicates that effective programmes involve much more than just relevant courses for individuals in need of language or literacy development. In reporting on British experience with 'industrial language training' for example, Roberts *et al.* concluded that:

> To be effective, the employer must accept the need for parallel training for key interlocutors such as supervisors, personnel and training officers, trade union officials and fellow workers. (1992: 20)

In the USA, educators such as Hull (1993) have stressed the need to look critically at the roles of literacy within work and ask:

> How much after all, depends on literacy itself? What else must we be concerned with, besides literacy, if we want to improve the conditions and products of work? (1993: 44)

Rather than just focusing on those with 'low language or literacy levels' – as identified by some general proficiency scale of dubious predictive validity –, a holistic, integrated approach is likely to involve an educational, support role with key people such as workplace managers, team leaders and trainers. It may, for example, involve helping to develop relevant and accessible vocational curriculum, facilitating effective teamwork, influencing assessment systems and having input into the development of standards or training plans.

If we accept that communication is a dynamic, interactive process, then it follows that the effectiveness of this process is greatly enhanced by increased awareness and strategies from all parties involved. In the new workplace of the 1990s, we are repeatedly reminded that the competencies needed to be effective include communicating, working in groups, negotiating and collaborating within the workplace and outside it. Management skills are increasingly consensual, team-oriented and dependent on supportive, mentoring skills. The blurring of hierarchical boundaries, greater use of communication technologies and focus on export markets have all meant that not only are we needing to interact more, but we are doing so increasingly with people of widely different sociocultural backgrounds, worldviews and communication styles.[4] In the multilingual and multicultural global workplace, the ability to adapt and successfully negotiate through these differences has become crucial.

As a number of workplace research studies have shown, communication difficulties are often due to varying cultural values, expectations and interactional patterns.[5] With the increasing emphasis on participatory work practices, effective intercultural communication is needed not only by trainers and managers, but also for effective teamwork on the shop floor and consultative processes such as training committees and consultative committees. Cultural values such as deference, the need to preserve harmony and show respect to older people and those in positions of authority, for example, need to be taken into account if appropriate strategies are to be developed to encourage full worker participation in a culturally diverse context. Similarly, predominantly Anglo-Celtic management could greatly benefit from becoming aware of the traditional collectivist, group-focused values shared by many of their workers, which, ironically, many team-based management strategies are endeavouring to develop. With the drive for niche marketing and exceeding customer expectations, workplaces are also realising the value of their employees' resources in reflecting the demographics of the markets they are seeking to capture.

At a more systemic level, to what extent should a diverse workplace accommodate non-native varieties of English? Should they, for example, adapt their training and assessment procedures to allow for those not so comfortable with print? Or should they devise different ways to consult and obtain employee input? To what extent can they use the cultural and linguistic resources of their employees to advantage when marketing their products and services to diverse local and overseas markets?

Collaborative development of industry standards may be a way of ensuring the results reflect more than a task skills, narrow, individualist monocultural view of competence, and are recognisable to those whose work they describe. Similarly, educators' input into the development of vocational curriculum can enhance their user-friendliness and consistency with the communicative requirements of the job. Helping to improve the appropriateness of training and assessment procedures and developing the skills of workplace trainers and assessors can greatly enhance the quality of learning for employees as well as the validity and fairness of assessment outcomes.

These roles are both formal and informal ones. A number of workplace personnel have, for example, commented on the value of having an external person there who is 'in the workplace but not of it'. They have noted the value of someone who is able to relate to different hierarchical levels, constructively question the prevailing assumptions and bring a fresh perspective. By extending and challenging narrow views of competence, and focusing on the person rather than just the task in question, educators can often assist workplaces value and use the rich diversity of skills and experiences of their employees, rather than seeing them as 'have nots'. To a great extent then, the workplace itself becomes the curriculum and the focus for reflection and change, rather than just a convenient, static, venue.

Educators' effectiveness then is greatly dependent on the extent to which they can work collaboratively and strategically with a number of different others in a role that facilitates learning, rather than delivers teaching. Such a role often involves challenging existing power structures and practices in workplaces, at the same time as working towards attitudinal shifts from key personnel, and inevitable dealing with passive – if not active! – resistance from others.

This strategic, collaborative competence needs developing, partly because it has, until recently, not been recognised in teachers' role descriptions or training programmes. An employer representative with a great deal of experience of workplace literacy practitioners remarked recently on our lack of skills in this area:

> Education providers need to review how they go about doing business. They are the only ones in the training market place who say 'I sold it but they didn't buy'. A lot of them don't seem to know how to get employers on side and to start where managers are at in terms of addressing their concerns while at the same time giving them an educationally sound service or product. They need to understand that any vocational training that happens in the workplace needs to be in line with the business goals and the rest will come. Otherwise it will be marginalised and ultimately useless.

Beyond the workplace

With the scope of the changes being implemented, and often driven by intermediaries and committees at a great distance from the reality of the workplace, the reach of workplace education needs to be wider than any particular organisation.

Fairclough in analysing discourses of power warns that 'when linguists take language practices at face value, they help to sustain this ideological effect and legitimise them' (1989: 92). He demonstrates how common-sense assumptions serve to sustain unequal relations of power. One prevailing assumption, for example, is that language can for all practical purposes be regarded as an equally available resource across a community. The many documents promoting competency-based training and their implementation at the coal-face indicate they assume a highly educated, native speaker level of English as the norm required to access these new opportunities.

If English is to be a significant determining factor in workers' job retention and promotion prospects, then, in Candlin's words, workplace education providers 'are no longer merely in a linguistic world but in one which relates to questions of fundamental rights and equities' (1992: 114). Through our understanding of language and its uses to maintain and create social structures, workplace educators have an important contribution to make in pointing out and challenging exploitative social relations that are reinforced through language. This contribution also extends to assisting in the development of more equitable structures.

Apart from provisions under general access and equity policies such as anti-discrimination legislation, recent vocational training policies in a number of countries clearly require increased access and improved outcomes for groups of people who have missed out on training and employment opportunities in the past. In Britain, the National Council for Vocational Qualifications Framework, for example, requires awarding bodies to ensure that competence specifications or assignments are not in any way discriminatory. Similarly, in developing standards and assessing competence, principles of equity and fairness have been built into the Australian process:

> 'Standards are to be expressed in a manner which can be understood in the workplace and training environment . . .
> . . . they must not directly or indirectly limit access by individuals on the grounds of age, gender, social or educational background'. (NTB, 1991: 18, 10)

> 'Assessment practices and methods within CBT must be fair and equitable to all parties concerned. Assessment must not directly or indirectly limit access by individuals solely on the grounds of age, race, sex, disability, employment status, social or educational background' (VEETAC, 1992: 16).

If those involved in developing standards, curriculum and training have a responsibility to address these issues, then what are some of the ways that workplace educators can assist in this process? At what point can they intervene in a supposedly industry owned and driven process to ensure that existing patterns of discrimination are not perpetuated through, for example, unrealistic expectations of competence in literacy?

Quite aside from the access and equity issues involved, there is a strong cost effectiveness argument. Realistic, accessible, standards and training programmes are more likely to reflect the diversity of the workplace and the outcome focus of competency-based principles than the requirement to read and write in abstract, technical English to demonstrate one's competence on a routine task. If resources are limited, it makes sense to use them strategically to develop responsive, user-friendly policies and programmes, rather than hope to address problems after failed implementation.

Over the last few years, there have been increasing examples of joint, collaborative projects between educators, industry and government agencies at the developmental stages of different training-related projects. In Canada, for example, a workplace advisory service has recently been set up to provide information to workplaces, government and media as part of ABC Canada. It aims specifically to raise awareness of workplace literacy issues, assist with initial workplace needs assessment and funding applications.

In Australia, Industry Training Advisory Boards (ITABs) have been established to develop industry standards and coordinate national vocational curriculum development. Specific language and literacy projects associated with these advisory boards have been a highly effective way of building recognition of language, literacy and cultural issues into the standards, training policies and plans developed for the industries covered by these boards. They have also provided a useful way of making contact with employers and assisting them in initiating specific workplace-based projects.

Similarly, a small number of unions in different countries have undertaken such initiatives as a way of increasing their members' skills in effectively dealing with cultural diversity rather than viewing it as simply a 'welfare' issue. Some union-based projects, for example, have specifically targetted training for bilingual representatives to increase their levels of confidence and competence in participating more actively in the workplace as well as in the union.

In the rest of this book, we will explore different ways that educators can influence critical communicative sites in the workplace, and look at case study examples of practice at the coal-face. As well as challenging discursive practices, many of the educators involved have helped to reframe ways of learning and working that value diversity, power-sharing and collaboration.

Far from perfect prescriptive models, or sanitised promotional examples of 'best practice', the case studies described represent attempts at the art of the possible, given the typical constraints of available skills, resources, insights and support. They attempt to illustrate the various tensions, ambiguities and conflicting pressures that educators commonly face in engaging with the 'praxis' of individual and organisational learning.

NOTES

1. Corrigan, J. and Kelly, H. 1993 Basic Skills at work – What happens when the funding ends?ALBSU No. 50.
2. Zacharakis-Jutz, J. and Dirkx, J. 1993 Unresolved Issues in State and Federally Funded Workplace Literacy Programs: Toward a rational perspective and policy. *Adult Basic Education* Vol. 3, No. 2 Summer.
3. See Mawer and Field, 1995: 27–8, Baylis, 1995: 43–44.
4. Sweet, 1989: 2, 3; Simosko, 1992; Peters, T. and Waterman, R. 1992, Karpin (The Boston Consulting Group, 1994).
5. Clyne and Ball, 1990, Willing, 1992, Scollon and Scollon, 1995.

PART THREE

FIVE

Establishing a workplace project – setting the ground for partnership

In the previous chapter, we defined the aim of workplace education broadly as being to promote the learning and development of individuals and to improve the effectiveness of communication, learning and management practices at an organisational level. If the workplace itself is viewed as the curriculum, then educators' effectiveness will be dependent on a range of factors that are much more complex than the design of appropriate teaching materials or learning activities. These factors include:

- the workplace's needs, expectations and readiness for learning;
- the ability of the educator to research the needs, see the opportunities inherent in the situation and present a viable action plan;
- the educator's negotiation skills and responsiveness to obstacles and opportunities as the project develops;
- the resources available.

Evaluations of successful programmes regularly point to the active ownership and collaboration of workplace personnel as crucial elements in this process.[1] This involves working together to create a partnership based on mutual trust and recognition of each other's different contributions. Inevitably, it also involves working through some points of difference and accommodating tensions and constraints. So how can this approach be reflected in the way that educators go about establishing a workplace project?

In this chapter, we explore some of the issues involved in researching workplace needs and setting the ground for a collaborative, responsive workplace programme.

1. INITIAL CONTACT

In the words of an industry training board representative, workplaces tend to think about a language/literacy strategy 'later rather than sooner'. It is often after some major problem(s) has occurred that language and literacy interventions are considered. Typically, these problems could be as a result of one or a combination of developments such as:

- an accident highlighting the lack of effective communication as being one contributing factor.
- a failed training programme, where people did not follow the content or the training methods used.
- production problems due to instructions being ignored or incorrectly interpreted.
- difficulties in introducing new work practices, such as quality assurance checks, self-managing work teams because of language, literacy or communication factors.

With the increasing visibility of workplace language and literacy programmes in industry, a number of workplaces find out about such programmes through industry contacts, forums or literature. In some situations, language and literacy programmes are considered as a way of preparing the ground for wider training or organisational change initiatives at a later stage. Whatever the reason(s) might be, it is crucial to establish at the outset who determined there was a language or literacy issue and whose problem it was considered to be.

The following two examples – one from a manufacturing, the other a health services context – typify the range of push factors:

Aus Tin is a well-established, medium size packaging/printing plant with three separate departments involved in the manufacturing and printing of packaging products.

In 1990, the company employed approximately 260 employees, of whom about 200 were production, 'wages', employees, working on the shop floor, and 60 'salaried' employees involved in administration, planning and managerial functions. The workforce was a highly stable one, with little staff turnover. While the production section of the workforce was culturally diverse, the administrative/managerial section was mainly Anglo/ Australian in composition.

The company had been gradually downsizing, actively undertaking cost reduction measures in order to remain competitive. With the general restructuring of awards, it was decided to introduce multiskilling and adopt team-based approaches to work design. It was also decided to gradually implement new computerised planning and production systems and seek international quality accreditation of company products. As the role of training was to be vital in implementing these changes, a new training manager position was created.

It was soon evident, as new forms of work organisation and technology were being introduced, that the full ramifications of restructuring were not clearly understood by employees, and there were doubts expressed (among management) as to the employees' capacity and willingness to embrace the new changes.

An external consultant, for example, had just conducted a training programme on a new production method at great expense, but the training did not promote the desired results. Closer investigation revealed that most of the employees attending the course had not been able to follow either the trainer or the manuals provided, mainly due to language and literacy difficulties.

The training manager contacted a provider with a request for an assessment of language and literacy skills – a language audit – as a way of establishing training needs in the company.

Franklin Hospital

Franklin hospital was part of an established community health service, along with a number of small, community-based specialist institutions providing specialised services such as Tresillian, geriatric or palliative care and emergency services to local communities. With restructuring, many of these small community hospitals were to be absorbed into larger impersonal institutions. Teams would be broken up, routines disrupted, jobs redefined. An appraisal system to identify strengths and training needs was to be introduced. While some staff saw the restructure as an opportunity, fears of job losses as a result of the restructure were rife.

Such fears were especially prevalent among the many overseas trained nurses working at Franklin Hospital. Loss of a familiar supportive team environment, the additional communication demands arising out of changed duties, appraisal and training were causing considerable anxiety.

The Equal Employment Opportunity branch of the health service was aware of the new demands and pressures experienced by these nurses. Improving English language skills was seen as the best course of action to enable the overseas trained nurses to cope with their changing work environment and an enterprise-based teacher was appointed to coordinate and provide language support.

As these brief examples illustrate, the workplace contact typically approaches a provider with an identified problem, and more often than not, a likely target group and a proposed solution. At the initial stages, central concerns from the workplace perspective include issues such as:

- How bad is the problem? How long is it going to take to fix it?
- How can we deal with all the language, literacy and technical training needs at the same time?
- How much disruption will be caused to work by the proposed training?
- What will they be able to do as a result of the training?
- How much is it going to cost? Will it be cost-effective?
- Is it more viable to sideline employees with low levels of skills in favour of more skilled employees or new recruits?
- Can we work with you (the educator)? Can we trust you? How will you fit in with the people and what we are trying to do?

Depending on whether the initial request originated from a 'training', 'operational' or 'affirmative action' workplace contact, there are often also issues within the company of convincing key personnel of the need for any kind of training, let alone in the area of 'general skills'. The legacy of previous experiences with training or other workplace change initiatives usually strongly influences personnel attitudes towards the desirability of yet another 'expert' intruding on their territory. As a result, the credibility and trustworthiness of the educator is critically scrutinised in these early stages. It is important, for example, that the educator is not perceived to be allied with any one particular faction, be it the training department, management, union or immigrant employees. Similarly, working to an open agenda and clarifying ethical issues, such as confidentiality, is helpful in gaining broad support and acceptance.

There are usually a number of possible starting-points for a workplace educator, ranging from the development of discrete courses to supporting the training of assessors or the negotiation of an enterprise agreement. While some may have obvious potential from the very beginning, others may only become clear after exploration and discussion. It is vital therefore that a proportion of time and resources is allocated to explore the field in the early stages. It is also important to treat initial proposals as tentative beginning points, rather than prescriptive directives.

2. RESEARCHING WORKPLACE NEEDS

The educators' ability to address workplace education needs depends to a great extent on the accuracy of their interpretation of the current workplace scenario and its potential. This in turn, to a great extent, depends on the rapport educators are able to establish and the support they are able to foster for educational initiatives. The ways that the 'need' and educator's roles are defined invariably determine the solutions that are later developed, whose problem it is and who has a responsibility to do something about it.

Humanistic traditions of research, such as ethnography (Hammersley and Atkinson, 1983) attempt to capture how people make sense of their world in their own terms, by observing and participating in these interactions. Ethnographers stress the exploratory nature of this approach, where 'data are not taken at face value, but treated as a field of inferences in which hypothetical patterns can be identified and their validity tested out.' Rather than imposing a frame of reference, ethnographers such as Silverman advocate an approach which allows definitions of phenomena to emerge from the data itself (Silverman, 1993: 24). Even when dealing with a familiar group or setting, for example, Hammersley and Atkinson warn against the tendency to 'go native' and encourage the participant observer to treat it as 'anthropologically strange in an effort to make explicit the assumptions he or she takes for granted as a culture member'.

For workplace educators this would mean adopting an 'emic' approach, which aims to explore the specific issues peculiar to a particular setting, rather than searching for problems that neatly fit any pre-packaged solutions they may have, or validating particular theories of language or learning. Yet, as Hammersley and Atkinson also observe, it is important for researchers to be aware of how their own values and those of their respondents can affect the findings:

'There are no pure data. All data are mediated by our own reasoning as well as that of participants.'

Similarly, Silverman (1993) points out how the validity of social research can be affected by factors such as the impact of the researcher on the setting (leading to a halo or Hawthorne effect), the values of the researcher and the truth-status of a respondent's account. He warns not to underestimate the embedded, situated nature of people's accounts, with their explicit and implicit agenda. Triangulation of different sources of data, for example, may increase the validity of the interpretation, 'but it is naive to expect that neat solutions will arise as a result.' (1993: 200). For researchers such as Miles and Huberman (1984), Silverman (1993) and Layder (1993), using quantitative research methods is essential in balancing the researchers' tendency to see confirming instances much more easily than unconfirmed ones.

How then, can workplace educators conduct exploratory research, which on the one hand has an emic, ethnographic perspective, and on the other produces valid, reliable data to guide what follows? Almost invariably, time and resource constraints mean that there is little scope for educators to engage in detailed observations, extensive interviews or statistical analyses. The action-oriented nature of the research means that explorations need to be strategically focused, and the findings have to take into account the multiplicity of audience and purposes.

One of the main purposes, for example, is to set the basis for a collaborative partnership based on mutual understanding, trust and goodwill. Rather than being a solo activity, initial research should aim to involve people from the workplace in defining their perceived needs and working out possible strategies to address them. On a practical level, enlisting the help of people familiar with the workplace and its practices is invaluable in determining where to collect typical samples of data and locating critical communicative sites. If the educator is perceived as an outside expert who diagnoses problems and prescribes solutions, it is unlikely that either the problem or the solution will be 'owned' by those concerned.

There are many advantages associated with workplace educators being new and external to the particular organisation. One can, for example, ask many seemingly 'innocent' or 'naive' questions from a range of stakeholders to obtain different perspectives on issues, in ways that would not be possible for an employee of the organisation. Such enquiry can often also encourage workplace personnel to examine their own assumptions, or ways of working that may no longer be appropriate. Another advantage of not being part of organisational structures is that one can relate to and easily move across the different levels, networks and factions without becoming aligned with any particular one.

Workplace programmes are often government-funded in some way, and therefore subject to particular codes of ethics. Making these explicit can be valuable in gaining the trust and support of different stakeholders. The confidentiality of individual assessments, for example, is a perennial issue that can usually be foreseen and negotiated at the outset. Identifying individual employees in the absence of guarantees of employment security can cause justifiable concern for employees and educators alike. Guarantees of confidentiality or security of employment at the beginning of the process is likely to generate more comprehensive and higher quality data.

Research focus

Initial research involves much more than doing a language and literacy analysis. Some of the reasons for undertaking a systematic analysis of the workplace, from an educator's perspective, would be to answer such questions as:

- What is the current scenario in terms of organisational goals and priorities, morale and resources?
- How informed are employees of workplace priorities and directions?
- What are some of the formal and informal communication systems? How effective are they?
- What are the current approaches to training and learning?
- What are the language/literacy requirements of jobs?
- What are some of the main barriers to effective communication, learning and work practices?
- To what extent are these barriers due to skill development needs? To what extent are they due to language/literacy/crosscultural factors?
- How is work currently organised? What changes if any are planned? To what extent is the workplace committed to investing in the skill development of its personnel?
- What are some of the high impact problems? What are some of the unused resources or unexploited opportunities in the organisation?
- What are some of the likely obstacles or constraints?

Understanding the interactional dynamics of the workplace is vital. Workplaces are not homogeneous entities, any more than any other institution, but rather a conglomerate of competing values and interests. Line managers' perspectives on training needs, for example, can be very different from that of their senior managers or safety officers'. As part of their early needs analysis, educators need to sort through the application of workplace reform from the visionary rhetoric and identify likely 'strategic alliances'.

Different workplaces may be using the same official rhetoric and symbols of quality, teamwork, customer focus and efficiency. The translation of these aims to everyday practice, however, is likely to be located at totally different points on a continuum. At one end, responsibility may have been totally devolved to the lowest level possible, following a learning organisation model. Mid-way along the continuum, there may be a strong focus on control and eliminating variability through a carefully documented, regimented system. Employees are typically multiskilled in that they can undertake a number of tasks, but they have little control or influence over their daily activities. As a result, they share little sense of responsibility for the ultimate result.

At the other end of the continuum, labels such as supervisors may have changed to team leaders, but little else has actually changed. Resentments from some ranks are common, for example, from employees forced to rotate, supervisors or quality people whose area of specialisation and privilege is being eroded. Employees in such workplaces tend to be very careful about what knowledge they share, and are often quick to point out that the 'new system' is to blame for any problems that occur.

Even in the most progressive workplaces, there are often pockets of scepticism, and resentment of change from people who feel they have lost through the process. Some of these losses may be an erosion of power, prestige, the disappearance of a profitable bonus system, or simply a sense of territory, predictability and control.

As Field and Ford (1995) point out, there are key aspects of organisational functioning that support or frustrate learning at both an individual and institutional levels. They identify the following four common aspects:

- employee relations, including employees' security, rewards and recognition;
- work organisation, including the various forms that an organisation can take, the links with other enterprises and agencies and the role of the supervisors;
- skill, training and learning, including training courses and a whole range of other approaches to skill formation;
- technology and information management. (1995: 22)

These aspects need to be considered in the context of learning across the enterprise as a whole, if language and literacy programmes are to be responsive and effective. There is little incentive for employees to admit to language and literacy development needs, for example, if their job security is in doubt. Conversely, the introduction of new technology or ways of working may legitimise the need for training which may have otherwise been considered superfluous.

At the individual level, educators have to also make decisions regarding whose competence they assess. For example, it is often assumed that only those with foreign sounding accents will have communication difficulties. At what level of the hierarchy do they stop – employees, trainers, managers? Do they focus on language ability, language use, or communicative competence? Do they observe someone performing a task, to establish if there are any difficulties due to language or literacy, or develop their own tasks or literacy events to be analysed in terms of discrete language/literacy competencies?

Discussing needs analysis in an organizational communication context, Downs (1988: 192) suggests there are five common errors that can be made in defining problems:

1. Not discovering a problem that actually exists – usually as a result of superficial or hurried initial research. Such problems may, for example, relate to the investment some people have in maintaining the status quo, or systemic problems that make it difficult to implement any changes. Not discovering such problems can reduce the validity of the findings and effectively sabotage any action taken as a result of the research.

2. Identifying a problem that does not exist – from the organisation or individual concerned. If, for example, adequate compensatory mechanisms have been developed to deal with difficulties some employees experience with written records, it is unlikely that identifying problems in this area will gain broad-based support.

3. Treating all problems as communication problems. Given the integral role of communication to different aspects of work practices, it is often easier for educators to attribute problems to inadequate communication skills rather than more systemic factors. Industrial accidents, for example, may be due to long shifts or poorly designed machinery rather than literacy difficulties. In a study of the metals industry, for example (Mawer 1993), the employees' lack of participation in work meetings had more to do with the way the meetings were structured, and perceived power relationships, rather than the linguistic resources at employees' disposal.

4. Trying to solve the wrong problems. This error is closely related to the previous one, in that incorrect analyses of problems will inevitably lead to unsatisfactory outcomes. In a particular government agency, for example, management introduced communication skills courses on the assumption that increased skills would enable employees to take on team-leader positions and other promotional opportunities. During the course, however, it emerged that employees' lack of ambition for promotion was mainly due to their perceptions of management

rather than their own lack of skills. Many simply did not want to be associated with the prevailing autocratic management style, and used lack of proficiency in English as a face-saving excuse.

5. Failing to probe deeply enough to understand the problem – there can be a vast difference, for example, between company policy as stated in mission statements and that implemented. Similarly, individual employees may have low proficiency on a standardised English test, but perform much more competently in their familiar work environment. Accepting things at face value can lead to superficial solutions or unrealistic expectations.

Downs suggests that these errors could be avoided by:

- making the search as comprehensive as possible;
- determining whether an observation of a certain phenomenon necessarily constituted a problem for the organisation or the individual concerned;
- testing different ways of characterizing problems, e.g. by formulating different definitions of the problem, involving relevant people in the process.

Within the given resource and time constraints, the appropriate focus for needs analysis then is a rather wide and comprehensive one. Its aim is to investigate the way that language and cultural factors limit individuals' ability to participate fully in their social environment. In suggesting guidelines for the analysis of discourse, Fairclough (1989, 1992), proposes three stages which attempt to include both micro (interpersonal, situational) and macro (institutional, societal) contexts. These involve description (discourse as text), interpretation (discourse as discursive practice) and explanation (discourse as social practice).

Often educators are most comfortable at the individual learner/classroom level, and therefore the 'problem' is defined in terms of individual needs and courses. While this may be appropriate in certain circumstances, such an approach needs to be balanced against more strategic ways of ensuring the most effective long-term outcomes for the workplace and its personnel.

Starting off by focusing on individual needs for instance – especially those with foreign accents – risks buying into a deficit model that targets those already vulnerable, rather than distributing the responsibility for effective communication across the whole workplace. Similarly, narrowly focused approaches may well provide text-types for learners to jointly reconstruct and approximate, but they risk oversimplifying the complexity and richness of workplace reality.

At the same time, it is important that educators focus strategically on critical communicative sites where improvements are likely to have a strong impact on those concerned. These inevitably will require educators to go beyond their own comfort zones as they get their hands dirty, have their ears assaulted by machine noise or struggle to follow documents such as competency schedules, training manuals or safety regulations.

Data collection

Selecting research methods which do justice to the complex, intertwined nature of workplace discourse on the one hand, and practical constraints on the other, presents real challenges. In practice, the methods used to collect data invariably depend on the particular circumstances of the organisation, its stage of development, the given time-frame and available resources. Hammersley (1992) points out, for example, that research methods should not be guided by an ideological commitment to one methodological paradigm or another, rather by the purpose of the research, the appropriateness of the method and the resources available. Nevertheless, the reasons for choosing a particular methodology – or combination of methodologies – should be made explicit. Miles and Huberman (1984), for example, stress that decisions on research methodology should be informed by the nature of the theoretical framework adopted.

In the Aus-Tin case study described earlier in this chapter, for example, the company was just beginning to address skill development needs in a systematic way, had little data on its personnel, and was in the early stages of establishing a training department. It was therefore appropriate to begin with an organisation-wide evaluation of the workplace's communication and training resources and needs. The term 'audit' was an extension of 'skills audits' that were being undertaken in workplaces seeking to document their existing skills and identify their training needs. Apart from providing a familiar frame of reference for workplace personnel, a 'communication skills audit' allowed for a broader focus than a training needs analysis, as well as enabling existing communicative resources to be recognised.

Similarly, a large-scale audit of the Australian motor vehicle industry was conducted in 1992 by the industry training board, as a precursor to the development of industry-based accredited vocational training pro-grammes. The study revealed, for example, that 71 per cent of workers did not have English as their first language, and 21 per cent had left school before the age of 15. It concluded that between 70 and 90 per cent had insufficient language and literacy skills to complete the proposed modules (Sefton and O'Hara, 1992). The study, while resource-intensive, resulted in radical modifications to the format and content of training programmes, and the development of an integrated approach to work-place education in that industry.

More typically, in an organisation with well established training poli-cies or limited training budgets, such an approach would not be appro-priate or feasible. As in the brief description of the setting in Franklin Hospital earlier, the choice in allocating resources may be between under-taking a thorough needs analysis, or addressing an intuitively felt need. In many instances, beginning with a small-scale 'pilot' programme can allow for ongoing research in informal ways and rapport building which can set the basis for further productive work.

Whatever the scope or time-frame of the analysis, it is likely that a range of methods will be required to obtain the necessary data. Social researchers such as Layder advocate a multistrategy framework in at-tempting to understand the complex relationships of macro (structural, institutional) phenomena to the more micro phenomena of interaction and behaviours (1993: 7–8). Qualitative and quantitative data are neces-sary both to complement and act as a check on each other, and highlight the links between the micro and macro dimensions.

In developing a methodology for researching the discursive practices of an educational institution, Candlin and Crichton (in press) draw the insights of critical linguistics and social research together into an 'eco-logical' framework which includes:

- text analysis – a combination of systemic functional and pragmatic analysis focusing on how discursive practices are textualised;
- ethnographic/'verstehen' perspective – to recover the lived experi-ence of participants, specifically in relation to how they interpret discursive practices;
- phenomenological/ethnomethodological perspective – makes explicit the resources available to participants as they engage in discursive practices;
- institutional/social organisational perspective – provides an account of the social, institutional and historical structures and processes which shape and are shaped by the discursive practices.[2]

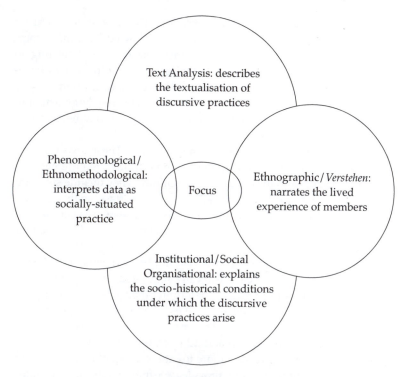

Figure 5.1: A framework for researching discursive practices
Source: Candlin and Crichton in Coupland, Sarangi and Candlin, (eds)
(in press)

Such an approach allows for the reflection of an emic understanding of workplace discourse and its social context and the foregrounding of tensions and dissonances. As Candlin and Crichton point out, the flexibility of such a framework also allows the researcher to use a range of data collection and analysis methods and make multiple cuts through the data to view it from different standpoints.

In a workplace context, there are a number of ways that such data can be collected. These include:

• A work-site tour with someone who has a good, general knowledge of the organisation. As well as providing insights into the work process, a tour is useful in appreciating general working conditions such as noise level, safety hazards, work organisation, use of computers, notice-boards, safety signs and general ambience. While such a tour is essential in the early stages, it can be somewhat overwhelming if it is too exhaustive. In a large organisation, it may be more useful to arrange for a short initial familiarisation, followed by a more comprehensive tour a little later to address specific issues relating to work process and organisation. It is also important to work out protocol and demarcation lines at this early stage, to avoid unnecessary tensions. Particular work sections or individuals may be reluctant to be observed or interviewed, or some information may be commercially sensitive.

- Collecting examples of written communication. These texts can provide a comprehensive indication of communicative requirements as well as insights into the organisational culture. They include standard procedures, handover reports, job descriptions, task analyses, competency schedules and training manuals. Notice-boards can usually provide examples of safety notices, meeting minutes and newsletters. Documentation such as organisational charts, mission statements, enterprise plans and leave forms may not be so freely available and may therefore need to be specifically requested. In collecting such sample texts, it is important to determine their intended purpose – as distinct from the functional one – and their level of usage. It is not unusual, for example, to find that many documents are not widely distributed, let alone read! Standard operating procedures are sometimes, for example, intended more to satisfy the quality accreditation inspection requirements, than provide user-friendly operational guidelines for employees.

- Observing and recording employees on the job is a very effective way of finding out first hand about communicative requirements, as well as different aspects of employee relations – such as morale and attention to safety issues. If possible, going through a mock induction, or being a worker for a day can yield extremely valuable data. Often, people will underestimate how much talking, reading and writing is involved in their work. There are also dramatic differences in individuals' communicative competence, depending on whether they are assessed at their work station, on familiar territory, or in an interview situation with generic assessment tasks. Labour turnover or rotation can significantly affect individuals' familiarity with tasks, and hence their ability to compensate for communication difficulties.

- Observing and recording regular meetings and training sessions is valuable in evaluating communicative requirements of trainees, as well as the strategies used by trainers and those conducting meetings. As well as providing an indication of current issues of concern within the organisation, such forums are useful for gaining insights into how decisions are made, and who some of the key people in the organisations might be, and how representative committees and training groups are in terms of their composition – ethnic, gender and sectoral representation.

- Interviewing employees about tasks they perform which entail oral interaction, reading or writing. Such interviews should also aim to gauge employees' perceptions of their own communication and training needs, understanding of company directions, and willingness to participate in training initiatives. For example, what strategies do they currently use to access information? In what ways have their jobs changed recently? What skill development and workplace change activities have they been involved in? With what effect?
- Interviewing supervisors, managers and trainers to gain their perceptions of communication and training needs in the organisation. How do training needs, for example, link in with job redesign? How do they perceive their own skill development needs? How successful have any new initiatives been? It is important here to also explore past experiences with skill development activities and their perceived usefulness.

Establishing good relationships with 'key informants' is invaluable both in helping to identify representative examples of discourse and workplace practices. Trainers, supervisors or less obvious personnel such as canteen attendants and security personnel can be rich sources of information as well as assisting in interpreting data already collected. They can be helpful, for example, in identifying communicative sites that are of critical importance or problematic to employees, or in explaining some of the background to particular practices.

Apart from the specific methods used, the skills of educators themselves will, to a great extent, influence the quality of the data gathered. In general, workplaces want to know that their particular circumstances have been understood, and that the person offering to help is credible, reasonable, and will act sensitively and efficiently. As well as effective interpersonal skills, educators' reflective and analytical abilities play a key role in this process. As Layder points out:

> Field researchers need the perceptual skills that allow them to inquire beyond the surface happenings of social life in order to detect the influence of structural factors. Secondly they need to be able to deal with analytic procedures which reflect this empirical depth. Thirdly they need to be sensitive to the theoretical implications of the underlying features of the empirical world. (1993: 70)

Data analysis and presentation

The needs analysis report will shape the recommendations and initiatives that follow. Yet the multiplicity of audience and purposes for such a report pose a number of dilemmas for educators in terms of its content, scope, tone and style. Lengthy reports, for example, are unlikely to be read by busy managers, so their contents need to be succinct and to the point. Not all types of analyses or findings will be appropriate for inclusion – long lists of text types or language functions for instance are of little interest to non-language experts, even though they may be critical in informing any subsequent curriculum development activities.

The language of the report needs to take into account the multidisciplinary audience it is addressing. Workplace personnel should not be expected firstly to acquire a sophisticated metalanguage in order to understand the research findings. It can seem somewhat ironic, for example, for a report focusing on the importance of effective communication to be full of academic jargon and lengthy abstract explanations.

The reliability and validity of the data need to be clearly evident as should the significance of the findings in terms of organisational goals or concerns. For example, if the analysis reveals that there is a lack of understanding of organisational change and directions among the workforce, the significance of this finding needs to be highlighted. Any change or training initiative is unlikely to be successful if its purpose and implications are not widely understood. In the same way, factors such as the importance of effective intercultural communication for teamwork should be clearly illustrated.

Any probing needs analysis is bound to uncover sensitive information that will need careful managing. For example, the 'needs' focus of the research can typically risk highlighting the deficits and problems of a usually vulnerable group of people, without identifying some of the often untapped resources. Examples of these include unused vocational qualifications, skills and experience or language and cultural resources. It may well be appropriate to document some of these alongside the needs assessments and suggest some of the ways these resources could be tapped.

Similarly, evaluating the effectiveness of current communicative practices needs to be sensitively handled. Critical incident techniques are usually very useful in illustrating the impact of ineffective communication on work practices, but they may need to be disguised, or cleared before being cited. In one particular workplace, for example, a memo produced by the personnel manager was publicly critiqued for its level of abstraction and formality. While the intention may have been to point out the need for 'Plain English' strategies, the public humiliation of the person concerned resulted in his systematically sabotaging the educator and her subsequent initiatives.

If particular systems have already been put in place at great expense – such as training programmes or documentation processes – there is usually much invested in their perceived effectiveness. For a variety of reasons, educators may need to work for incremental change within the given parameters, rather than recommending more 'radical', albeit pedagogically sound options.

The needs analysis phase may well need to be accompanied by some awareness raising activities about the dynamics of workplace communication. Information about other effective workplace language and literacy projects, for example, can be helpful in raising awareness of different possibilities, and the resulting benefits. Publicity information in the form of videos or short case-studies is useful in this regard. It is often necessary to debunk some common myths, such as the perception of literacy as a quantum, discrete skill rather than the notion of multiple, evolving literacies. In the Aus Tin example outlined below, an awareness/briefing session at the very early stages of the project was useful in highlighting changing literacy needs, and the importance of effective communication in enabling the company to achieve its organisational objectives. Rather than perceiving the proposed language programme as a 'quick fix' to particular employees' difficulties, the workshop encouraged participants to reflect on their own contributions as employee representatives, trainers and managers in facilitating communication and participation.

The process of presenting the findings itself should invite the input of workplace personnel in working out the significance of the findings, and planning the follow-up. Written modes of communication alone do not allow for such interaction. It may be appropriate, for example, to present the findings in a summarised format, and follow up with a joint discussion with key workplace representatives. Presenting a range of options or tentative recommendations, for example, allows people to discuss and ultimately own the final proposals. While language and literacy educators offer specialist knowledge and skills, they are often not in a position to prescribe appropriate action plans that fit the particular local conditions. Such plans should therefore be developed in close collaboration with the different parties involved – such as managers, trainers, supervisors and employee representatives. In the next chapter, we examine some of the ways of developing realistic, responsive action plans.

In the following examples, we return to the two workplaces described earlier, Aus Tin and Franklin hospital. The first account outlines a detailed needs analysis that was undertaken at Aus Tin as a precursor to the establishment of a integrated language and literacy programme. In contrast, a group of employees – overseas trained nurses – had already been selected for a communication skills course at Franklin Hospital. Catherine O'Grady describes how she and a colleague used an ethnographic approach to redefine the initial problem and involve management in developing strategies to improve communication in the hospital.

CASE STUDY 1. AUS TIN – ASSESSING THE COMMUNICATION SKILL NEEDS OF A CHANGING WORKPLACE

Following the request for a 'language audit', and a preliminary site visit, a meeting was organised between Aus Tin management, union representatives and the workplace education provider. The workplace educators (a manager and two part-time project officers) explored the reasons for requesting a 'language audit' and the expected outcomes of such an exercise. Initially, the aim seemed to focus around the need to survey the significant proportion of immigrant employees to assess their language and literacy skills and arrive at a more precise picture as to their skills and abilities to cope with the changes ahead.

The educators suggested widening the focus beyond a particular group of employees, to include the whole communicative context of the workplace. The workplace personnel involved in these early discussions were receptive to this wider focus, and in fact considered ways that the audit could inform other issues they were dealing with – such as career path planning.

A workplace consultative committee had recently been established in the company with four management and eight employee representatives. A three-day search conference was being organised for the committee to consider the implications of workplace changes and develop a strategic plan for the years ahead. The project officers suggested preparing an audit brief to present for discussion by the committee at the search conference. This presentation included a short cross-cultural training session which aimed to raise awareness of how language and cultural factors impinge on communication and the management of change in a multicultural workplace. The experiential, interactional nature of the session was useful in sensitising the committee to the issues involved before presenting them with the audit proposal.

The rationale for the audit was discussed in the context of the strategic plan the group had developed during the search conference. Ethical and practical issues such as confidentiality, target groups, voluntary participation, coverage of night shift were also discussed.

In relation to confidentiality, for example, management was keen to have access to information on employees' skills and experience to aid in career path planning. However, there were also legitimate concerns at the potential misuse of data regarding employees' language and literacy proficiency, especially in times of economic downturn. A compromise was reached, where individual employees' written consent would be sought at the end of the interview for the release of certain information (relating to personal background, experience and career path interests) to management.

At the end of that session, the following objectives were developed for the audit :

1. To assist Aus Tin identify the communication proficiency levels of its employees.
2. To document the employment related skills and experience of plant employees as part of a career planning process (e.g. unrecognised overseas qualifications, informally acquired skills).
3. To identify the training requirements of a multicultural workplace in the light of industry restructuring.
4. To identify the significant issues in communication processes in the company to improve their effectiveness, (formal and informal communication networks, attitudinal factors).

Given these objectives, the term 'communication skills audit' seemed more appropriate than 'language audit' because of the wider scope of the exercise and the inclusion of skills, knowledge, experience and attitudes in the assessment.

It was also agreed by the committee that participation in the audit would be on a voluntary basis and would involve all levels of management across the three shifts. A clear memo, stressing the purpose, voluntary and confidential nature of the survey was to be issued jointly by the consultative committee members. The committee members also undertook to encourage employees informally to participate.

This session was strategically important from a number of points of perspectives. There was a recognition of the need to take into account the linguistic and cultural diversity of the workforce in the strategic plan of the company. There was also understanding and support for the audit as well as a degree of ownership gained through consultation. Last, but not least, the project officers had established their professional credibility as a provider and been accepted by the committee. The session was later described by the training manager as 'a benchmark in the process of integrating language and literacy education with other workplace initiatives'.

Audit methodology

In addressing the whole communicative context of the workplace, it was crucial that, as well as pointing out problem areas and language 'gaps', the audit accurately documented the resources already existing in the workplace and gave due recognition to the fact that many employees perform complex tasks despite little training and an imperfect command of English. It was also vital that the assessment tasks reflected realistic work-related communicative demands.

The audit process consisted of individual interviews (see Figure 5.2) where employees were asked to complete:

1. A questionnaire covering personal details, skills, qualifications, work history, training and perception of training needs and communication processes within the plant.
2. A global and task-based assessment of communicative competence in a work-related context. All the participants were involved in some form of assessment, depending on their language levels and position of responsibility:
   (a) Oral Interaction (for employees of non-English speaking background). A criterion-referenced assessment was made of the employees' ability to follow simple and complex instructions, describe an event taking into account sequence, cause and effect, justify a course of action and express an opinion, give information and ask for assistance and use repetition and repair strategies to facilitate communication;
   (b) Reading and Writing (all employees, depending on level of literacy). A criterion-referenced assessment was made of the participants' ability to interpret safety signs and symbols, follow written instructions, extract information from texts and tables, fill in forms and write short reports;

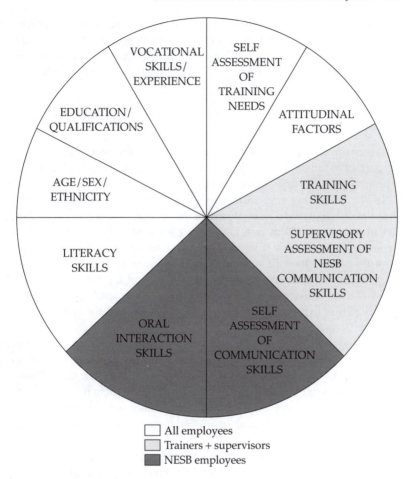

Figure 5.2: Individual assessment
Source: Barton and Mawer in Mawer 1991

    (c) Training Skills (for supervisors, leading hands and employees with identified training responsibilities). They were assessed on their ability to give clear, logical instructions that would be understood by an employee with limited English.
3. A self-assessment communication skills questionnaire dealing with the same areas previously covered.
4. A questionnaire for management and leading hands dealing with the communication skills of the employees under their supervision.

The assessment tasks were based on an analysis of communication requirements arising from workplace changes such as the moves towards multiskilling, teamwork and the integration of quality monitoring processes into all aspects of work. They were validated by workplace personnel.

Audit findings and recommendations

In assessing the communicative competence of the workforce, it was important to reflect the dynamic, interactional nature of workplace communication in the assessment tasks.

In the 'following oral instructions' task, for example, participants were asked to listen to a set of simple instructions and a more complex set in order to perform two tasks. They were told they could ask for repetition or assistance if needed and were assessed on their ability to complete the tasks with varying degrees of support.

As Figure 5.3 indicates, with appropriate levels of support e.g. explanations and demonstrations, all the employees were able to complete a technical task expressed in language that was beyond the range of the majority's comprehension.

Compared with the simpler task where nearly 40 per cent were able to follow independently the instructions, only 10 per cent were able to achieve the same result on the second, more complex task. These statistics reflected the reality of communicative interaction on the shop floor, where employees reported substantial amounts of time wasted in repeating instructions and overcoming misunderstandings due to ineffective communication.

This discrepancy also had significant implications not only for particular employees' needs to upgrade their communicative competence, but also for trainers and supervisors' roles in facilitating effective communication and skill acquisition.

Using a variety of indicators, the audit findings revealed that about 20 per cent of the total workforce sample had a very basic general command of English, inadequate for their changing work-related communication requirements. A further 23 per cent had adequate English for day-to-day communication requirements but would experience considerable difficulties following meetings or formal training programmes. The majority of employees with training responsibilities (76 per cent) were also identified as needing further training in training and presentation skills.

The audit confirmed many of management's impressions regarding the nature of the workforce. There were over eighteen different nationalities,

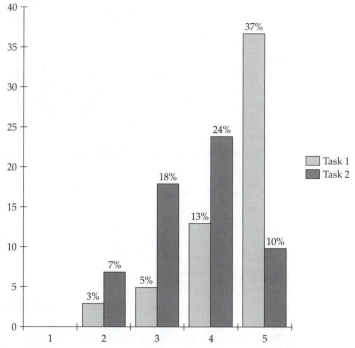

Rating Scale
1. Considerable difficulty in doing task despite demonstration and help by assessor.
2. Able to do task with demonstration, explanation and help.
3. Able to do task with repetition, explanation.
4. Able to do task with minimal help.

Figure 5.3: Following oral instructions

with most immigrants being long-term Australian residents (over twenty years) and long term employees (over six years). The employees were mainly male, with 75 per cent having had ten or less years of schooling. Those from a non-English speaking background, especially women, were consistently found to occupy the more junior positions in the company.

However, the audit also revealed that there was a broad technical and vocational knowledge and skills base in the workforce which had been acquired through a variety of formal and informal channels.

Contrary to management perceptions, the vast majority of the workforce (95 per cent) were highly motivated to maximize their training and promotional opportunities and identified computer and technical skills and English skills as priority areas. They did, however, express strong reservations about previous training and a strong preference for practical, hands-on training to more theoretical, abstract, formal modes of instruction.

The findings also revealed a general lack of awareness of the company's organisational structure and internal policies, especially in relation to restructuring initiatives. Formal channels of communication were found to be inadequate in disseminating information in the plant, partly due to literacy barriers.

Based on these findings, a range of recommendations was made, which included:

- specific literacy courses with a strong vocational or skill-linked focus;
- trainer and supervisory training;
- reviewing of consultative mechanisms to make them more accessible;
- the integration of communication skill competencies in the development of enterprise competency standards;
- reviewing of training programmes to make them more practical and closely integrated with on-the-job learning;
- adopting a plain English approach to writing memos and training manuals;
- greater utilisation of skilled overseas qualified employees.

A summary of the findings was presented at a meeting of the consultative committee, supervisors and managers where there was considerable discussion of their implications. Questions were asked, for example, as to how to prioritise training:

> Do we address basic skills, higher skills or trainer skills?
> How long will it take to raise the skills of the employees to a level where they can access training?
> What are the implications for future recruitment practices??

Overall, there was wide acceptance of the report and support for its wide-ranging recommendations. The implementation of the audit recommendations evolved over a three year period. While the general framework was consistent with the recommendations made in the audit, the timing and scope of the changes introduced were inevitably shaped by a range of internal and external factors. These included the priorities established in the company strategic plan, economic factors impacting on productivity and efficiency, attitudinal shifts in the organisational culture, changes in management and educational personnel and the availability of government subsidies.

The audit procedure was fairly complex and time-consuming, however, the multifaceted nature and comprehensiveness of the approach helped to ensure the results were both reliable and valid. The balance between 'expert' objective assessment, self-assessment and supervisory assessment, for example, was appropriate in an adult context where people were being encouraged to develop more analytical skills and autonomy. The active involvement of management, trainers, union and employees in the planning stages ensured that the educators were working to a common open agenda and that joint ownership was established from the start.

As a result of this audit, there was potential for the involvement of workplace educators in a multipronged, systematic and focused way that was well integrated into mainstream training activities. With the positive rapport established through the audit, there was management as well as grassroot support for this involvement.

CASE STUDY 2. INVOLVING NURSE UNIT MANAGERS IN IMPROVING COMMUNICATION AT FRANKLIN HOSPITAL

As the educator appointed to Franklin Hospital became familiar with the workplace environment, she realised that the language support for the overseas-trained nurses needed to be complemented with cross-cultural training for colleagues and managers of English speaking backgrounds. Through her observations of on-the-job communication she noted:

- little interaction between staff of an English-speaking background and overseas trained nurses; the social chatter and humour which cemented working relations among the Australian born staff was lacking, affecting teamwork.
- medical staff and nursing managers tended to direct instructions to nurses of an English-speaking background, especially in emergencies. This undermined the confidence of the overseas nurses. The Australian born nurses also resented the increased workload.
- communication practices were inappropriate in this culturally and linguistically diverse workplace. Rapid idiomatic speech was the norm in the busy, urgent environment; overseas nurses seldom asked for clarification; their colleagues seldom checked to confirm if they had been understood.

- while the overseas nurses spoke English fluently, difficulties arose out of different communication styles, unfamiliar accents and confusion about the roles and relationships expected at work.

At a meeting with key health service personnel including staff development managers, and the Equal Employment Opportunity coordinator, the educator floated the idea of an cross-cultural training programme to complement language classes. This would provide a forum for staff of English speaking background to explore their role in improving on the job communication and supporting their overseas colleagues in the language and culture learning process. It was recommended that management be targetted initially for this training as their commitment and support would be critical to further staff training. It would also be essential if strategies were to be implemented to improve intercultural communication among staff. Support was gained for a series of workshops for Nurse Unit Managers (NUMs) and Directors of Nursing.

Developing the training

The educator invited colleagues specialising in cross-cultural communication to present the training programme, collaborating closely with them to research and design the workshops. Research confirmed many of the educator's observations and provided the basis for a relevant and practical training programme. This research involved:

- surveying Nurse Unit Managers about their experiences communicating with staff of different language and cultural backgrounds;
- discussion with overseas trained nurses to gain further insight into their perceptions of workplace communication;
- collection of transcripts of workplace communication, incidents of misunderstanding and the identification of issues to be explored through case studies.

Most of the Nurse Unit Managers were concerned that instructions and information were not clearly understood:

> Staff of non-English speaking background often give the impression they understand when in fact they don't.

> It is often difficult to know how much my communication is really understood.

Despite their unease, they seldom checked understanding. Saving face appeared to be an issue for all concerned. Whilst the NUMS did not wish to draw attention to possible language problems, the overseas nurses were reluctant to imply that their managers were difficult to understand.

> My supervisor is very difficult to follow. When she asks if I understand I sometimes say 'yes'. It's easier that way. Then later I check with a friend.

In the communication courses, the educator assisted nurses to develop the confidence and communication strategies to ask for clarification appropriately. The cross-cultural training sessions would provide the opportunity for the NUMs to critique their own communication style as well as to explore ways to create an atmosphere in which people were comfortable to ask for clarification.

Many of the communication difficulties raised during research were *pragmatic* in nature and occurred despite the apparent fluency of the speakers. Cross-culturally words and phrases can often carry unintended meaning. Some overseas nurses, for example, were perceived as abrupt and curt and these perceptions fuelled stereotypes and reinforced divisions:

> I often observe apparent abruptness on the part of one staff member to another; particularly from staff of X background. This certainly causes ill feeling.

In addition, staff did not share the same view of appropriate roles and working relationships. Different assumptions about appropriate behaviours were a source of tension and misjudgement. For example, many overseas nurses found the teasing, irreverent humour of their Australian born colleagues abrasive and rude. They themselves were seen as reserved and distant. Many criticised them for remaining within their own group.

Team meetings were a source of frustration for NUMs who expected nurses to identify problems and suggest changes in hospital procedures. Many overseas nurses were uncomfortable with this role. They expected their supervisors to provide direction. Suggesting improvements in practices, even when encouraged to do so, felt inappropriate and disrespectful.

It emerged during research that some nurses believed they had experienced prejudice from patients. Despite considerable distress, they had not raised this with their managers.

Based on these research findings an initial training programme was developed for NUMs. It aimed to:

- deepen understanding of the sources of misunderstanding and misjudgement in their culturally diverse workplace;
- provide the opportunity to look critically at their own communication and to develop strategies for improvement;
- explore ways to support the overseas nurses in the culture and language learning process;
- open discussion about prejudice in the hospital and identify their role in dealing with it.

Developing training activities

The incidents and issues raised during the research phase were a rich resource for the development of relevant materials and activities. Shift handover, for example, emerged as a particularly critical communication site. As one shift finished, a nurse would give a brief oral report to update incoming nurses on patient issues. Nurses finishing shift were tired and the handover report was often rushed. There was great potential for misunderstanding.

A transcript of a shift handover, collected by the educator was the stimulus to enable participants to critique their style of communication as well as current procedures for handover. The activity is presented here together with feedback provided by the workshop participants.

SHIFT HANDOVER

This is a short transcript of a shift handover. The nurse making the report is Australian-born. Some of the nurses taking over the shift are of non-English speaking background

Australian-born nurse:

In 215 is Mrs G. She came in around half past one, and she's for total hip replacement tomorrow first thing, at 8 in the morning. Now it's going to be necessary to get in touch with the orthopaedic surgeon in residence. He'll have to come over and examine her. OK? And she brought in two blood slips with her. One's for an HB. group, and save serum and the other is for U's and E's. She's going to need an iodine test and I've taken the precaution of getting cot sides because of her age. If she fell out it'd be really serious. She's a frail little old lady. She's really shaky and nervous and a bit at a loss to know what on earth's happening to her. She'll need a lot of reassurance.

During the shift handover you notice a number of nurses of non-English speaking background listening quietly. However, following the handover, you observe two of these nurses consulting with each other.

During the day a number of incidents indicate to you that these nurses have misunderstood parts of the handover report.

What's happening here and why?

What suggestions could you make for more effective handovers?

The NUMs analysed the transcript in small groups and discussed some of the ways that shift handovers could be improved. The following are some of their responses to the two questions:

What's happening here and why?
- overseas nurses aren't following and they aren't seeking clarification. Probably don't want to appear foolish
- Australian-born nurse doesn't invite clarification
- abstract language
- ambiguous language
- superfluous language
- not organised logically... all over the place
- lack of specifics about the situation
- colloquial to the workplace ... overseas nurses often have different jargon
- too rushed!

What suggestions could you make for more effective handovers?
- allocate time for the handover, allow for some shift overlap
- create a calm, unrushed atmosphere
- detailed written report is needed so it can be referred to later
- nurse should refer to written record during handover
- nurse should invite people to check and clarify
- present the information in chunks, asking people to comment, and check after each part
- don't take it for granted that everyone understands the jargon

- avoid colloquialisms
- be precise, cut the superfluous talk; it only distracts.

To explore the issue of possible patient prejudice, a case study was developed to provide NUMs with the opportunity to discuss the issue and explore their role in dealing with it. It is presented below together with feedback from the NUMs participating in the workshop.

DEALING WITH POSSIBLE PREJUDICE: CASE STUDY

In your unit is an efficient and talented nurse of non-English speaking background. Recently you have received a few complaints from patients who say they have difficulty in understanding her because of her accent. One asked for an 'Australian nurse'.

What issues does this situation raise?

What action would you take?

In response to the first question, the workshop participants suggested the following issues:

- nurse's self-esteem is at stake;
- possible racism; need to ascertain this;
- need to know more about history and experience of the patient;
- is the nurse intelligible?
- what is an 'Australian nurse'?
- health of the patient might affect tolerance to other accents;
- noise level? elderly slightly deaf patients may have real difficulty understanding;
- are patients of the same background? caste/class differences may be at work.

In discussing what action they would take, the NUMs were aware of the need to balance concerns for patient welfare against those of the nurse. A wide range of suggestions were made, and a fruitful discussion followed on their relative merits and consequences:

- provide moral support to the nurse; let her know her skills are valued.
- explore the particular circumstance, ascertain whether the nurse's accent presents difficulty to people in general; maybe this isn't prejudice but a genuine difficulty.
- speak to the nurse and patient individually to get their feelings;

- ask nurse about her perceptions;
- if nurse is difficult to understand support her to overcome pronunciation difficulties; suggest courses; support her attending courses;
- ascertain who the patients were; commonalities could give insight into the nature of the difficulty;
- if patient is very old and infirm or particularly belligerent, consider moving the nurse away from the patient – in doing this ensure that the nurse knows she's valued;
- where bias or prejudice is the issue, counsel the patient; explain that the nurse is qualified and a valued professional in the hospital. Point out that the nurse is an Australian and might be very hurt by the patient's attitude.

As the workshop progressed, it became clear to participants that a variety of factors contributed to the communication difficulties experienced in the hospital. Language and cultural differences played a part in this process, and the NUM's recommended steps to ensure that all staff received training in cross-cultural communication. In addition, nurses of non-English speaking background needed encouragement and support to continue their language learning.

The NUMs also recognised that hospital procedures and practices were often inappropriate within the context of a culturally and linguistically diverse workplace. These practices had emerged out of a very different workplace culture, where nursing staff and clientele had been almost exclusively of English speaking background. If the hospital was to overcome communication difficulties and fully benefit from the skills of all nurses, norms and practices needed to evolve to accommodate the diversity of its staff. This was especially important as restructuring occurred and staff had to deal with a greater variety of tasks, functions and patients. The NUMs recommended that procedures such as meetings and shift handover be carefully reviewed in the light of staff diversity.

NOTES

1. See, for example, Mikulecky, L., in Hirsche, D. and Wagner, D. (eds) 1993 for an evaluation of US and Canadian workplace literacy programs, and Baylis, P. 1995 for an evaluation of the Australian Workplace English language and literacy program; Department of Employment, Education and Training, 1996. *More than Money can say – The Impact of ESL and Literacy Training in the Australian Workplace*, DEET: Canberra.
2. Crichton, J. 1996. Issues of Intertextuality in the Marketisation of English. Unpublished Ph.D. thesis: Department of Linguistics, Macquarie University.

SIX

Strategic beginnings

More often than not, the natural starting-point for workplace language programmes is a course for a particular group of employees, usually those with the lowest levels of competence in English. Where there is no history of a learning culture in the organisation, this may well be appropriate, but in other situations, it may be neither the most appropriate or effective strategy in the long term.

As we saw in the previous chapter, the reason for carrying out a systematic needs analysis is so that what takes place as a result can have maximum impact on the workplace's communicative and learning practices. The role of the organisational context is crucial in shaping what is appropriate and feasible. Successful ways of working in one situation cannot usually be simply transplanted into another, regardless of similarities in personnel or work processes.

While particular ingredients – such as sufficient funds, support from management, employees, relevant curriculum and competent educators – are always necessary, they are not sufficient to ensure the success of a programme. The frustrating situation at Optiboard, as told by the educator involved, is a case in point:

Rumour has it that the Optiboard project was the brainchild of some late night networking at a function. Certainly those involved in the project agreed it had not been well conceived, and often wondered why it had hung on for so long before finally biting the dust.

Optiboard was a branch of a large national printing company, with an evident need for language and literacy courses, given its highly multicultural workforce. When the project was announced by the training manager from the interstate head office, operators were keen and grateful for the opportunity to learn more English. Although many had been in the company for a number of years, the noisy environment had made the learning of spoken English at work very difficult. Supervisors and leading hands had regularly lamented the fact that miscommunication often led to waste and damage of the expensive printing and cutting equipment.

While the management of the local Optiboard had given the project its blessing in principle, it soon became apparent that running courses in a factory where orders were filled *just in time* was hugely inconvenient. Signs moved from one machine to another as they were cut, glued, printed and packed. As regular deadlines approached, tensions ran high, and even the managing director would be on the factory floor assisting with production. The absence of any one operator at an English course led to massive hold ups, lost production and profound and menacing displeasure from head office. As one leading hand commented:

> It's no use letting them go to learn English if we get shut down, and they lose their jobs. No one will thank us for that!

Different scheduling arrangements were tried over a period of months, with little success. It was then decided to try releasing learners in pairs for one hour twice a week, but this too proved impractical. Despite the noise, the educator then tried working alongside the operators and teaching at the same time, but when the pressure was on, this too proved to be a distraction, and a brake on production.

Notwithstanding these difficulties, company management was unwilling to advise head office that they needed to terminate the project. Government funds had been received to assist with the project, and both the education provider and company manager persisted with half-hearted attempts to accommodate the project. Some months later, to almost everyone's relief, the contract came to an end. The costs to all concerned had been high. The employees whose learning opportunities had been whittled to nothing felt disillusioned with management that had seemed to promise so much. Both factory management and the educator had to come to terms with a sense of failure and the waste of precious government funding.

In this chapter we look at some of the strategies involved in planning for success and the integration of workplace language programmes into mainstream activities rather than their marginalisation. Some of these involve:

- developing an action plan;
- negotiating roles and responsibilities;
- supporting and publicising the project;
- setting up monitoring and evaluation mechanisms;
- maximising the impact of courses.

DEVELOPING AN ACTION PLAN

In principle, action plans are more likely to succeed if they are collaboratively developed following the research phase – once data has been collected, analysed, and some rapport established. However, in practice, this is not always possible. With government subsidies of workplace language programmes, for example, funding for particular activities is sometimes granted on the basis of demographic details, or an intuitively felt need, rather than a comprehensive needs analysis. In situations such as these, educators may need to work within the given constraints to modify existing proposals.

Timelags between the submission of proposals and their approval can also significantly affect the viability and relevance of what has been proposed – seasonal factors, production pressures, changes in technology or personnel can often make pedagogically well-laid out plans unworkable. In one particular instance in the construction industry, bureaucratic delays in approving a project proposal meant that by the time funds were available to start the project, the actual building project had been completed and its workforce dispersed! In the pharmaceutical company example later in this chapter, changes in personnel and delays with the development of industry standards both meant that the original plan needed substantial reviewing.

Sometimes, the potential for particular strategies may not become evident until a 'settling in' time in the workplace. The collaborative development of training programmes, for example, usually requires some rapport and trust to have developed, as well as time for the educator to have become familiar with workplace requirements.

One of the greatest tensions in planning an integrated approach to workplace language and literacy comes from needing immediate results on the one hand, and planning for long-term effectiveness on the other.

The readiness of the workplace – in terms of timing and available resources – also has to be taken into account. Both educators and workplace personnel need to realistically assess strategic starting-points, and their likely outcomes. Given the pace and nature of changes in the workplace, and short-term funding arrangements, three-yearly, lock-step action plans, for example, are unlikely to work. Neither are radical transformations of workplace practices likely to occur after a short course – or even a series of courses.

Linking in to current initiatives – whether it is the development of Standard Operating Procedures, the introduction of team-based approaches or the training of trainers – makes sense in a number of ways. It helps to legitimise the programme as a mainstream concern and demonstrate its value in assisting different workplace personnel to achieve their particular goals, such as improving quality. It also enables learning opportunities to be more easily integrated into daily work, rather than being regarded as merely 'chalk and talk in the training room'. A course on 'Report Writing for Team Leaders' or 'Using Operational Procedures' for instance, is likely to gain more support than a 'Basic' or 'Functional literacy' course. Furthermore, because of the existing support and commitment for initiatives such as quality or safety, meaningful, visible outcomes tend to be produced relatively quickly and painlessly.

In the same way, having more than one point of intervention is usually necessary for a number of reasons. Firstly, it is virtually impossible to adopt an integrated approach to workplace language programmes without seeking to influence a range of systems and practices – from training and assessment strategies to document design and communication practices. Secondly, it is vital that the programme is seen to focus on the whole communicative context of the workplace – from team leaders to trainers and employees – rather than those in an already vulnerable position because of their accents or lack of formal education. If from the beginning the educator's role is perceived as 'the basic skills teacher who runs literacy classes', it becomes much more difficult for him or her to be involved at a later stage with trainers or the design of technical courses. On a pragmatic note, being involved simultaneously in more than one activity allows the educator to become more familiar with the workplace, and enhances the probability of at least one of these activities being successful!

As in other types of change initiatives, the success of language and literacy programmes is more likely to be enhanced by small, experimental projects rather than overly ambitious ones. These pilot projects tend to generate support without being over-threatening. Tom Peters, a well known writer on organisational change advises supporting fast failures on little projects:

> The best approach to a major reform ... is to test bits of it ... for a few weeks or months. Small-scale tests, and accompanying small scale failures, are the only building blocks for efficient and effective long-term, full-scale success. 'All at once' implementation, without such tests and failures is a recipe for disaster. ... (1987: 266)

Equally disastrous in its potential is a 'literacy-led' workplace change programme. Key aspects of organisational functioning (such as employee relations, work organisation, approaches to skill formation, technology and information management) certainly need to be taken into account, and the project needs to be strongly aligned with workplace goals and priorities. However, the educator's role is primarily one of facilitating learning and change, not driving it. While it might be appropriate sometimes to provide models of effective learning or communication, the educator's role, in Silverman's (1993) words, is to 'facilitate changes which mobilise the innovatory capacity of people' rather than being the main performer. If the programme is to be effective in the long term, it must be owned and driven by the workplace, rather than an 'outsider expert'.

As argued in the last chapter, collaborative, 'emic' approaches to researching workplace practices and needs are particularly valuable in providing the groundwork for a responsive and realistic action plan. The following example from a pharmaceutical company illustrates such an approach where the project aims and activities evolved over time to suit changing priorities and circumstances.

Merck Sharp and Dohme (Australia) Pty Ltd is a subsidiary of the US pharmaceutical company, Merck & Co. Inc. and is one of the major national manufacturers and exporters of pharmaceuticals.

The company was aware of the need to upskill their production employees as part of the process of modernisation and expansion of its Sydney site – with a workforce of 500 people, of whom 140 people are involved in the production area. With the forthcoming development of competency-based standards and curriculum for the pharmaceutical industry, quality accreditation to ISO 9000 series and introduction of new technology, it was evident that such changes could not be implemented without effective English language, literacy and numeracy skills.

The company sought government funding to employ a full-time educator on site for 12 months. At the time funding was sought, the aim of the project was to:

> incorporate language and literacy competencies into the training programs offered to MSD's production/maintenance employees and the explicit teaching of those competencies to employees needing such assistance.

In the interval between the development and approval of the project submission, a number of changes occurred. Delays occurred with the process of developing national competency-based standards for the industry, so that standards and curriculum were not available for implementation at the start of the project.

The situation within MSD had also changed in that the original contact personnel who had been involved in initiating and negotiating the project were no longer with the company, and the anticipated full-time appointment of a training officer did not materialiee. Following a preliminary needs analysis, the project objectives were modified to reflect these changes, and set the basis for a multifaceted approach, that addressed language and learning needs throughout the plant. The project aimed to:

1. Contribute to the planning of training at MSD with respect to language, literacy and numeracy, communication and cross-cultural issues.
2. Contribute to delivery of training at MSD with respect to language, literacy and numeracy, communication and cross-cultural issues.
3. Contribute to MSD workplace culture and communication strategies.
4. Liaise with industry and other practitioners to promote and disseminate information from project.

Specific performance indicators were developed for each of these objectives. During the twelve month period, the educator worked simultaneously with different occupational levels in the organisation. Activities relating to the project included:

- Evaluation and input into training programmes in respect to Plain English and language and literacy issues;
- Assistance in the development of specific inhouse training modules e.g. *Documentation for In-Process Checking;*
- Assistance with the development of Operator Instructions, user-friendly signs and information around the plant;

- Development and delivery of section-wide training modules to address specific needs e.g. *Calculator Skills* to improve reconciliations of product (approximately 80 employees);
- adaptation and delivery of a short communication course dealing with interpersonal and cross-cultural issues – attended by over 200 employees in cross-sectional groups;
- Development and delivery of short training modules to supervisors and team leaders e.g. *Writing in Plain English, Train the Trainer* (with a focus on language and literacy issues);
- Support for trainers delivering in-house courses e.g. *Introduction to Good Manufacturing Practice*;
- Language/Literacy/Numeracy support for 60 employees from different areas through regular weekly group or individual sessions;
- Individual or group tutorial support for employees undertaking specific internal or external courses e.g. *Introduction to Good Manufacturing Practice*;
- Informal support on the process line to assist individual employees;
- Educational counselling and referral of employees to appropriate external training courses.

The strategies adopted by the project focused on addressing immediate workplace needs in a constructive, collaborative way. The short course on calculator skills, for example, was in response to problems with reconciliation records in the packaging section. As part of multiskilling, the mainly female, immigrant operators, were issued with calculators and asked to assist in monitoring the output of their section, but there were significant problems in achieving consistent, reliable figures. The course was designed in collaboration with workplace personnel and offered on a voluntary basis to the whole work section. At the same time, changes were made to standardise the equipment and procedures used. One of the problems, for example, related to the use of widely varying calculators, with confusing keyboard layouts and symbols.

As an initial project activity, it was highly successful from a number of perspectives: it cost-effectively addressed a business problem, and raised managers' and supervisors' awareness of literacy issues and of the importance of consciously planning for changes in work organisation and skill development. Offering the course to the whole section helped to legitimise the need for skill development in response to changing operational procedures, rather than 'deficiencies in basic skills'. The course's impact in generating a positive attitude to learning and establishing the project officer's credibility were significant in ensuring the success of the overall project. As one employee commented:

> The calculator training made people comfortable with her because they realised she's here to help, and that it's OK to have a go.

Working simultaneously with different levels of management in the organisation was strategic in raising language, literacy and numeracy issues as part of the organisational agenda, while at the same time improving employees' spoken and written skills across the company. The short communication course for example was offered to all employees in cross-sectional groups, which enabled many of them to interact for the first time. In an evaluation of the project, these courses were cited by a number of respondents as significant in changing attitudes and helping to create an environment that was supportive to learning and people.[1]

NEGOTIATING ROLES AND RESPONSIBILITIES

Supportive, collaborative relationships can easily deteriorate into frustrating power-struggles if there is no clear understanding of roles and lines of communication. The respective contributions of workplace personnel and educator(s) need to be clearly understood, and agreed, early in the life of the project. It is essential, for example, that there is a shared understanding of the role of the educator *vis-à-vis* workplace management and training personnel. This applies especially to more process-oriented projects which do not consist of discrete, easily quantified activities such as the delivery of a series of training sessions.

In Australia, for example, there has been an increasing trend for providers of workplace education to appoint or second an educator to the workplace for the duration of a project. The educator becomes known as 'project coordinator' 'literacy consultant' or 'enterprise-based-teacher'. While there is clear value in an educator being based full time in an organisation, there are a number of issues which usually need to be carefully considered.

The first one relates to the match between the project's preset aims and objectives, and the particular skills and experience of the educator(s) appointed. Some educators may have highly developed skills in particular areas, such as discourse analysis cross-cultural communication or assessment, but less experience in areas such as numeracy or computer-assisted learning. In many situations, a team-approach to workplace provision offers distinct advantages. It offers a higher quality service for the workplace concerned. It also provides educators with a practical professional development opportunity and reduces the professional isolation which can result from being 'outposted'.

Secondly, the status of the educator(s) *vis-à-vis* the workplace needs to be clarified. There are delicate issues relating to educators being 'in the workplace but not of it'. It is not unusual, for example, for educators to find themselves treated as workplace trainers with responsibility for technical content they have no expertise in. Working conditions often also cause some concern if educators are wholly based in a workplace, as entitlements and leave conditions can vary markedly. Primarily, educators' effectiveness should be measured by the quality of services and outcomes achieved, rather than the hours spent on-site.

The physical facilities provided can also influence the way the project and the educator involved are perceived. In many workplaces, there are territorial divisions between the air-conditioned, comfortable, carpeted 'white office dweller' culture and the more noisy lino-covered operational areas. Practicalities of access and comfort often need to be balanced against those of possible isolation or influence. Is it better to be located in the comfortable training department – if one exists – but have less interaction with operational personnel? In a smaller workplace, is it more important to be located close to the operational manager or the safety or personnel officer? While needing to be in a central, visible place, educators will inevitably also need some privacy and quiet thinking space.

To avoid frustrating situations such as that which developed at Optiboard, some of the key factors for success should be made explicit, and agreement reached on different parties' contributions to this. The active and public endorsement of the project from senior management, for example, is essential for any new initiative to succeed. This endorsement relates to more than just agreeing to release employees for training, and providing adequate facilities. It also involves supporting changes as a result of insights gained or skills developed. There is little point in developing new skills if employees are not then encouraged to use them and are rewarded for doing so. In fact, it can be counterproductive, for people can easily become cynical if they perceive the rhetoric of workplace participation and teamwork to be hollow.

SUPPORTING AND PUBLICISING THE PROJECT

Obtaining support for any new venture is difficult, especially when one is unfamiliar with the workplace and its networks. Relying on formal strategies alone, such as newsletters or memos, is unlikely to generate much in the way of support, or enthusiasm. More interactive approaches – such as team-meetings, or tool-box sessions – tend to be more effective, and allow for discussion of sensitive issues or concerns. The support of senior management and key personnel – such as line managers, consultative committee or union representatives – is usually vital in such forums. Publicity information about other projects in the form of videos, or short case studies can also be useful here in presenting the benefits of such projects in similar workplaces.

In general, new initiatives are likely to be more successful if the concerns of different parties have been acknowledged and addressed. Particularly in workplaces which have not had an established training or learning culture, these concerns may go unvoiced, and not become apparent until major problems have developed. Such issues often relate to workplace pressures, personal anxieties, and perceived costs and benefits. Workplace managers, for example, tend to be typically concerned about issues such as:

- What are the immediate benefits likely to be in terms of quality, productivity, safety, efficiency?
- How much is it going to cost? Is it value for money?
- How will it impact on operations? How do we organise release time?
- Can this person work with us? Are they too pushy / academic / industrially naive? Have they done this type of work before?
- Can they work around our operational pressures / shift arrangements?
- What extra work will this mean for us? How much help / supervision will they need?
- Can they relate to the different groups in the organisation?

The concerns of middle levels of management are often a little more immediate and personal. It is not unusual for supervisors and team leaders to be uninvolved in making decisions on training activities, yet they play a key role in determining their success or quietly sabotaging them. Middle managers are typically already operating on minimum staff, struggling to meet more demanding production schedules. Their concerns tend to relate to issues such as:

- Who will do my people's jobs while they are away? How long will it take?

- Why don't they go to training in their own time? I learnt the hard way, why shouldn't they?
- I don't have time to be involved in this. We find a way to get by, do they really need training?
- Is this a way of weeding people like me out?

Employees and their representatives are often concerned about the relevance and perceived rewards or incentives associated with training. Being nominated as 'needing English' can have a negative impact on one's job. For those with limited or negative formal learning experience, lack of confidence in their own ability is often a major factor. For employees with relatively high status in the organisation, there can be as much resentment as a recognition that it might be worthwhile, if loss of face is involved. From their perspective, questions such as these are common:

- What will I have to do in the training?
- Why do I have to go to school now? I am too old to learn. I will look stupid to my workmates/partner/children.
- When/where will the training take place? Who will do my job while I am away?
- What will I get out of this? I've been doing the job for ten years. It's not likely to change.
- What happens if I say no? Is my job on the line? Is this a way of weeding out people like me?
- What will I be able to do as a result of the training? Will I get more money? A recognised qualification?

In planning the project, it is important that these concerns are acknowledged in the way that different activities are structured and presented. The links with other workplace initiatives, for example, need to be transparent, so do the incentives and safeguards associated with participating. Language and literacy issues will often only be relevant to the extent that they are perceived as necessary to achieving a particular work-related goal. If the need for skill development, for example, is not evident, it is unlikely that the project will receive a great deal of support. Conversely, if job security is a real issue, employees will be understandably reticent to admit to a training need, especially in 'basic' skills, such as language and literacy. In some workplaces, input from bilingual employees, union officials or participants from projects at a similar workplace has been very useful in explaining the project and outlining some of the benefits.

As Knowles (1978) points out, people tend to feel committed to a decision or activity in direct proportion to their participation in influence on its planning and decision making. Personnel who play a key role in supporting or undermining the project – such as supervisors – need to be involved early in the life of a project, to ensure that the content and structure of various project activities are relevant to their needs, as well as those for whom they have responsibility. In this way, at least some of the almost inevitable disruptions to operations caused by the project will hopefully be compensated for by improvements in work-related tasks and interactions.

This consultative process need not necessarily be time-consuming, but rather focused and well planned. In the following example, Julia McCall outlines how, given limited time-frame and resources, she worked to enlist the support and involvement of hospital supervisors in a communication skills course.

CASE STUDY – ENLISTING THE SUPPORT AND INVOLVEMENT OF SUPERVISORS IN A WORKPLACE COMMUNICATION SKILL COURSE AT CHISWELL HOSPITAL

As in many other hospitals, the various departments of Chiswell Hospital such as cleaning and catering were being streamlined and merged to increase efficiency. With fewer personnel, staff could no longer be spared to show their workmates what to do when telling them did not work. Similarly, memos became more commonly used rather than word of mouth for passing on messages.

Various incidents had highlighted the need for communication skills training. A cleaner had entered a room in the process of being fumigated because she could not read the 'Do Not Enter' sign on the door. Another had only just been prevented from responding to a patient's request for a glass of water because she had been unable to decode the 'Nil By Mouth' sign over the bed.

The 'Customer Focus' initiative, which stressed the importance of gratifying clients as well as completing workplace tasks, was also leading to an increased awareness of the need for politeness strategies among Hospital Assistants. People who could only say 'You move please' needed to learn the more indirect 'Could you possibly move?' and so on.

After suggestions by staff, the hospital superintendent approached a workplace language and literacy provider with a request for a communication skills course for employees in the commercial services division. A sixty hour course was negotiated over a twelve week period.

I photographed signs around the hospital, watched cleaners at work and talked to Nurse Unit Managers to establish what needed to be learnt. From the outset the language needs of the clientele appeared to be diverse with learners coming from the laundry, food preparation, cleaning and engineering departments. After the individual needs analysis, it was clear that the language levels and backgrounds of the learners were incredibly varied too. Although many people came from farming backgrounds in Yugoslavia or Portugal, had little formal education and had been in Australia for more than fifteen years some had recently come from China and Thailand and had completed high school. While some of the learners could not read or write in English but had effective, if idiosyncratic oral communication skills, others had difficulty making themselves understood at all.

I reluctantly recommended splitting the group into two reasonably homogeneous groups of learners, knowing that in doing so I was reducing their teaching hours from four per week to two. It was clear that if significant language gains were to be achieved, learning needed to be supported outside the classroom, because two hours a week was simply not enough. Workplace supervisors would need to play a part too.

It was with this thought in mind that I decided to change my usual format for the pre-course supervisors' meeting. Instead of using the two hour session to brief supervisors on the history and nature of workplace language and literacy courses and gather information on typical communication breakdowns, I decided to concentrate on providing them with some sort of analytical framework which would perhaps allow them to identify strengths and weaknesses in the communication skills of their employees. It would also help them to make sense of the communication tasks that I would be asking learners to get their help with. Perhaps most importantly, it would give them an insight into the multifaceted and complex process of learning English in any new context.

I took Halliday's (1978) register variables of field, mode and tenor and provided a brief explanation of each, using workplace data to illustrate what I was saying.

Having explained that the *field* of language was its subject area and each workplace had its own field, I went on to elicit examples from the various departments – e.g. *mangle, steam hose, imprest sheet* from the laundry, *menu, nil per mouth, assembling room* from food preparation, *detergent, Lemex, mop and bucket* from the cleaners and so on. The supervisors were amused to realise that some parts of the field of language that they had come to take for granted as commonplace were inaccessible to outsiders e.g. 'stripping trays' was meaningless to anybody who did not work in the food services department.

I went on to say that 'field' was an area of strength for most NESB learners and in fact they usually had to teach the teacher some of their work words. I pointed out, however, that it was one thing to be able to apply the correct word to an object or substance and quite another to understand the full implications of the word, and that while people had been able to identify workplace items from photographs in the interviews, further probing uncovered a dangerous lack of understanding of the meaning of the words that were serving as labels. A yellow bag emblazoned with the words 'Contaminated Waste' was shrugged off by more than one interviewee as 'rubbish'. 'Detergent' elicited the comment 'make floor smell nice'. While neither response was actually wrong, it was clear that for the learners the words they were using were not functioning to their full extent. It seemed that 'Contaminated' was not setting in motion a train of associations (danger, disgust, Chernobyl, caution, distance) that would protect the workers and 'Detergent' was prompting a cosmetic job rather than a thorough one. I stressed that employees were by no means ignorant of the functions of the yellow bag or the detergent but that for them the words had no 'aura' and were not helping them to do their jobs correctly.

To illustrate the point that language influences thought and hence behaviour I went on to recount the experience of the linguist Benjamin Whorf[2] who, as a young man, worked as a fire prevention officer for an insurance company in the USA. He noticed that a number of fires were caused by employees smoking in the vicinity of apparently empty petrol drums despite being warned not to do so. In fact, although the drums were referred to as empty they were full of highly flammable fumes. It appeared that people went on smoking near the petrol drums because the word 'empty' used to describe the drums influenced the way people thought about them, even to the extent of overriding warnings provided. In the hospital's case, the language in use was adequate and should have directed employees to do the right thing but their understanding of it was incomplete.

I explained that one of the functions of the courses would be to broaden and deepen employees' knowledge of the particular fields of language relevant to them in the workplace and asked for the supervisors' support in doing this.

I then went on to explain the register variable – mode – as the channel through which communication took place and explored some of the different ways of communicating in the different service departments of the hospital. Although the spoken word in face-to-face encounters was the predominant mode of communication (with only engineering services using the phone), written communication was important to a greater or lesser extent in all departments. Food services had to read the partly handwritten patient menus and rosters as well as job descriptions, laundry services had imprest sheets and order forms to complete while the cleaners had to understand directions and warnings on the fluids they used. All these areas were seen as highly problematic and workers' inability to cope was generally ascribed to an inability to read. In fact, though difficulty with reading constituted a problem for most people, it was compounded (particularly for the cleaners) by the use of words on labels and warnings which they would be unlikely to have heard in the normal course of a working day, e.g. *'odour'* rather than smell, *'generous amount'* rather than a lot of, *'use neat'* rather than 'don't mix with water' and so on.

By highlighting some of the differences between spoken and written English I hoped firstly, to make less inexplicable the ignorance of common English words displayed by long-term migrants who had learned English through speaking only and secondly, to alert supervisors to the need not only to read but also to paraphrase workplace texts for those who could not access them for themselves.

Owing to time constraints in the meeting described above, the register variable of tenor was touched upon but not fully covered. However, had there been sufficient time, *tenor* would have been explained as the way in which the power relationship affects both written and spoken communication, and some of the common workplace relationships explored. The patient/cleaner, patient/food services person encounters were of special interest, as service people, in the course of doing their jobs, often have to give directives and intrude on personal space. The distinction between direct and indirect requests and commands causes particular difficulties for employees whose native language is not English. They needed to master the more deferential and roundabout ways of getting people to do what they needed them to do.

Although I was unable in two hours to explore and analyse all the communication needs of the hospital assistants with the supervisors, I found the framework provided by the register variables extremely useful for teasing out and comparing the different language used in the four departments. It provided an orderly way of moving through the range of data available (e.g. What are the main modes of communicating in a) cleaning b) the laundry c) food services d) engineering?).

The concepts of field, mode and tenor, once explained, were straight-forward enough to be understood by the supervisors and seemed to engage their interest.

They were ready to offer specific examples of frustrations and mis-communications occasioned by the limited English language skills of the workers and I was able to respond by formulating objectives for the course. As a result of this session, supervisors were able to see the class as firmly set in the workplace matrix and myself as sympathetic to their problems. The rapport established led to ongoing contact and during the course various supervisors either looked in or made contributions to the sessions. Some also agreed to assist in assessing learners in real life situations such as 'reporting a problem' and give course particip-ants feedback on their skills at communicating clearly.

SETTING UP MONITORING AND EVALUATION MECHANISMS

Part of developing an action plan involves setting up a mechanism to discuss progress and issues of concern on a regular basis. As well as providing a way of supporting the project, such a group provides the basis for evaluating how effectively it achieves its set aims.

Besides representing the different parties (education provider, man-agement, employees, trainers) such a group should ensure it has enough authority to act on the information received. In workplaces where train-ing committees are already in operation, it may be preferable for such a committee to adopt this role, rather than creating a separate mechan-ism. In this way, issues of language and diversity can be more system-atically addressed as part of mainstream skill development activities.

Some of the roles that such a committee would play include providing guidance, troubleshooting practical problems – relating, for example, to the release of employees – supporting the programme by encouraging participation, arranging for necessary resources and giving feedback on different initiatives.

Evaluation is usually needed for a number of purposes and by dif-ferent individuals and organisations. One of the primary reasons is to provide feedback on how to improve current and future activities. Another is to determine whether the programme has achieved its agreed objectives and assess its impact on the workplace and the learners. Evaluation is usually also necessary to satisfy the accountability require-ments of funding agencies. Almost inevitably, these diverse purposes will require different criteria and evaluation methods. These should be jointly agreed at the beginning of programmes, rather than as an after-thought. Where possible, it is preferable for the final evaluation to be undertaken by an independent party – or at least validated from a number of perspectives – to provide an objective assessment.

As far as possible, a broad cross-section of workplace personnel should be involved in developing evaluation criteria and methods. If line management and potential learners, for example, are involved, there is a greater chance of a shared understanding on indicators for effectiveness and how to measure them.

Agreeing on appropriate indicators of effectiveness can pose a number of challenges. For example, if one of the central aims of the programme is to integrate language, literacy and cross-cultural issues into a workplace's communication, training and management practices, it can be difficult to identify discrete indicators. Successful programmes often greatly enhance and positively influence other initiatives such as teamwork, quality monitoring or customer service, rather than providing separate, quantifiable outcomes. By the same token, other factors, such as employee relations or reward systems, can also significantly impact on such initiatives.

Also, it is often difficult to find the appropriate balance between qualitative and quantitative evaluation. Qualitative evaluation – which reports on individuals' views about the programme – is useful in gaining feedback on programme relevance and learner satisfaction, but can often result in little more than subjective 'happy sheets'. It can also be influenced by factors such as different parties' interests in seeing the programme as either successful or unsuccessful.

On the other hand, quantitative evaluation or 'hard' data – such as course enrolments, achievement of particular competencies – can be highly reductionist in accounting for the differences the programme has actually made to the learners and to training or communication practices in the organisation as a whole. Yet it is usually these quantifiable measures which are needed for continued funding.

Often programme outcomes, or their relative importance, change in response to unforeseen factors, such as disruption to work schedules, or the introduction of new initiatives. As the adult educator Brookfield (1986) points out, such improvisational ability should be regarded as crucial to successful practice, rather than an unprofessional deviation. Responding to changes may greatly enhance the relevance of the programme in the workplace, but unless such flexibility has been inbuilt into the evaluation process, the final results may be devalued for going off of the originally specified track.

As far as possible, evaluation criteria should be sufficiently broad to reflect programme goals and yet allow for responsiveness and incidental learning. Some of the basic aspects needing to be addressed in evaluation include:

- reaction to the programme – Do employees (learners, line management, trainers, etc.) express satisfaction with the programme? Have they actively participated, or regularly attended training sessions?
- learning – Have learners demonstrated gains in communicative competence as identified in the programme objectives? What else has been learnt as a result of the programmes?
- transfer – Has there been a transfer of learning to the daily work situation? To wider contexts?
- results – Have there been improvements in work, training or communication practices?

Quantifying and attributing 'results' can be a challenging exercise, but a useful precedent can be found in a comprehensive national Australian study of the impact of ESL and literacy training. It identified five areas in which the effects of training had been most keenly felt.[3] The evaluation instruments used a combination of objective and subjective data relating to the following:

- direct cost savings – in worker time, unproductive labour and maintenance costs.
- access to and acceptability of further training
- participation in teams and meetings
- promotion and job flexibility
- the value of training – in increased worker morale and employee relations.

Meaningful comparisons of progress can only be made if baseline data is gathered at the beginning of programmes. Rather than reporting simply on improvements in learners' communicative competence, points of comparison should highlight its impact on daily work. For example, reporting on employees' increased familiarity and use of work instructions, understanding of company directions, or participation in work activities is more likely to be of interest than lists of competence statements. Similarly, improvements in trainers and team-leaders' ability to communicate effectively, the user-friendliness of training manuals and written communications should be included. Critical incidents are a particularly useful way of illustrating gains in these areas and should be (sensitively) documented in the early stages of the programme for later comparison.

Documenting how learning has been applied to wider areas, such as family life and broader social settings, is also useful to illustrate achievements due to increased confidence or improved morale. Learners often comment on their increased ability or willingness to initiate interactions with their children's teachers at school, or become involved in social activities at work.

Frequently programme effectiveness is best evaluated some time after completion. Indicators such as learners' ability to successfully complete other training programmes or gain promotions are dependent on more than just the effectiveness of the programme. It can take quite a while for learning to translate into significant quantifiable outcomes. As a personnel officer from a manufacturing company observed:

> From the communications skills course, and other vocational courses
> that we have had running here now over the last two years, I can see
> some real benefits. Some of the people are now trainers, some involved in
> Occupational Health and Safety committees, in computers, in quality, they
> are helping to work out the graphs, they are on the consultative committee,
> they are a lot more active, and they are taking more interest and more
> control of their working life.

If such long-term evaluation is not possible, it should be at least pointed out that some of the benefits of the project will not become evident immediately, and may be dependent on follow-up strategies.

MAXIMISING THE IMPACT OF COURSES

There are many situations where language and literacy courses may be the logical starting-point in a workplace project. In organisations where there has not been a strong focus on structured skill development, for example, such courses provide a valuable means for workers to build up their confidence, formal learning, teamwork and problem-solving skills. Apart from providing a broad base for skill development, workplace communication courses can often give an opportunity for employees to become familiar with proposed changes at work, organisational goals and priorities. They can also act as a valuable forum for employees to interact more informally with their managers and trainers.

From the educator's perspective, courses can provide a comfortable starting-point, especially for those with little experience of workplace education. They allow the educator to become familiar with the workplace and its idiosyncrasies, as well as to experiment in small ways with different approaches to integrating language and literacy.

However, such courses can become quite limiting, especially if they represent the sum total of an educators' contribution to a workplace. Dramatic improvements in learners' overall competence in English are unlikely to occur after a short course, and the prospect of a series of long courses is not viable in most workplaces. Developments in employees' communicative competence usually need to be matched by modifications to general communicative and training practices in the workplace if significant improvements are to result. These modifications are unlikely to occur, if the educator confines her/himself to a training room, with a selected group of employees.

Maximising the value and impact of courses involves more than just using authentic workplace materials, or designing courses around particular workplace tasks. It involves making strategic decisions at different stages of planning and delivery to integrate different aspects that are often rigidly compartmentalised – such as learning and working; language, literacy and technical skill development.

These decisions need to be informed by workplace considerations as much as pedagogical ones. For example, selecting prospective learners involves considerations of what is educationally, industrially and practically possible. While voluntary participation in courses is usually encouraged, there may be some situations where particular employees need to be approached and encouraged to participate. Especially in workplaces with little initial support, it may be necessary to select a group of learners in terms of the potential impact of the first course, rather than the long-term needs of particular employees.

Having a homogeneous group of learners is usually highly desirable from an educational perspective, but selecting learners according to occupational or sectional groupings may have equally beneficial outcomes. In the Merck, Sharp and Dohme example above the calculator skills course was offered to a 'mixed-ability' work-group as a way of introducing some to formal learning, and legitimising the need for developing language and literacy skills as work practices changed. It was possible for the whole section to be offered such a course chiefly because of its short duration. At Chiswell Hospital on the other hand, the disparate educational background, stages of competence in language and work sections made the initially proposed group unworkable. Learners who have problems with copying letters of the alphabet can't be easily accommodated in a report-writing group. Dividing the group along proficiency lines was a difficult, but necessary decision.

Factors such as the timing and location of the courses can also play a major role in determining their success or otherwise. In some workplaces, such as road maintenance or construction gangs, it may be administratively efficient to release employees for a whole working day, on a fortnightly basis, but from an educational perspective, such an arrangement can have a disastrous effect, unless the course is carefully designed to cater for such intensive sessions. Similarly, holding training sessions at the end of a long working day, or with a group of employees on night or rotating shifts can pose logistic and methodological challenges.

The location of the course often provides clear signals as to its status within the organisation. Improvised spaces at the back of the canteen, for example, can be clear signals of marginalisation if such a venue is not usually used for 'real training'. By the same token, employees may not feel comfortable initially in using the company boardroom, if it has been previously out of bounds.

The actual content of the courses needs to be negotiated in close collaboration with the different parties involved: managers, supervisors, trainers and employees. Learning activities which allow learners to make the links with the communicative demands of their work, and to apply the skills learnt will obviously have greater relevance and impact for both learners and the workplace. Small problem-based projects – where learners identify a problem and work together to arrive at a solution – can be particularly effective. In one workplace, for example, employees critically reviewed safety notices and operational instructions. In another, they were asked to develop for the first time, a flow chart for processes in their section and talk about their role in the process.

The direct and indirect involvement of workplace personnel is essential if the courses are to lead to changes in daily work practices. Depending on the situation and available resources, they can be involved in different capacities: by contributing workplace materials, reviewing course content, providing input and feedback as the course progresses or helping to set up peer tutoring partnerships to supplement course time. Particular workplace personnel, such as managers, supervisors, trainers or safety officers, could be invited to address learners on particular issues of interest, or co-present sessions on specific work-related topics. Even less obvious people, such as canteen attendants, first aid, security or pay officers can also play a valuable role in providing learners with opportunities to practise their skills – provided they are well-briefed and willing to help!

Courses usually provide a valuable opportunity for the educator and workplace personnel to develop a rapport and the basis of a productive collaborative relationship. In the following example, we return to Aus Tin, and briefly outline some of the courses that were conducted following the communication skills audit. The educators involved in conducting the courses had not been part of the audit exercise, and therefore needed to familiarise themselves with the workplace and its personnel.

Communication Skills Courses at Aus Tin

Following the communication skills audit undertaken at Aus Tin, it was decided to offer a series of language and literacy courses, as a precursor to the technical training courses which were yet to be developed. Due to production and budgetary factors, only one course could be offered at one time, and consequently a choice had to be made regarding which group to target.

For political reasons, it was essential to get broad acceptance from all levels of the organisation for the first such course and to have successful, immediate outcomes as a result of this 'pilot' if any further courses were to follow. It was also evident that outcomes would need to be expressed in quantifiable, production efficiency terms rather than human resource terms, partly because of the prevailing work culture, and partly because of the difficult economic situation.

For all those reasons, a course was offered to ten employees who had intermediate literacy and oracy skills, and who held more responsible positions on the shop floor, e.g. production maintainers and mechanics. The stated aims of the ten week, forty hour course were to:

- develop participants' literacy skills to enable them to participate more effectively in the workplace, access company training and multiskilling opportunities.
- increase participants' understanding of the changes occurring as a result of restructuring and workplace reform.

As part of the course, a series of workshops, involving one of the section supervisors was conducted to introduce the participants to the new computer-based production and planning system in the workplace.

A significant and innovative component was the introduction of a work experience opportunity for each participant where for half a day per week for six weeks, they worked in a different section of the plant where they had indicated an interest e.g. despatch, administration. These practical opportunities for multiskilling were strategic, both in legitimising the course as an integral part of the company's response to a structural concern of equipping people for new jobs, and in allowing for more informal interaction between different people and sections in the plant.

The course was positively evaluated by both management and the participants involved, with noticeable improvements being observed in communication, confidence, increased participation at work, quicker understanding of instructions, better morale and team spirit.

As a result of the successful pilot, another two sixty-four hour courses were offered that year, followed up by the full-time 'Enterprise based' appointment of the teacher the following year, who conducted two further thirty-two hour extension courses for the lower level groups . These courses had a strong literacy focus and catered for employees identified by the audit as having only a very basic command of English.

While the general aims of the course were similar to the first one, there was a considerable focus on the development of the employees' confidence in their ability to learn, and strategies for formal learning. In developing literacy skills, the teacher used authentic workplace texts as well as more general material, so the employees were able to immediately transfer the skills learnt in class to their working situation.

As company specific training materials became available, the educator was able to design specific support materials and integrate them into the courses, so that the employees were in a better position to access the technical training. Examples of these included abbreviations on factory orders or practising basic computer functions.

There was again a work experience component to the course (half a day p.w. over eight weeks), which enabled some of the employees to develop skills in other areas of the plant. One employee, for example, was able to learn how to enter production data on the computer as a result of the course. These skills were subsequently formally recognised and used by her department.

The educator consulted a great deal with the supervisors and peers of the employees to gain their support and active involvement in the courses. She also gained considerable credibility with both employees and management by spending time on the noisy shop floor observing and finding out about the employees' jobs. Through this informal networking she was able to obtain and provide feedback on the learners' progress and integrate any new developments in work organisation into the course. As a closer rapport was established and formal technical training introduced, the educator was increasingly consulted regarding the accessibility or appropriateness of particular texts, or ways of communicating certain concepts.

Key personnel were invited to attend the course to observe or talk to the employees about a specific issue. As a way of informing others of the work being covered in the course, some of the learners' work was, with their permission, displayed on the plant notice-board.

At the end of the courses, formal presentations were held, to recognise and celebrate the gains made by the course participants. The presentations were organised and catered for by the participants, with the teacher and training manager's assistance. The course 'graduants' were issued with certificates and made short speeches. These presentations soon became an important, highly valued ritual which also provided a rare opportunity for key management personnel in the company to informally interact with the employees in a different setting.

Short articles about the English courses were published in the company's national magazine, as well as other journals. Copies of these were distributed around the plant and (proudly!) displayed on notice-boards.

The following worksheets illustrate some of the work covered in the courses and the progress made by one of the participants over two courses (almost 100 hours). V., was typical of the group in that she had completed primary school in her native Italy and received no further formal training. She, in particular, needed a considerable amount of encouragement to enrol in the course, and seemed very apprehensive in the early stages. At the first session, she came with her name and address written for her on the palm of her hand, as she could not reproduce these independently.

After approximately six sessions, she was able, with a considerable degree of encouragement, to produce the following text. The beginning of each sentence was provided by the teacher:

```
MY NAME iS  v
I COME FROM  ITALY.
I CAME TO  AUSTRALiA iN 1958.
I WORK aT
I aM a  PROCESS WORKER.
MY SUPERViSOR)S NAME iS N
I hAVE 3 chilDREN.
                        28/8/91
```

V.'s story

Later in the course, she was independently able to produce the following 'story' about her work, with the teacher assisting only with the spelling of two or three words she had difficulty with:

```
        MY WORK    31/10/91

I WORK AT
WE MAKE
ShAViNg cREAM, PAiNT,
OVEN cLEANER AND OThERS.
I WORKiN ThE ROUNDROOM.
I START WORK AT 7 o'cloek.
FiRST I WORK ThE WEiDER
FOR 1 hoUR. ThEN I goTo ThE
PALLETiZER.
AFTER ThAT, I goTo ThE WATER
TESTER AND SEAMER.
WE hAVE LUNch AT 12 o'cLoek.
AFTER LUNch WE go BAck
To WORK,
UNTiL 3 o'cLock eoMES.
```

V.'s work

As the literacy levels improved, the course focus drew more on authentic workplace texts. The following is an extract from one of the work-specific exercises developed by the teacher, which V. was able to complete successfully:

Operating the Slitter

OPERATE SLITTER TO CUT BODY BLANKS

1. Put on   scrap and remove
2. Follow correct   body blanks
3. Check for   starting procedure
4. Square cut   defects, scratches and burrs
5. Check for   safety gloves

FOLLOW CORRECT STARTING PROCEDURE

1. Press   responsible person
2. Start   start buttons in correct sequence
3. Inform   welding wire when machine is warm
4. Turn on   automatic control and conveyor line if
               no welding problem exists

By the end of the course, all the participants (including V.) were able to undertake the following communicative tasks:

- identify the main areas of the workplace from different types of diagrams
- identify key stages in the production process
- read a simple flow chart, diagram and graph
- find important information on factory orders and tickets
- read workplace abbreviations
- follow a set of simple written instructions
- fill in basic factual information on a variety of forms
- use a variety of reading strategies to find important information in a memo

In evaluating the usefulness of the course, the employees made the following comments:

'I've learnt many things. I didn't want to learn before, now I do.'

'It has helped me with my job. I understand many things now.'

'I couldn't write nothing before. Now I can write lots of things, and spell words. My reading was O.K. but I can read better now.'

Many also reported a transfer of their learning into more general areas. One employee, for example, commented that she was now better able to understand her children, whose English was more fluent than their Croatian.

The supervisors and managers' evaluations focused on both the quantifiable and the qualitative gains:

'They've improved so much. They are a lot more relaxed and confident.'

'I asked them to do a job, I started to explain how, and one said "Oh, I know how to do this! We did it in class!". She proceeded to do it perfectly.'

'Individual productivity has increased by 20 to 30 per cent and there has been a major improvement in communication. Additionally, because there is now more interaction on the shop floor, employees are taking a broader interest in their work and the company generally, are suggesting more efficient methods of doing jobs and are prepared to work in areas other than those to which they were originally assigned.' (Plant Manager)

'They all fill in their own leave forms now.' (Pay Officer)

As technical training was introduced, the supervisor/trainers also commented that the employees who had attended the English course seemed more receptive and comfortable in the learning environment, and were able to participate more actively than those who had not.

While there were many significant gains made through the English courses, there were also some difficulties and unanticipated negative repercussions. English courses were the first type of formal training generally offered to production employees, at a time when the implications of workplace reform were still unclear to the majority of the workforce. It involved time release (initially for 50 per cent of training time) which impacted on production schedules, already operating with little margin. Some managers were dubious about the value of the courses and resented, for example, the use of the relatively plush conference room by 'wages' staff.

For almost twelve months at the company, language and literacy courses were the only training available for production employees, as the technical courses had taken much longer to organise than originally anticipated. This was perceived by some as favouritism, and led to some resentment, until other training opportunities were made available.

These opportunities included the comprehensive technical training programme, as well as wordprocessing and numeracy courses. The educator was closely involved with the numeracy teacher, and was able to inform the syllabus content because of the needs analysis undertaken.

The English courses had met the objectives that had been set, and it was felt that the workforce's basic level of English proficiency had been vastly improved. After an evaluation of the courses, it was decided that for the next phase, different forms of learning arrangements were more appropriate. An Individual Learning Program and a Distance Learning Programme were established for those employees who wished to continue after completing the courses and those who had previously been unable to access the language and literacy courses. These included nightshift employees, employees from a third department in the company, who had for a number of industrial and managerial reasons not been involved in any form of training. The learning materials for these programmes include general literacy as well as specific, bridging, materials for technical training and workplace specific materials.

NOTES

1. For more details, Mawer, G. 1994. Language, Literacy and Numeracy at Merck Sharp and Dohme (Australia) Pty Ltd: Evaluation Report of an Integrated Approach. Foundation Studies Division, Western Sydney Institute of TAFE, NSW and Merck Sharp and Dohme.
2. Carroll, J.B. (ed.) 1956 Language, Thought and Reality: Selected Writings of Benjamin Lee Whorf, Cambridge, Mass. MIT Press.
3. Department of Employment, Education and Training 1996 *More than Money can say – The Impact of ESL and Literacy Training in the Australian Workplace*, Canberra.

SEVEN

Development of competency standards

Competency-based standards are the focal point for national approaches to skill development and recognition: they provide the benchmark for identifying and rewarding skills, developing new job descriptions and establishing career paths, ways of organising work and criteria for recruiting and promoting employees. Standards also form the basis for developing curriculum, accrediting training programmes and assessing learners.

Mismatches between what it actually takes to perform competently at work and the description of that competence in industry standards can therefore have wide ramifications: for the individual concerned, their workplace and more widely for education, training and industrial parties. Inequities in standards can, for example, impact on the way employees' skills are recognised and rewarded, and whether existing bias is addressed or reinforced. Narrow standards almost inevitably lead to narrow approaches to skill formation and work organisation. Rather than facilitating a system that recognises and develops the skills needed for work in the midst of change, standards can become just as constraining as the hierarchical, Fordist models of work they are seeking to replace.

As individuals and organisations attempt to develop standards, or apply them, they often find themselves needing to deal with a number of thorny conceptual, industrial and practical issues. Typical ones include:

- Can standards meaningfully capture more than the quantifiable, routine 'task skills' and still be outcome focused?
- How can standards be nationally consistent and yet locally relevant and meaningful?
- Should standards set minimum criteria or optimum ones?
- How can standards reflect and reward the diversity of skills and resources that individuals bring to their work?

- How can the standards development process be used to redress present imbalances in terms of what skills are recognised and developed?
- Should competence in language or literacy be explicitly addressed in industry standards? If so how? If not, how else can it be addressed?
- Do standards automatically translate into curriculum?

Language and literacy educators are usually not involved in the process of developing national industry standards, as this is undertaken primarily by the relevant industry parties (through Lead Industry Bodies in the UK, or Industry Training Advisory Bodies in Australia). They are often more likely to be involved in the process of customising national standards for use at local workplace level, or developing a curriculum based on established standards. So they are often working within an already established framework.

In this chapter, we briefly discuss some of the main issues relating to the definition of competence and the standards development process. We explore some of the ways that language and literacy educators can influence the development of useful, inclusive standards in the workplace.

IDENTIFYING AND DEFINING COMPETENCE

Competency-based – or outcome focused – approaches to standards and skill development have been promoted as offering many advantages over traditional approaches based on seniority, inputs or length of training courses. Some of the main positives include:

- providing a clear and consistent statement of work requirements (rather than sets of implicit assumptions of what is required);
- recognition of the skill requirements in occupations previously deemed unskilled;
- a basis for recognising prior learning (RPL or APL) and current competence (RCC), thus enabling portability and recognition of competence, regardless of how or where it was gained;
- the possibility of incremental achievement via statements of competence (rather than needing to complete an entire qualification before any credit is given).

For traditionally disadvantaged groups, such as individuals with limited formal credentials or facility in English, competency-based approaches potentially offer a more empowering and flexible means of having skills recognised and rewarded.

Governments, industries and education and training sectors adopting competency-based approaches stress that competence should be defined broadly rather than narrowly, and should attempt to be future-oriented in terms of the skills needed and the way that work is organised. In Australia, for example, competence has been defined as:

> the specification of the knowledge and skill and the application of that knowledge and skill within an occupation or industry level to the standard of performance required in employment. (NTB, 1991: 7)

> The concept of competency focuses on what is expected of an employee in the workplace rather than on the learning process; it embodies the ability to transfer and apply skills and knowledge to new situations and environments. This is a broad concept of competency in that all aspects of work performance, and not only narrow task skills, are included. It encompasses:
> - the requirement to perform individual tasks (task skills)
> - the requirement to manage a number of different tasks within the job (task management skills)
> - the requirement to respond to irregularities and breakdowns in routine (contingency management skills)
> - the requirement to deal with the responsibilities and expectations of the work environment (job/role environment skills). (NTB, 1991: 18)

A particular set of terminology has also developed: competency standards are built up from a collection of *units*, which in turn are made up of *elements*. As the following diagram shows, related *performance criteria* are developed for each competency statement to specify the required level of performance. The *range of variables* indicate the conditions or limits that apply to that performance, while the *evidence guide* indicates the context and evidence required for assessment purposes.

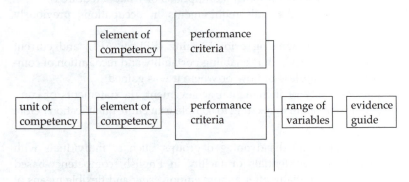

Figure 7.1: Components of competency standards
Source: Adapted from NTB 1992: 34

In Australia, an ambitious target was originally set to develop standards for 90 per cent of the workforce by the end of 1995. Even with a subsequently revised target of 80 per cent by the end of 1997, this accelerated pace – compared with other countries – has meant that quality has often been sacrificed for expediency. Standards have often been set by outsiders to the actual coal face with little systematic empirical research, piloting or evaluation. By its own admission, the National Training Board, in endorsing standards, has opted not to 'get it right first time', in favour of having a rudimentary system in place sooner rather than later:

> We have gone for . . . speed rather than for too high a quality level
> initially . . . and a review within 2 years. Thus the standards you are seeing
> will all have deficiencies, commonly of being overly task based and not
> grappling as well as they will in future with underlying competencies such
> as communication, problem-solving and so on. (Godfrey, NTB, 1992: 4–5)

This approach has meant that the standards developed to date have generally reflected a narrow conception of their intended uses and users. Despite having adopted a broad definition of competence, work has been typically dissected into artificial, task-based categories which are out of step with workplace realities. Some of the essential key elements that contribute to the development of a highly skilled, flexible workforce and effective work practices, such as teamwork and contingency management skills, have been underemphasised, if not totally ignored. The narrow focus on discrete tasks and individual skills, for example, is out of step with more fluid, team-based, ways of working. Research and practical experience indicate that at an individual level, aspects such as 'stance', 'perseverance' 'reliability' and 'mindwork' can be just as – if not more – important as the possession of a high level of technical skills or knowledge.[1]

Yet attempts to deal with 'softer', 'higher order' or 'key' competencies have been problematic. In Australia, for example, a national framework consisting of seven key competency strands was adopted in 1992.[2] Industry parties are required to identify key competencies as part of the standards development process, either in an adjunct or integrated way. These were defined as:

- Collecting, analysing and organising information
- Communicating ideas and information
- Planning and organising activities
- Working with others and in teams
- Using mathematical ideas and techniques

- Solving problems
- Using technology.

An eighth key competency – *Cultural Understandings* – was under consideration for some time, but not adopted.[3] Industry use of the key competencies has not, to date, been extensive. Apart from methodological challenges in identifying and describing competencies such as organising ideas and solving problems in precise, measurable terms, there have been a number of industrial and resource implications of recognising and therefore remunerating and developing skills in seemingly 'non-core' areas. Employers typically do not see their responsibility as providing a general broad education in 'generic skills' or theoretical concepts, especially given the high costs of curriculum development and training delivery.

These considerations have been particularly relevant in accounting for competence in English as part of competency standards – an issue which has been the subject of much debate in countries such as the UK and Australia. Do skills in English constitute a competency in their own right, or as the Australian National Training Board put it, are they a central enabling requirement for competency?[4] In a country such as Australia, with one of the world's most linguistically diverse workforces, is it not discriminatory to specify English language competencies? How can such competencies be established at an appropriate level, when communicative contexts are by nature often fluid and dynamic? In many work situations, there may be little need for language, be it English or otherwise, to perform a particular task. Industry parties in Australia have strongly argued that specifying a 'minimal general level' of English language and literacy for particular occupational classification levels could discriminate against a significant proportion of the workforce who are currently performing their work competently.[5] On the other hand, if English language and literacy skills are not identified, how will they be addressed in curriculum development, or allocated sufficient resources? With the increasing communicative requirements of work, is it not appropriate to set specific standards so that this competence can be acknowledged and developed?

Difficulties with unrealistic communicative requirements of developed standards and pressure from education sectors have led to a ministerial policy decision in 1994 that:

> Standards should encompass all aspects of competency, including
> underlying knowledge; ability to transfer skills to new applications;
> and language literacy and numeracy competencies (ANTA 1994 (b): 9)

This decision was followed by a small number of government-funded projects to support the development and review of industry standards, and to develop methodological tools and resources to assist this process.[6]

The ministerial decision is also likely to influence debate in the related area of bilingual skills. If competence in English can be regarded and rewarded as an essential requirement at work, could not the same apply to bilingual competence in particular work contexts? Up to now, bilingual skills may have been recognised as valuable and rewarded through supplementary allowances, but they have been seen as belonging to particular individuals, rather than being an essential component of the work. This contrasts with the establishment of a Languages Lead Body in the UK in 1993 and the development of a competency-based National Language Standards framework for the use of foreign languages at work.

Quite apart from the issue of accounting for language and literacy in industry standards, competency-based approaches to language learning have themselves been hotly debated since their introduction in countries such as the USA in the 1980s.[7] The points of criticisms have been very similar to those made against their use in industry standards: checklists of behavioural objectives fail to capture significant areas of competence such as critical thinking, the ability to learn from experience and the ability to organize information which are key skills needed for the acquisition and application of knowledge. A narrow focus on the teaching and assessment of job-related language risks reducing language learning to a mechanistic behavioural task rather than one requiring the creation of meaning. Language, it is argued, is a highly complex skill and cannot be equated with the mastery of isolated behaviours: the whole is greater than the sum of the parts.

Another major criticism has been the flow on effect of reductionist approaches to describing language to reductionist curriculum and assessment practices. Auerbach (1986) and Tollefson (1986) have both strongly argued, for example, that the use of competency-based approaches in refugee programmes in the USA restricted learners to menial and lowly paid positions, rather than empowering them to be active members of their new country. In Australia, the adoption of spoken and written texts as the basis for describing language competencies in some accredited courses has been criticised as lacking both construct and empirical validity.[8] The value of separately accrediting language and literacy competencies in a vocational education and training system has also been questioned.

It is evident, therefore, that things are very much in a state of flux as far as standards are concerned. In Australia, many industry standards that were among the first to be developed are currently being reviewed as part of the requirements of new National Training Packages, which contain endorsed competency standards, national vocational qualifications and assessment guidelines. The aim of the review is to ensure they relate more closely to workplace realities and reflect a broader notion of competence, encompassing aspects such as communication, teamwork and cultural diversity. Similarly, at local enterprise level, many organisations are developing their own competency schedules, with reference to national standard frameworks, as a basis for establishing training plans and skills-based pay systems. Endeavours in the language and literacy fields are also producing competency descriptions of language outcomes, such as the National Reporting System (Coates *et al.*, 1995) that can be used nationally to specify particular language requirements and account for learner progress.

It is likely that educators will find themselves more involved in the standards development process both at local workplace level, and as part of collaborative national projects. In the next section, we explore some of the aspects of this process and the ways that educators can contribute to the development of more responsive, inclusive standards.

THE STANDARDS DEVELOPMENT PROCESS

Because industry standards form the basis for skill recognition and development, there are usually strongly competing priorities and agenda needing to be balanced in the process of developing them. Skill relativities and career paths, for example, are major issues for industry parties in setting the framework for how work will be organised and skills rewarded. Ways of integrating a focus on quality, safety and flexible work practices are also important considerations. The process of achieving national consensus among the different factions of industry – employers, unions, small and large businesses – can be tortuous, with many compromises needing to be made between visionary ideals and pragmatic constraints.

It is not surprising, therefore, that communicative requirements or issues of cultural diversity or access and equity become minor considerations alongside these other factors. Because of the high stakes involved, and pressures of time and resources, there tends to be little involvement of the 'grass-roots' in these processes, in preference to officially sanctioned representatives, and little empirical testing of the validity of the standards finally produced.

So to what extent can educators be involved in this process? What influence can they have? It depends very much on how early they can be part of the initial development or subsequent adaptation and review process, and how they define their role. In Australia, for example, a small number of government funded language and literacy projects have enabled educators to work collaboratively with those involved in developing industry standards. These have ranged from relatively small-scale workplace-based projects to national reviews of existing standards.[9] Educators' contributions in these collaborative ventures have varied from an awareness raising and facilitation role, to providing analytical tools for identifying communicative requirements and reviewing the clarity of expression of the final competency statements.

The selection and preparation of those involved in developing standards, for example, can greatly influence the outcomes. One way of building awareness of language and cultural issues into the process is to ensure that those involved reflect the demographics of the present and potential target groups. This can often be difficult as employees with less facility in English tend to self-select out of forums like focus groups because of their unfamiliarity and general lack of confidence with formal group methodologies. Briefing sessions, for example, can be valuable in engaging their active participation and input, so are particular provisions such as the use of bilingual assistance, or the judicious selection of participants to ensure that operators do not feel inhibited by the presence of their supervisors.

Awareness raising for those involved in developing standards extends to more than just highlighting the communicative aspects of work. It also includes challenging assumptions about how competence itself is defined and some of the ways narrow descriptions and parameters can inadvertently be discriminatory. It may involve raising awareness of policy requirements in terms of bias, access and equity issues. For example, in a particular industry, most employees may currently be full time, male and have English as their first language. Despite this existing scenario, the standards should accommodate a very different workforce and other work arrangements that might occur in the future. Similarly, requirements for particular modes of communication e.g. through written reports, may be discriminatory if they are not an essential part of the work.

The processes and methods used to develop standards are obviously important aspects that affect the quality of the final outcomes. It is often difficult to analyse one's work in terms of competencies, especially for groups whose skills have traditionally been undervalued. The 'Umm to Aha' phenomeon coined by Cox *et al.* (1991), for example, noted the value of a facilitative group process in providing a framework for women to help uncover their 'hidden skills' by reflecting on life, work and educational experiences. For employees operating in a second language, such reflection and identification can be even more daunting.

The starting-point for identifying competence can often be limiting in itself. Approaches focusing on tasks, for example, tend to almost inevitably result in a step-by-step list of task skills. As a more traditional standards developer saw it:

> You plan the work, prepare, do it and then clean up.

Such an approach greatly undervalues the capacity of the individuals doing the work, and their relationships with their fellow-workers and customers. Re-conceptualising the nature of the work to identify 'what it takes' to be competent at work tends to bring out a more holistic view of competence. In identifying ways of discriminating between the performance of work by a competent employee and one not so competent, underlying knowledge, contingency management skills, and higher order skills such as communication and problem solving then come to the surface more easily. Task management and contingency management skills, for example, are usually integral to tasks, but often receive little attention.

Analytical frameworks and tools highlighting the contributions of individuals to work can therefore be very useful in focusing attention on more than simply the 'skills mix' required to perform a task adequately. Critical incidents, for example, are particularly useful in this regard as they help in highlighting specific aspects of competence in a way that draws on and affirms employees' ways of knowing and working. Similarly, an explicit focus on job/role environment competencies is essential if employees are to have more than a narrow, Taylorist approach to their work and career path. As one standards developer put it:

> We've tried to build in an awareness of the before and after, whys and
> what ifs of work into the actual standards, so people have a spatial relation
> of where things sit, what the whole process is about, what else there is
> going on that might be of interest or relevance to them.

An explicit focus on job/role environment competencies also enables standards to address work practices and organisational values – which is often where indirect discrimination occurs. Competencies that, for example, require employees to apply equal employment principles and demonstrate an appreciation and accommodation of difference would enhance the inclusivity of work performance as well as organisational work practices.

The wording used to describe the competency descriptions is also important. Draft competency descriptions are often rewritten after a standards development workshop to make them more concise, consistent and authoritative. The requirement to 'report problems with work' for example can find itself translated as 'variations and constraints affecting work requirements are identified and reported to nominated person so that appropriate corrective action can be taken'. This can result in their being unrecognisable by both the workshop participants who originally drafted them and their intended users.

A recent British review of NVQ standards pointed out similar problems. A detailed study[10] analysed all two million words (!) of the NVQ database of accredited qualifications and compared them with current English texts drawn from newspapers, books, magazines and broadcasting. They found two major areas of difficulty. The first was related to readers' unfamiliarity with standards documents, due to their complex, innovative conceptual basis. The second area of difficulty, however, was due to sixteen problematic linguistic features identified. These included: ambiguity, words used in unfamiliar combinations, unfamiliar words, lack of precision and cumbersome sentence structures.

Given the standards' role as a 'critical communicative site' for recognising employees' skills and determining their career paths, it is difficult to justify their further mystification through unnecessarily complex language. Interestingly, it is only very recently that the impact of abstracted, technical descriptions of competence on accessibility and user-friendliness has been taken into account by the Australian National Training Authority. As a result, the new National Training Package guidelines have been changed, requiring that:

> competency standards should be written in clear, simple, user-friendly language so as to be readily understandable to trainers, supervisors, potential employers and trainees.[11] (ANTA: July, 1997c: 35)

Educators can greatly contribute to the development of inclusive, usable standards by focusing attention on the wording used.

The following example from the NSW Community and Health Services industry training board illustrates how some of these considerations were taken into account in developing standards in a 'green field site' where no formal standards had existed for the largely female, culturally diverse workforce. From the beginning, the project aimed to develop standards that were 'relevant, understandable, useful and credible for both workers and organisations'.[12] As the project manager put it:

Before developing standards, we had a workshop for people to explain what standards were for and the importance of ensuring that our process was empirically based. We used a mixture of critical incidents, questionnaires, and workshops. We also targeted particular occupations and particular demographics within our industry, and used bilingual help where needed. It was constant validation.

People were excited about the opportunity to identify what it is that they do, and competencies such as like cultural understandings, interpersonal skills, advocacy and communication continually appeared. The identification of what made someone competent in these areas was challenging and crucial to the diverse services provided e.g. working with aged people from diverse backgrounds, refugees who had suffered trauma; Aboriginal and Torres Strait Islanders, street kids.

It was also important to express the competencies we developed in ways that people understood and owned them.[13]

Following the development of the draft standards, they were validated by further observations and consultations with workers in the field and broader industry consultations. As a result of this intensive, collaborative work, the competency statements have captured some of the essential elements of good practice in ways that are meaningful to the industry, individual worker and patient. Some of the competencies for caring for aged persons, for example, include supporting their interests and needs within legislative requirements, taking time to establish and develop rapport and taking into account individual and cultural differences when communicating with them.

A recent national project in the warehousing and distribution industry (NBEET, 1996) has produced a useful model and a set of practical, methodological tools for developing standards that incorporate language and literacy competencies. While providing a clear systematic approach based on explicit principles, the authors emphasise throughout the report the need for a contextualised, collaborative approach:

There are a number of options and combinations of options that can be used to incorporate English language and literacy explicitly into industry / enterprise standards. There is no single formula for every industry or enterprise. (1996: 34)

Another resource – *Workplace Communication in National Training Packages: A Practical Guide* Fitzpatrick and Roberts (1997) – has been recently published by Language Australia to assist with the development of English Language Literacy and Numeracy inclusive Training Packages. It provides a step-by-step guide to identify, and incorporate communicative competence as part of industry standards. It provides a framework, for example, for the different purposes of communication – procedural, technical, personal, cooperative, systems and public communication.

The guide also provides specific examples of how language and literacy requirements can be integrated into the different components of competency descriptions (such as units, elements, performance criteria, the range of variables and underpinning knowledge and skills). This integration also enables some of the new changes in organisational culture, such as teamwork, an increasing focus on quality and customer relations to be made more explicit.

The following example of standards development is a detailed look at an early attempt to develop competency schedules for Aus Tin. This initiative took place at a time when national standards had not yet been developed for the industry, although a general framework had been endorsed. At the local level, concepts such as quality and teamwork were beginning to be considered as viable options, and were yet to be systematically implemented. The competency descriptions, therefore, were incremental rather than visionary in scope. The value of the example lies probably more in the description of a locally-stituated response, rather than providing a prescriptive model for the development of comprehensive competency descriptions.

DEVELOPING WORKPLACE COMPETENCIES AT AUS TIN

Following skills audits and task analyses undertaken at Aus Tin, and the restructuring of different work functions, the organisation needed to identify the competencies needed, to inform both skill development initiatives, and ultimately, the development of a skills-based pay system. A taskforce made up of the training manager, a technician, a supervisor and the language educator was formed to begin this process. The educator's role was to identify the oral and written English competencies necessary for the particular jobs as to well as ensure that the schedules developed were expressed in an accessible format.

Together, they attempted to come to terms with a number of critical issues. They were keen, for example, that the competency schedules reflected a broad definition of competence, which took into account more than just task-skills. A considerable amount of time was spent therefore exploring different approaches to defining and identifying competence, and different ways of 'packaging' the descriptions. Deciding on clear, consistent and useful categorisation principles was problematic: should, for example, safety and communication be integrated into all aspects of the job or should they be emphasised as a separate entity? Should competencies be described as they apply to the present jobs and organisational structure or assume that the company's plan for integrated, semi-autonomous, computer literate teams was operative? The competencies were being developed at a time in the company when the implications of new technology, multiskilling and team structures were still being teased out.

Another issue was the degree of detail to include in the competency schedules. Some of the taskforce's early work resembled 'how to', procedural training manuals rather than succinct competency standards.

The greatest challenge proved to be the reconciliation of different perspectives on the same work function, and defining the competencies in a way that employees were able to recognise their work. In describing a particular operational process, for example, the technician's focus was typically on the correct technical sequence, and the most efficient operation of the machine. The quality assurance manager's priorities were, predictably, on the quality of the product, the standardisation of the process and the measurement and recording of quality checks.

The section manager, on the other hand, was concerned with accountability and productivity issues, while the training manager emphasised analytical skills, as well as effective problem solving and teamwork. The production employees, however, were strongly focused on the procedural aspects, in a holistic, intuitive, rather than a systematic lock-step, fashion. They were typically very familiar with the idiosyncrasies of particular machines, for example, and keen to point out that this aspect of competence was crucial.

These different perspectives had significant implications, both in terms of their linguistic realisation and the emerging emphases they favoured. For example, in outlining the process of packing components into paper bags, the section supervisor had provided the following account in his task analysis:

1. Check the measurement of a given number of tops/ends per bag on the frame of the packing station and adjust the number of tops/ends packed to meet stated production requirements as per instruction sheet, without error.
2. Sort torn, split, dirty and/or unacceptable packaging materials to correct production standards.
3. Use appropriate gauges, given access to the *Working Instructions Production Inspection* book, conduct quality checks on 4 tops each hour during normal production and report any deviation from acceptable quality immediately to responsible staff.
4. Check 4 tops/ends per bag for visual defects at the packing station and take appropriate action to report any deviation from acceptable quality immediately to responsible staff.

These four steps constituted part of a ten-step process. The quality assurance manager, in his account, itemised the various gauges (aperture, countersink, etc.) and emphasised the need to understand the reasons and record the results of the checks. The training manager, on the other hand, was keen for the ability to differentiate between critical and minor defects to be explicitly stated as a competency, and the actual setting of the packing frame to become part of the packer's responsibility.

Observing production employees and getting their input was vital to developing the competencies. The packers of components, in their account, for example, referred to the 'unacceptable packaging materials' as 'bad' or 'torn paper bags'. Even though they did not have access to the *Working Instructions Production Inspection* book, they correctly carried out the necessary checking and recording functions, but referred to the gauges by the number on the form rather than the name. When asked, they could not explain why they were carrying out the checks, except that they knew it was important for the final quality of the product for the components to be 'good ones'. They could expertly differentiate between visual faults that 'did not matter', and those that made the components 'no good' and consequently needed to be reported.

The educator's concern in this exercise, as mentioned earlier, was to identify the oral and written English competencies necessary for the particular jobs, the implications for language support that may be needed at the workstation, for the training skills of supervisor/trainers as well as ensuring that the schedules developed were expressed in an accessible format.

The taskforce attempted to strike a balance between the use of lay, simple terminology and the more, precise, but unfamiliar technical jargon. It recognised that with multiskilling and training, employees needed to acquire new and more abstract lexis to perform their day-to-day functions. So, there was a conscious effort to introduce 'high currency' words and use them in a consistent way e.g. specifications, critical defects, conduct, record. Conscious attempts were made to avoid unnecessarily complex expressions and terminology, when others were equally functional. The draft schedules were 'walked through' with different employees to ensure they were accurate and useable.

Table 7.1 shows the relevant part of the competency schedule for the process of packing components, after taking into account the various perspectives mentioned above. The last column contains the oral and written competencies identified, and was not part of the company's competency schedule. Its purpose was to inform the development of an industry-based language syllabus framework and support materials.

The taskforce decided to identify separately key competencies such as teamwork and communication, as well as incorporating and cross-referencing them as part of the different aspects of work. In this way they were contextualised, but at the same time more visible for training purposes.

For each occupational classification, communication competencies were identified in a way that attempted to realistically reflect the work requirements. These competencies were set at a minimal, threshold level, which emphasised communicative and strategic competence, rather than just grammatical competence. The performance criteria and range statements sought to reflect the interactional aspect of communication, the collaborative nature of teamwork and distribute the responsibility for effective communication across both parties in the interaction.

In the competency area dealing with teamwork, for example, (Table 7.2.), the performance criteria for 'working effectively as a team member' (6.2) included 'asking for assistance from others in solving work problems' as well as 'assisting others'. In the competency area dealing with following instructions (2.2), the range statement places a significant responsibility on the 'instructor' to give instructions clearly and encourage feedback.

The identification of competency standards on the basis of empirical evidence ensured that they realistically reflected the work requirements. Such a process was also valuable in providing a valid, comprehensive basis for the development of assessment methods and criteria as well

Table 7.1: Packing Components–technical/language competencies

Packing Components

Element	Performance Criteria	Lang/Lit/Num. Competencies (Teacher's only)
1. Machine Setting and Maintenance • Set packing frame ruler to required length using hand tools	• Use supplied tools to adjust ruler to adequate tension • Following instruction sheet, count required number of components into the packing frame, adjust and mark frame	• Reading/interpreting instruction sheet: tables, grid format, numbers • Numeracy – match numbers, horizontal, vertical

2. Carrying out Quality Assurance Checks
• Conduct QA visual and size checks and record outcomes
• Report critical defects to responsible team member
	• Check for defects in compound, damaged curls, dirt, grease or scratches
	• Given appropriate gauges, conduct all size checks as listed on final inspection sheet
	• Identify critical and minor defects as per manufacturing standards
	• Record correct information on final inspection sheet
	• Identify appropriate person(s) to contact when reporting critical defects
		• Inspection sheet: names of gauge (e.g. countersink), reasons for test
		• Sequencing language
		• Record information in appropriate box
		• Reporting critical defect:
		  – getting mechanics' attention
		  – lexis e.g. lip, rim, diameter adjectives – cracked, defective dirty, scratched, minor, critical, torn, split, dirty, scrap adverbs – too much/not enough
		  – clarification strategies: what do I do if? What about?
		• Record defects, note form

Table 7.2: Extract from Teamwork and Workplace Communication Competencies for Packer of Components (ASF level 1)

Occupation: Production Employee (ASF1)

Packing Components – Competency Unit 6. Working effectively as a Team Member

Competency element	Performance criteria

6.2 Contribute effectively as a team member	• Can list main team roles
	• Can talk about own role in team and how it affects the rest of the team
	• Work cooperatively with other team members
	• Assist in solving work problems
	• Ask for assistance from others in solving work problems
	• Participate in team discussions and decisions:
	  – Listen to other ideas
	  – Ask questions to check understanding
	  – Accept disagreement without taking it personally
	  – Contribute ideas and thoughts

Packing Components – Competency Unit 8. Workplace Communication

1. Handle Job Related Information

Competency element	Performance criteria
1.1. Follow Instruction Sheet to set a Packing Frame Ruler 1.2. Follow Final Inspection Sheet to conduct Q.A. Checks and record outcomes 1.3. Report critical production problems 1.4. Ask for help or information when necessary 1.5. Respond to requests for help or information from Team Leader or fellow workers	• see 2.1 • Recognise layout of form, key items, abbreviations • Fill in sheet correctly (see 3.1) • Identify who to contact • Can explain nature of problem • Can explain reason for request • Ask for repetition or explanation if necessary • Respond to request or explain why unable to respond

Table 7.2: Cont'd

2. Follow routine instructions

NB. Instructions should be: – given in clear, plain English
　　　　　　　　　　　　　– broken into small logical steps
　　　　　　　　　　　　　– backed up by demonstrations and explanations
　　　　　　　　　　　　　　of difficult terms
Instructor should be supportive, encourage employee to check and give
appropriate feedback.

Competency element	Performance criteria
2.1. Follow instructions for packing components 2.2. Demonstrate ability to ask questions 2.3. Participate in informal work group	• Perform each stage of instructions correctly • Use verbal and non-verbal communication to interrupt, ask for repetition, explanation and indicate understanding see competency area 6

as supporting language curriculum. The competency descriptions themselves underwent further refinement and review as they began to be
used to determine training needs and for recognition purposes.

NOTES

1. See, for example, Scott. G., 1991, 1996, Marsick V. and Watkins K. 1992, Hirsche, D and Wagner, D. 1993.
2. Mayer Committee 1992: 8.
3. Centre for Workplace Communication and Culture, 1994.
4. NTB, 1992: 43.
5. NBEET, 1993.
6. A national pilot study was undertaken in 1995/6 into the treatment of language and literacy in competency standards for the warehousing indus-try (Australian Language and Literacy Council, 1996). This resulted in the design of a model to assist the standards development process. The follow-ing year, a practical guide was developed to assist in the development of English language, literacy and numeracy inclusive training packages (L. Fitzpatrick and A. Roberts, 1997).
7. See, for example, Auerbach and Burgess, 1985, Auerbach, 1986, 1987, Tollefson, 1986.

8. See, for example, Brindley, 1994, Williams, 1994.
9. Large-scale projects have included a national pilot study into the treatment of language and literacy in competency standards for the warehousing and distribution industry (National Board of Employment, Education and Training, 1996) and the development of a practical guide for the integration of English language, literacy and numeracy into National Training Packages (L. Fitzpatrick and A. Roberts, 1997).
10. J. Channell and M. St John, 1996. The Language of Standards. *Competence and Assessment No. 31*, February 1996: 2–5. Department of Education and Employment, Cambridge.
11. Australian National Training Authority, 1997c.
12. NSW Community and Health Services Industry Training Board, 1994. Direct Care Workers in Aged Care Services: National Competency Standards Development Project, Bulletin No. 1, p. 1, April. NSW Community and Health Services Industry Training Board: Sydney.
13. Cited in Mawer and Field 1995.

EIGHT

Collaborative development of vocational curriculum

THE ROLE(S) OF VOCATIONAL CURRICULUM

Curriculum development is often described as a pedagogical exercise with a series of clear steps: tasks are analysed to identify the necessary knowledge and skills and logically sequenced learning activities are then developed to help learners acquire and demonstrate competence in these areas. In reality, however, curriculum never exists in a value-free context, and is therefore greatly influenced by the values and priorities which different parties bring to its development and the expectations they have from its ultimate use.

This is particularly the case in a workplace context where pedagogical considerations are often secondary to more pragmatic and instrumental concerns – often 'bottom line' outcomes. These concerns affect the content, process and importance given to curriculum development. As one union representative put it:

> Curriculum is about the management of conflicting interests, whichever way you look at it, it's political. Companies often see teachers as a passive way of getting across a particular set of values, and teachers can be pushing their own barrows too. There is a need to make the different agendas explicit so the parties can negotiate.

Depending on the priorities of those involved, vocational curriculum can be perceived as any one or more of the following:

- a prepackaged product, to be delivered in a variety of settings with minimal change to achieve standardised outcomes. Vocational curriculum here is typically seen as the solution to skill gaps and variations that may arise due to changes in personnel or work practices such as job rotation. It makes the work more fool-proof.
- a management tool for achieving significant change in work practices and organisational culture. Vocational curriculum here is typically

seen as an opportunity to change the way employees regard their work and hence the contribution they make to the workplace. Concepts such as quality, teamwork, and commitment to enterprise goals are usually crucial elements of such curriculum, and the process of learning as if not more important than the content.

- a threat to carefully guarded 'secret knowledge' and 'tricks of the trade'. Traditionally many employees have gained power and status by hoarding particular knowledge and skills. Making such information publicly available to all and sundry through manuals and training programmes threatens these hard-earnt territorial bases and places further risk to job security.

- a means of obtaining formal recognition of vocational skills, and as a result, increased pay and/or job advancement opportunities. As a result of industry restructuring, the link between skill and pay levels has made access to vocational curriculum a bread and butter issue for many employees – regardless of the inherent merit or otherwise of its content.

- a vehicle for teaching general skills and increasing learners' confidence through a familiar vocational context. For many years, language and literacy workplace education providers have used the workplace as a useful context for helping employees acquire language and literacy skills as well as become more actively involved in their work and general community.

- a way of increasing business for education and training providers. With the increasing privatisation of vocational education and training, viable curriculum is not only that which meets immediate client needs, but also that which can be easily marketed as a commodity to other clients and provide a competitive edge against other providers.

These different priorities affect the 'currency', status and content of the curriculum developed. While employees may value nationally recognised and accredited curriculum, for example, employers will be more interested in the relevance of a curriculum to workplace needs and concerns and the achievement of organisational goals.

Given these conflicting priorities, how can educators negotiate their own and others' interests in developing a curriculum that is meaningful to the workplace and its employees? Within the usual constraints of time and resources, what can educators do to maximise the learning and change potential of a workplace curriculum? We explore some of these questions in this chapter and look at some strategies used to develop a relevant, multifunctional curriculum in different workplaces.

COMMON PROBLEMS WITH VOCATIONAL CURRICULUM

Vocational curriculum for lower skill classification levels is a relatively recent phenomenon, as jobs at these levels have been traditionally regarded as 'unskilled'. Skill development in these areas, therefore, has tended to be informal and *ad hoc*, with the 'buddy' or 'sitting by Nellie' approaches being commonly used to impart the necessary knowledge and skills.

It is only in recent years, with the introduction of new technologies, flexible work practices and more stringent quality standards, that skills in 'non-trade' areas have been recognised and formalised. Task analyses, skills audits and process control documentation and industry competency standards are all examples of attempts to analyse skills which were often previously implicit or simply assumed to be 'common sense'. Designing vocational courses in these new areas – such as the *Vehicle Industry Certificate* or the *Engineering Production Certificate* in Australia – has usually been undertaken by technical specialists from the related trade area, with little involvement from the actual 'coalface'. Most industry specialists see their responsibility as transferring their technical expertise into competency-based terms in an acceptable curriculum format. Issues to do with key competencies, communication, cultural values, where and how the learning is to take place are usually secondary to the technical content of the curriculum – if they are considered at all.

As a result, curriculum products have often been a dilution of existing trade or technical courses, rather than attempts to address workplace production needs, emerging work practices or learning issues. In some instances, for example, specific units of industry standards have been automatically translated into discrete training modules, or 'knowledge' modules have been separated from 'skill' modules. Such 'Taylorist' curriculum seems to assume that work can be compartmentalised into categories such as 'quality concepts' as distinct from monitoring quality or reporting on a problem at a team meeting and working together for a solution.

Theoretical classroom-based training often results in 'chalk and talk' teaching methodologies, where the language of learning becomes academic, and unrelated to the real concerns of the shop floor. Rote learning and reproduction of facts through written tests often become the main indicators of learning rather than the actual application of new knowledge and skills. The effectiveness of team members, for example, ends up being assessed by their ability to list 'key active listening elements and factors limiting group effectiveness' rather than their involvement in any communicative team-based activity.[1]

Another frequent complaint has related to assumptions curriculum developers often make about learners and learning. Notions such as the desirability of 'life-long learning' may be becoming more popular in education and training circles, but many working adults feel they have finished with formal learning. National Australian surveys, for example, indicate that many experienced workers don't see themselves as in need of any training (ABS, 1994).

The assumed 'normal' or 'standard' learner has often been a very narrow subset of the actual target group – learners are assumed to be proficient in spoken and written English and comfortable with formal classroom learning, despite ample demographic evidence to the contrary. In Australia, for example, issues to do with the language, culture, gender and lack of access to education are usually defined as minority issues. This is despite the fact that they concern about 70 per cent of employees in the first three (non-trade) levels of the National Standards Framework.[2]

Many prospective learners of vocational curriculum are not native speakers of English, or they have been out of formal education for a long time – usually with negative experiences of formal, classroom-based learning. Typical learning activities such as taking notes, reading manuals, interpreting graphs, presenting written assignments are usually daunting and foreign to them – especially when packaged in educational, competency-based jargon.

It is commonly acknowledged that learning about a particular aspect of work will often involve more abstract and complex language than that which is actually required to perform the task in question.[3] This is particularly so if the aim is for the learner to be competent not only in simple procedural aspects, but also the 'why, how, and what if' aspects of the work. This degree of abstraction and complexity can become a significant obstacle for learners, who may be dealing with new concepts through the medium of a second language in an unfamiliar, formal learning situation.

There can also be a number of cultural assumptions in curriculum that many learners find foreign, if not offensive. Teamwork and communication modules often use a variety of simulation games whose intent is not at all clear, prescribe particular 'acceptable' ways of behaving, or extol the virtues of unfamiliar concepts such as 'synergy' and 'paradigm shifts'.

Even with language and literacy support, the mismatch between the expectations of the curriculum designers and the intended learners can make the teaching/learning task highly problematic. Initial attempts to deliver the Vehicle Industry Certificate in Australia are a case in point:

> When nearly half the workforce were having problems with the training program that had been designed specifically for them, one has to question the program.
>
> This is especially so when it is apparent that employees that cope with complex work processes are being redefined as incompetent in the classroom: that in fact the problem may lie with the training program, the learning materials, the performance criteria, delivery strategies and/or the assessment methods. Investigation showed that these had been designed, developed and delivered without taking account of the learning needs of the potential participants. Only half of the equation had been considered. (Sefton, 1993: 40–1)

In such cases, the literacy programme itself can work effectively to further marginalise employees by denying their intuitive ways of doing and knowing, in preference for more objective, sequential, hierarchical, text-dependent methods. In describing the experiences of female African American hospital employees, Gowen (1991) graphically relates how the literacy programme alienated participants because of assumptions about competence, knowledge construction and assessment which saw them as 'deficient'. A whole repertoire of relational skills and intiative were ignored, while sequential acquisition of knowledge through procedural texts was foregrounded:

> While management thought productive and co-operative employees must focus on text, the women believed the most efficient way to execute their jobs and to gain information was through oral, face-to-face communication, contextualised in the particulars of the moment. As a housekeeping aide explained: 'What does he know? If I did my job the way he [the black male manager] said, I'd never finish'. (1991: 443)

Reactions of employees to inappropriately designed curriculum range from withdrawal to passive resignation or outrage. Gowen, for example, describes how the women in the hospital programme resisted attempts to define, measure and change their ways with literacy – efforts which they felt aimed to control and silence rather than empower them. The following comments from participants in different Australian industries reflect similar reactions:

> I don't understand everything and I feel stupid – I don't want to go to any more training. Operator – manufacturing.

They think they've got to give us all this theory first, then we can get on to what it means. It is so boring! Operator – chemical and oil industry.

Why are you locking me in this classroom? If you don't like the way I work, sack me, but don't tell me I have to sit through this airy-fairy rubbish!' – Leading hand to manager.

We had a walk out the first time we tried to run a course. The guys felt we were setting them up, because they couldn't see how all the reams of paper related to their jobs. Section supervisor – building industry.

One of the difficulties is that there is often little trialling of curriculum before its accreditation and implementation. This is partly due to time and resource or administrative constraints. Often it is not until the 'fast trackers' have been through the first courses, that problems with language, learning and cultural assumptions are discovered. A common response in these sorts of situations is to ask for the skill 'deficiencies' to be 'fixed up' – through basic skill or literacy courses – before employees are able to access the unchanged training modules.

At an organisational level, mismatches between the content of training programmes and the ability to apply it to the 'curriculum of the workplace' can also be problematic. The degree to which learners can apply their newly developed skills depends greatly on the willingness and ability of key people in the workplace to provide them with the opportunity. The following two contrasting comments illustrate how contextual factors can be as – if not more – important in determining the perceived effectiveness of the curriculum:

After the hygiene and sanitation module, a lot of the workers put effort into putting their skills into practice. They became much more aware of hygiene factors and set down their own house rules as a result. It was very successful because it was their first effort of going back to the educational process after a long time. (Food processing production manager)

There is no point giving skills to people at the lower end if their line management are also not trained. People cannot apply the skills they have gained if their work practices have not changed. I've seen many instances where they try to apply the quality concepts they learnt and their manager says 'I'll tell you when it's wrong. Go back to the line'. This creates cynicism and frustration. (Union official)

As these two comments indicate, key aspects of organisational functioning such as those identified by Field and Ford (1995) can effectively block or facilitate what learning takes place: employee relations, the way work is organised and rewarded, how information and technology are managed. Educators usually have little influence on these aspects but can utilise their existing learning potential in the way that workplace curricula are developed.

In many instances, educators may be working with already developed, nationally accredited curriculum, rather than developing their own. Nationally developed curricula offer many advantages: they tend to be less resource intensive in that they can be bought as 'off the shelf' products – without workplaces having to engage in the tortuous process of curriculum design, development and accreditation. They usually also offer learners a nationally recognised credential. However, these considerations usually have to be balanced against factors such as relevance to local needs, and the organisational benefits of employees being actively involved in identifying and addressing their workplace learning needs. Workplaces which have developed their own curriculum, have used this process as a vehicle for driving 'cultural changes' in the ways that work is organised and skills recognised and rewarded. Employees are often 'trained up' in task analysis, curriculum development, presentation and training skills. Collaborative approaches like this are time and resource intensive, but the returns are well worth it in terms of increased employee participation and commitment, and improvements in productivity and morale.

Even in workplaces where resources are not plentiful, the customisation of 'off the shelf' curriculum, and strategic involvement of workplace personnel can greatly enhance the development and use of skills. Rather than passive consumers of glossy training packages, employees can be involved in critically reflecting on their work through active, enquiry-based learning, and together shaping new ways of thinking and doing work.

INTEGRATED APPROACHES TO SKILL DEVELOPMENT

Integrated approaches to developing and using skills involve more than just making links between the technical and more communicative aspects of work or learning and applying new ways of doing things. They are more about taking into account the learning potential of individuals and the organisation, and finding ways of taking this potential forward. Learning, then, is more than an activity that individuals undertake in a group situation. The content and processes of the curriculum are rather integrally linked to system-wide processes of change: changes in the way people regard their work, their roles and working relationships.

Some of these approaches may be through formal training programmes, but they will not be confined to the learning that happens in
classrooms or training rooms. Formal training programmes may provide unique opportunities for reflecting, exploring and experimenting
with ways of applying that learning to work. But they are only the
starting-point in terms of allowing new knowledge, skills and attitudes
to become part of everyday working practices. In the next chapter, we
discuss some of the ways that educators have exploited the informal
learning potential of their workplaces in a wide variety of almost
idiosyncratic ways.

Educators cannot pretend to 'empower' individuals or achieve a
'literacy-led' transformation of an organisation's culture. However,
the process and content of the curriculum can to a large extent help
develop an environment that facilitates changes in such directions.
Learning strategies that promote critical reflection, interaction and
groupwork, for example, can provide tangible ways of reflecting the
rhetoric of organisational learning objectives and set up relationships
and systems that support learning. Language teaching in particular has
had a long tradition of learner-centred, needs-based, collaborative curriculum development and holistic, interactive approaches to learning.
These often stand in stark contrast to mechanistic, behavioural objectives of vocational training, where theory is often divorced from practice,
or learners' life experiences are ignored. Yet the trend in recent years
towards competency-based approaches to language learning and more
visible accountability risk eroding these holistic, humanistic orientations
to curriculum development and teaching practice.

Focusing on individuals' overall learning needs, rather than a detailed task analysis is likely to result in more meaningful and effective curriculum. For example, there may be a need to focus initially
on communicating the reasons for change and exploring new ways
of individuals perceiving their contribution at work differently. Many
employees know surprisingly little about the overall structure of their
workplace, its goals or the pressures on their particular industry. Similarly, many employees have had little opportunity to interact with
managers or fellow-workers from other sections and have little understanding of the different aspects of the work process and the roles of
specialist sections.

The development of learner motivation and confidence is also likely
to be a major focus of integrated approaches to learning. The characteristics of the target group must be taken into account if the curriculum
developed is to be relevant to their needs. Aspects such as learner

competence in language, study and research skills, prior knowledge and experience need to be factored into the curriculum if learners are to be framed for success rather than failure.

More than likely, a variety of different paths or support options will be necessary to enable learners to achieve the same outcomes. Some of these options may, for example, include tutorial support, team-teaching or distance learning. Standard curriculum provision then becomes what ever is needed to provide successful outcomes for all learners, rather than catering for a mythical subset of 'normal' learners.

One of the major challenges in developing an integrated curriculum is finding the balance between the relatively accessible 'shop-floor' language and more prestigious 'technical' and 'management' discourses. As one workplace trainer succinctly put it:

> We're developing training manuals, and it seems to me that it's our choice basically whether they end up looking like the Financial Review or a comic book. I reckon the blokes here would rather have a comic book version.

As employees take on a greater range of tasks, and become more involved in making decisions about their work, there is a corresponding quantum leap in the knowledge, skills and communicative requirements of these new roles and functions. The language of the shopfloor is, in many situations, not the language of power and influence. So, while 'comic book versions' of vocational curriculum may be accessible they can also, in the long term, be restrictive and reductionist. Employees need to become familiar with the new lexis and concepts underlying their expanded roles, if they are to be actively involved in shaping their working lives.

The design of *Work Instructions* and *Standard Operating Procedures* are a typical example of this dilemma. These documents have become a common feature in many workplaces. For quality assurance auditors, they attest to the fact that processes are in place to ensure the quality of what is produced. They are also used to ensure that consistent standards apply as employees rotate around different tasks or shift arrangements.

Yet it is common to find such procedures lengthy, full of technical jargon in very tight print, or tabular format. Despite the many hours and resources put into their production, they are seldom used – even where such forms are designed to be filled in by employees. In one typical workplace, employees routinely ticked the appropriate boxes on the forms at the end of the shift, with no thought or reference to the instructions or checks in question.

Collaborative, employee-centred approaches to developing vocational curriculum tend to produce more than just accessible training programmes or work instructions. They also provide practical learning opportunities, affirming employees' competence in their work, and increasing their confidence in themselves as learners, workers and trainers. They also engender greater commitment to the processes and products of learning.

With their understandings of language and learning, educators can play a vital role in facilitating this collaboration. For many employees, the process of developing a vocational curriculum can be a strangely foreign and frightening experience. As one employee put it when approached about developing training programmes:

> They want me to help write up the instructions manual. I know how to do the job, you come, I show you, but I don't know how to write about it in a book!

The complementarity of skills that educators and employees such as these bring can be harnessed to great effect. In a pharmaceutical company, for example,[4] the educator provided some training in Plain English, and with management support, encouraged work teams to establish consistent formats for more user-friendly procedures. The teams developed flow-charts of the process, with a brief summary of different operational roles. They worked together to write down the instructions and display them in a visible, accessible way. As one of the team members related the experience, there was obvious pride and ownership of the process:

> We took on the ideas of Plain English we'd got through the training and decided we'd write the instructions step by step, laminate them and put them up on top of the machine, for everyone to 'see, alongside clear diagrams'.

Even where employees' spoken or written English is quite limited, their competence in their work can be harnessed to develop their confidence in learning and communicating. In the integrated approach to the Vehicle Industry Certificate, for example, learners were encouraged to use their first language in the training context, where necessary. Standard English was regarded as a long-term aim rather than a necessary prerequisite for skill development:

> Learners were encouraged to think, write and speak in their first language, to analyse, categorise information, solve problems, acquire and share new concepts. This encouraged them to participate at a more sophisticated level than they would otherwise have done and facilitated the acquisition of English language and literacy, as well as generic skills underpinning

analytical thinking. While learners were encouraged to work in their first language if that was more convenient, the eventual final product and presentation was made in English. . . . In validating and enhancing the first language, it also affirmed positively the ethnic origins and cultural diversity of the learners' (Sefton, R., Waterhouse P. and Deakin R. (eds), 1994: 107).

The following two case studies are examples of collaborative, learner-centred curriculum development in two very different settings. The first example outlines the development of a comprehensive set of training modules at Aus Tin which were to be accredited, and form part of a skills-based pay system. In the second example, Julia McCall describes how she worked with hospital personnel to strengthen the impact of her increasingly marginalised language and literacy classes, and increase the confidence and ability of her learners to access their vocational training. In both, contextual factors and the need to build learners' confidence in their own learning ability strongly influenced the content and process of curriculum development.

CASE STUDY 1. DEVELOPING TRAINING MODULES AT AUS TIN

As with many companies prior to restructuring, there had been little emphasis on systematic training within Aus Tin, and minimal infra-structure to support or document the informal training that had been undertaken. The aim of the training materials project was to develop a comprehensive set of technical modules that took into account the organisational and technological changes brought about by restructuring. A major focus of the project included the use of diverse learning strategies to accommodate the individual and structural needs of the workplace.

A project team consisting of two external technical and a language educator was appointed to develop these modules. A training seminar was conducted for the writers by a consultant specialising in 'whole brain'[5] learning strategies. The seminar dealt with the content of the training as well as the typical learner profile of the workforce, and the learning preferences expressed in the audit. It also identified the range of learning strategies that could be drawn on in the design of the training modules, within a competency-based framework. These included the use of symbols, experiential exercises, audio/visual reinforcement, as well as a considerable degree of hands-on experience with a machine simulator or actual workplace equipment. The instructional design principles that would be used for the technical modules were discussed and agreed to. It was also decided that the training materials would be written in Plain English, with support literacy materials for those that required it.

The writing team worked with company employees for approximately four months, observing them at work and seeking their help in producing technical training modules on different sections of the plant. The final results, though, were disappointing for a number of reasons. Firstly, the magnitude of the project had been underestimated, in terms of the number of modules to be developed. Secondly, the writing team had difficulties in determining their role relationships, both within the team itself and with company personnel. When trialled, many of the learning activities developed were inappropriate for the intended employees – this was possibly due to the team members' preference for traditional learning styles, and familiarity with more literate, technically aware learners.

A critical factor related to the prevailing workplace culture. Key workplace personnel who had the technical expertise were resentful and suspicious towards the writing team. They were reluctant to share the expertise they had with outsiders (who in their eyes lacked credibility), so it could be documented for other (less skilled) co-workers to access. Even though there had been some consultation over the development of the training plan, some of these employees were not willing to share their 'trade secrets' when job security and reward systems were still unclear. As one such employee put it a year or so after the event:

> We had this supposed group of experts who came in here to write manuals to tell us how to do our job! They had a you-beaut-plan that they were going to carry out regardless of what we thought of it or what we wanted . . . and they expected us to come to the party, No way! They could figure it out for themselves if they were so expert!

Without these employees' active cooperation, the technical writers were unable to obtain significant information. The main outcomes of this project were the production of a number of technical modules at various working draft stages, which could be further developed and trialled.

The following year, the training manager was successful in obtaining further government funding to complete the production of these (and other) modules and assist in the training of workplace trainers. Aus Tin contracted the educator involved in the original audit and competency standard project, in addition to the already existing full-time educator.

A small taskforce was formed within the company to continue the development of the technical training modules begun the previous year. This taskforce was established by drawing on internal personnel, both from within the plant and the wider national company network. It included the training manager, two team leaders (supervisors who were designated workplace trainers) and a technical expert co-opted from within the national company network, and the educator.

In collaboration with members of the taskforce and the quality manager, the educator edited some of the draft introductory modules and assisted in the further development of technical training modules and Standard Operating Procedures to comply with quality accreditation requirements. She was also responsible for developing support literacy materials which were either integrated into the modules, or used (and often extended) in the concurrent English courses or Individual Learning Programme. These literacy materials were developed to cater for different levels of competence in literacy and could also be used for individual study.

There was a conscious attempt to focus on active rather than passive learning strategies and to develop learners' understanding of the concepts underlying different procedures in the production process. The training manager, particularly, was keen to emphasise quality and effective teamwork concepts and encourage the development of the 'higher order' competencies such as organisational and analytical skills. Problem solving and group work activities, for example, were built into the modules, so that learners needed to work together as they applied new knowledge and skills to real workplace tasks. As far as possible, assessment tasks were designed around typical workplace problems, using faulty samples or common workplace scenarios.

While adopting a 'Plain English', user-friendly approach to the training modules, it was essential not to oversimplify or significantly alter the technical content. As employees took on a greater range of tasks, they needed to become familiar with the technical, mechanical, quality, mathematical and computer lexis and concepts underlying those expanded roles.

Yet most learners at Aus Tin were typical of manufacturing industry employees in that they had little formal education and limited communicative competence in English, were not comfortable in a formal, print-dependent learning environment and were encountering training manuals, computer terminals and measurement gauges for the first time in their working lives. There was understandably great apprehension towards the new 'competency-based' training programme that would inevitably define their career path progression.

There was a deliberate attempt therefore to facilitate and enhance the learning process, whereby the necessary lexis and concepts were progressively introduced, explained and reinforced, without over simplification of the content. This process involved capitalising on the learners' existing knowledge and experience of the production process, the use of hands-on practice with authentic materials and equipment. A disused piece of equipment, for example, was used to simulate an aspect of production, while real samples of products were used to illustrate particular points.

It also involved considerable use of 'easification' devices. This term was coined by Bhatia (1983) to refer to the process of providing additional access structures around or within the text to foster practical reading strategies to enable the reader to decode the text for themselves. These devices were extensively used in the presentation, and sequencing of information, as well as the lexicogrammatical structure. They included the use of diagrams, flowcharts, the highlighting and foregrounding of key information and revision exercises, such as crosswords, to reinforce the technical lexis and concepts introduced.

The training materials produced by this taskforce were validated by the Quality Manager and various section managers for accuracy before being trialled by learners and employees involved in the communication course for accessibility. Modifications were made as a result of this feedback.

Developing standard operating procedures

An interesting dilemma arose over the development of Standard Operating Procedures, which are an emerging 'genre' resulting from the push for accreditation of products against recognised International and Australian Standards (3900 series). The original source documents were technical manuals originally designed for use by the quality manager and section managers as reference documents. They were often highly abstract, technical and relied on a considerable degree of assumed knowledge of the field. It was essential, for the purposes of quality accreditation, that the employees become familiar with the content of these source documents as the responsibility for quality monitoring and troubleshooting was devolved. However, they were inaccessible in their original format for this new group of users.

The quality manager, particularly, was highly reticent to make any alterations because of the quasi-legal status of the documents, and concerned about any dilution in content that might occur as a result of 'translating them' into a more reader-friendly version. However, he also acknowledged his frustration at the fact that employees were not referring to the procedures, and he feared they would not be able to answer the quality inspector when the company was audited, as part of the accreditation process.

As a way of raising awareness of some of the conceptual and literacy 'hurdles' that had inadvertently been constructed for employees to negotiate, the educator designed the following operational procedure for the taskforce to review:

Operational procedures

1. Select suitable heat-resistant receptacle and undertake specified Q.A.checks (check for cracks, mould, adhering dirt) and take corrective action as required.
2. Follow procedural instructions to select correct prepackaged sachet from the available range and undertake visual Q.A. checks for seal. Position in receptacle, ensuring tag is securely placed exterior of rim.
3. Using correct implements, and following specified safety procedures, heat water to requisite temperature (within the range of 98°–100°). Transfer sufficient amount to fill receptacle to indicated levels (to a tolerance of 5 mls), as indicated on customer order form.
4. Ensure sachet is immersed and agitated to allow for required colour density uptake.
5. Following customer order specifications, undertake requisite Q.A.checks on required optional additives (visual, olfactory), select and use appropriate tool to measure and incorporate additives to liquid compound.
6. Taking necessary steps to follow safety procedures and minimise waste, extract and discard sachet into appropriate scrap receptacle.
7. Record outcomes on Final Inspection Sheet and Daily Production Schedule prior to transport to designated delivery point.

Most of the group were unable to work out that these instructions referred to making a cup of tea, and were quite amused to look at the way that a simple task could be couched in grandiose, technical language. This was contrasted with a diagrammatic representation of the same procedure:

Figure 8.1:

The group discussed the advantages and drawbacks of both ways of setting out similar information. While the pictorial version was easier and quicker to read, for example, it tended to oversimplify the procedure. Aspects such as the need for correct water temperature, waste disposal, safety and record-keeping had been missed. In a real workplace procedure, these were important elements. Terms such as *heat-resistant, receptacle, tolerance and immerse*, may be ones that employees needed to become familiar with if they were a necessary part of the task.

The group explored ways of developing a procedure that was a compromise between these two extremes – retaining essential elements, while ensuring clarity.

This diagram illustrates one of the original instructions for the measurement of the 'diameter over bail ear' of a particular type of product. This extract is relatively accessible as it deals with simple go/no go gauges rather than some of the more sophisticated measurement gauges:

Diameter over Bail Ear Check

Reason: Customer requirement for handle fitment.

Test to be conducted hourly, using the G 198 Go/No Go Gauge:

a. Using the No Go face, present the gauge to the bail ears, holding the gauge as horizontal as possible. The gauge should not fit over the bail ears.

b. Using the Go face, repeat the above If the ears will not fit between the edges of the gauge, the can is REJECT. If the ears fit the gauge, the can is ACCEPTED. Slight drag may be encountered if the bail ears are at maximum or minimum tolerance, but this should not be so great that the gauge has to be forced over the bail ears.

Following observation of the actual check being carried out on the shop floor and consultation with the quality manager and section team leader, the instructions were modified to the following:

DIAMETER OVER BAIL EAR

We use this gauge to make sure the can is the right size to fit the handle. Use the G198 GO/NO GO gauge to measure the diameter of the can with the bail ears attached.

1 Use the GO side of the gauge and fit the gauge over the can. (Do not force the gauge to fit over the can). The can should fit between the 2 edges of the gauge.

2 Use the NO GO side of the gauge and fit the gauge over the can. It should NOT fit over the Bail Ears.

This test is carried out every hour

YOU NEED TO BE ABLE TO . . .

- CARRY OUT inspections at the packing station using the GO/NO GO gauges
- SHOWING how each gauge is used correctly
- in the CORRECT ORDER of checks

- DESCRIBE what is to be done if a check shows that the final product is faulty

Figure 8.2: Modified instructions for diameter over bail ear check

These modified instructions were developed as part of a module dealing with quality checks, and it was agreed that both the original 'official' instructions and the modified ones would be displayed at the work stations.

This collaborative approach to the development of the technical materials was effective in giving the project a higher degree of credibility and more local ownership than the initial developmental phase had enjoyed. A significant reason for this related to changes in the prevailing work culture, with less reticence on the part of key personnel to share their expert knowledge. Some training modules (which had been edited by the educator in the early stages of the project) were conducted, and met with positive feedback, from both trainers and learners. It was therefore easier to build on the positive momentum generated by the implementation of the training programme.

However, there were also some significant drawbacks in this arrangement. Firstly, the project had to deal with frequent interruptions due to production problems as the key personnel involved in the taskforce were needed to troubleshoot or replace absent workmates.

The validation of the training modules produced was a time-consuming but essential part of the process. On occasions, for example, there were inconsistencies between technical procedures as written in manuals and accepted practice on the shop floor. These were often because short-cuts or alternative ways of achieving the same results had been devised by the employees, or in some instances, the reasons for particular procedures were not understood, and they tended therefore to be ignored. These inconsistencies needed to be satisfactorily resolved.

Furthermore, while the taskforce members were very competent in technical matters, such as troubleshooting, their level of competence did not extend to the identification of the skills they wanted to develop in learners, nor were they able to translate the content of the training into manageable, accessible learning activities. As in any multidisciplinary team, it was essential to develop mutual respect and an understanding of different members' perspectives for the taskforce to work effectively and arrive at constructive solutions to problems. One satisfying aspect of this process, from the educator's perspective, was to observe the increasing awareness and skills that the other members themselves developed over time, so that they were able to identify difficult or inconsistent terminology, and suggest specific learning objectives and suitable learning activities. As they began delivering the training modules, their 'ownership' of the contents was evident in their enthusiasm and the way they followed up learners' application of skills at the different work stations.

CASE STUDY 2. INTEGRATED TRAINING IN THE CLEANING DEPARTMENT OF A SYDNEY HOSPITAL

I'd been teaching a small group of cleaners in an outer suburban hospital of Sydney for six months when I realised that I had got to change my approach if literacy and language training were to continue, and actually make an impact on the Domestic Services Unit as a whole. My little class was lovely – passionately enthusiastic and delighted with their own progress but harassed by the pressures of work left undone because of the classes and needled by the jokes of their colleagues about them going 'back to school' ('The teacher'll give you the stick if you're late', 'Have a nice bludge', etc.). I myself was getting needled by the way anybody else's training in the hospital always took precedence over mine when it came to the use of training rooms, and the way it was always the literacy class that had to go scurrying about for somewhere to sit down and learn. We became quite used to using a tray of salt instead of a whiteboard to write on but the students and I both felt the lack of interest in and respect for what was for all of us groundbreaking stuff. They were at last learning to write and I was learning to use Computer Assisted Language Learning programs to teach them.

The need for a formalised training programme for all cleaning staff was evident, particularly with increasing trends for multiskilling and job-rotation in the hospital. Very few of the staff had received formal cleaning training of any kind and while most had acquired a high degree of competence from learning on the job they lacked the theoretical understanding for why things were done in particular ways – such as the reasons for not mixing different cleaning compounds. The head of General Services and the manager of the cleaning staff had been planning a four-day training programme for their thirty-five cleaners for some time and quickly became enthusiastic about the idea of including a language and literacy component.

Researching and designing the course

Initially I was a little daunted by the range of learners that my language and literacy training would need to encompass. About 75 per cent of the cleaning staff were from non-English-speaking backgrounds with 25 per cent being born in Australia or the United Kingdom. Literacy skills ranged from more than adequate reading and writing to very little reading and no writing at all. Though most of the cleaners spoke sufficient English to communicate fairly effectively on day-to-day work issues, around 50 per cent were unable to read English with any kind of ease or fluency. This meant that the potential of the training manual as a teaching tool was strictly limited.

It was felt that by integrating the language training into the departmental cleaning training, those with language support needs would not be marked out and those who had been reluctant or unable to admit to requiring help would be able to come to terms with their own needs at their own pace. By homing in on terminology specific to the various areas of cleaning practice, with a particular focus on synonyms (e.g. neat, undiluted, straight) and formal/written language (e.g. insert) as opposed to informal/spoken (put in) we hoped to facilitate access not only to the training manual but also to instructions and notices around the hospital. An integrated approach would also provide an opportunity to explore cross-cultural issues, and typical breakdowns in communication that occurred due to obscure expressions like 'getting the ward up to scratch' and 'it's a vicious circle'.

The Computer Assisted Language Learning programs that I had been experimenting with had great potential, as they provided shells of exercises into which language of any sort could be poured.[6] The spelling program, for example, could be filled with words like contamination, uric acid encrustation, faeces, thorough, susceptible and so on. The tense testing sentences could be based on interesting cleaning situations involving scrubbing, dusting and wiping. There was a multiple choice testing program that could be tuned to testing knowledge of cleaning practices. Moreover, people could work in groups at their own level and pace, thus enabling the simultaneous training of a range of learners. Computers were soon going be used in the hospital to monitor waste disposal, and such a program could be useful in removing some of the terror and mystique that computers held for most employees. By spreading the original language learners through the groups, they could help teach others how to use the computer programs.

We decided that the best way to implement the plan was for me to attend and record each of the four-day sessions of cleaning training alongside the cleaning staff and develop a follow-up session with a range of activities to reinforce and clarify the content of the 'cleaning' session as well as begin to explore the language involved. I would then provide sessions to the staff in three groups of around ten each.

Our approach was influenced by the Action Research model proposed by Kemmis and McTaggart (1988) in which action is framed in terms of a cycle of planning, action and observation, reflection and replanning. A constraint on this was the need to provide sessions that were as nearly identical as possible to each of the three groups on each of the four topics, so that everyone could emerge from the training having experienced similar input. Each module, however, was designed in the light of responses to the previous ones and the final module that had been planned was in fact jettisoned because participants expressed a strong interest in exploring in more depth an issue that had formed part of the third module.

A second principle drawn from Kemmis and McTaggart concerned beginning small and gradually involving an increasing circle of people from the department. At the outset there was simply an agreement between the language teacher and the mainstream trainers that the mainstream and language sessions be linked together but, due to time constraints, each should be planned separately. The language teacher would sit in the first mainstream training session of each module and draw material from that upon which to base subsequent language support sessions. However, as the course progressed, evaluation and discussion of issues arising from both mainstream and language sessions became an informal weekly event that often branched off into debates on issues relating to cleaning practice or language theory. The language teacher and the mainstream trainers gained insights into each others' field of expertise as a result.

The skills of other members of the department were harnessed as the need for them became apparent. The cleaning supervisors, for instance, had essential roles in the project, taking on the complex task of timetabling the sessions and providing clarification on cleaning practice to the language teacher. Early on the participants themselves were introduced to the concept of integrated training and advised of the experimental nature of the programme and how the project could be of value to other hospitals and workplaces. They were regularly asked to provide comments and insights into how they had personally been affected by the training and how they saw the department gaining from it. By the evaluation stage of the project most of the department felt that they owned it and many people wanted to read the final report.

Structuring the integrated skills training

Four modules of cleaning training, each two and a half hours in length, were planned by the Department Manager and Deputy of General Services:

1. Cleaning equipment and compounds
2. Dust control, mopping, carpet and vinyl care
3. Bathrooms, isolation, wall and glass cleaning and the cleaners' room
4. Sanitation procedures, bedmaking and ward tidy

(In the event, as mentioned above, the fourth session was replaced by a more thorough discussion of infection control.)

Each of the first three modules was presented by the General Services trainers to each of three small groups of participants (up to ten). As soon as possible after each mainstream training session each group was provided with a language focused follow-up session run by me (who, as mentioned above, had myself attended one of the cleaning training sessions and prepared materials relating to it). Although the second and third modules followed the same pattern, it was decided that for the fourth module mainstream and language trainers would present together to the three groups.

The mode of delivery of the training varied throughout the course as the trainers assessed how the trainees were receiving the material, and moved from a fairly formal lecturing style through to discussion of issues and question and answer sessions and eventually experiential learning activities.

Presenting the sessions

Given the range of communication skills of the participants in each of the groups, the format I developed for the language support sessions needed to have cleaning knowledge and skills as their superordinate focus with exploration of the English language and teasing out of meanings as subordinate. By organising the sessions this way it was hoped that all participants would share enough common ground to find relevance and not feel in any way patronised. I also had to take into account the sensitivities of those who could not write at all and make sure that my activities did not expose their perceived inadequacy to the rest of the group.

Activities that were exceptions to this principle – in that there the primary focus was language – were short presentations on pragmatics (the function of indirectness in language) and semantics (the Whorf Sapir hypothesis and how connotations of words affect our actions). These two segments were included because it was felt that they offered new and interesting insights into language for everyone including even the most proficient of native speakers.

The recipe I have come up with was a curious blend of play, experimentation and solemn learning. Activities were short and varied in the extent to which they required concentrated listening to the presenter, cooperation or competition with other trainees or solo study. Because some participants could hardly write anything in English, writing was kept to a minimum, though not totally excluded from the sessions. Reading either alone (worksheets) or in groups around the computers (computer assisted language learning activities) was, however, the backbone of various activities, with support being provided to the less able readers by co-trainees or the language teacher.

I began each session by asking people to get into groups with the injunction that they make sure at least one person in each group could write in English. I then explained that I had prepared a quiz on the previous training session for them, but before doing it, they needed to review what they had learnt. One person in each group took notes and after a few minutes I gathered in the pooled information, teasing out any confusions and supplementing where necessary. Often the clarifying and supplementing was done by members of the groups as they knew far more about cleaning than I did. Just to keep my end up I sometimes threw in a bit of spelling to the review sessions and explained oddities like the two u's in 'vacuum' and the double c in 'accident' and 'success'.

After this we moved on to 'Soil of the Century' a heavily derivative game in which two teams of cleaners vie for points to win the prize – a $2 Scratch lotto ticket.

Round one was mostly vocabulary-based. I had sets of three words on an overhead projector slide which I read aloud and then gave everyone plenty of time to read for themselves, e.g. susceptible, infectious, contaminated and then provided the question e.g. 'Which of these words means can catch a disease easily?' When the answer was provided I explored the other two words with the group. This round was interpersed with other purely technical multiple choice questions concerning such things as appropriate treatment of stains, etc., thus avoiding a purely language focus.

Round two featured an invented character called Cassie who does everything wrong as demonstrated by this sample question:

It was a beautiful spring day and Cassie was working in the Children's ward. 'Poor little things' she thought as she said hello to a couple of kids with asthma in their oxygen tents, 'It must be boring for them. Never mind, I'll use my special way to make the windows nice and clean for them, so at least they can see the trees and flowers outside.' And she got out her cloth and bottle of methylated spirits, and started wiping the windows.

What did Cassie do wrong? (She used methylated spirits, of course, which could be very dangerous, especially around oxygen tents.)

This round provided an opportunity to reinforce principles of occupational health and safety and left everyone with a smug sense of superiority!

Round three was 'What am I?' and allowed for the highlighting of workbased vocabulary that, although useful, tends to get sidestepped in practice e.g. 'pile' (of a carpet) 'grout' and 'slurry', (the slosh of cleaning solution on a bathroom floor before it gets mopped up).

After any contentions about marks had been resolved and the scratchy had been scratched by the winning team, we moved on to a practical exercise involving a small amount of writing for those who were able to do it. For the session on cleaning chemicals, this involved identifying by smell and listing on a form eight liquids including floor cleaner, ammonia, whisky, water and metal polish. Most people were unable to identify all of them thus allowing me to stress the importance of clearly labelling cleaning compounds. After this the learners used PH testing strips to categorise the liquids into acid and alkali and then the relative harmfulness of the different chemicals to the skin and the hospital environment was explored. For dust control we again identified a range of samples of dust and dirt (e.g. a bit of bloody tissue (simulated), a cockroach leg, a cobweb, sand, etc.) and evaluated them on a scale of ten as unhygienic, unaesthetic and damaging to the hospital environment. For both these activities a form was supplied for learners to complete. People who couldn't write usually coopted the help of people who could which enabled me to identify those needing extra help in a private session of their own. Because the writing is peripheral to the experiments nobody feels more than slightly awkward about not being able to write. They have, after all, completed the body of the task which is to identify and evaluate the substances.

After this everybody went for a coffee and I turned on my three Macintosh computers and selected a range of programs to engage the interest of all participants. One computer had a crossword with all the words relating to cleaning (Crossword Magic program) – quite challenging for native speakers to guess and literacy learners to spell. The second had a note to a supervisor in which all the words have been blanked out (Storyboard). Learners got a brief glimpse of the text and then got to reconstitute it word by word. This tested the spelling and grammar of the less proficient writers and provided quite an amusing memory exercise for the others. The third computer was dedicated to 'Practise your Skills' the Hypercard program mentioned previously, which focuses on making appropriate language choices. Interestingly, even these exercises can be designed to involve using professional judgement as well as knowledge of the language. The Dust Control session included an exercise in which learners had to fill a space in a sentence with WILL, CAN or COULD. Some of the sentences were:

Sand _____ eventually damage a carpet in a high traffic area.
If nurses dispose of sharps in yellow rubbish bags these _____ cause injury to cleaners.
A lighted cigarette end in a rubbish bin _____ burn down the hospital.

Selection of the correct word elicits a round of applause or a personalised message e.g. 'Fabulous Flavia!' from the computer. Nobody to date has found this patronising or offensive!

As people drifted back from their cups of coffee they settled into a reading exercise drawn from the training manual and processed by a clever CALL program named Wordweaver[7] which allows the teacher to take a text and have it treated in four different ways. Exercise 1 splits all the sentences in half and mixes the second halves up. Students have to connect the parts relating to the reasons for instructions in the process, e.g.

Never mix cleaning compounds because	this contaminates the contents
Never top up from one bottle to another because	you can create dangerous gases and even cause explosions

Exercise 2 gives the students the sentences in the wrong order and requires them to number them correctly (especially useful for checking understanding of procedures.) Exercise 3 allows the teacher to replace keywords with a space and list the words underneath the exercise e.g.

Never _____ cleaning compounds because you can _____ dangerous gases and even cause _____.

create   mix   explosions

The last exercise has the words of the sentences jumbled up, and, depending on the length of the sentence, can be extremely difficult. This is useful for anyone who finishes the previous three exercises very quickly. It is also a useful exercise for advanced learners of English who are inclined to omit articles and auxiliaries.

The overall effect of doing these exercises is both to absorb the information contained in the sentences and to raise awareness of the various language features chosen for emphasis, e.g. the balance of a good prohibition consisting of a command + *because* + reason.

The mood of the group during this stage of the session was in marked contrast to that of the other segments. Everybody was quiet and serious and if individuals helped each other it was done very quietly. In between feeding new worksheets to people as they finished the exercises, I usually worked alongside anyone who was having difficulty at this stage.

After about half an hour the group moved to the computer of their choice, and groupwork began again as they worked out what was required by the different exercises. Interestingly some of the more proficient students often opted to work with the less able ones on the simpler exercises, seemingly preferring a peer tutoring role to doing a puzzle for themselves.

If there was time at the end of the session everyone came together to watch a bit of the video of the original training session and I noted any problematic words and phrases on the board which got explained just before everyone headed off home.

Assessing and evaluating the course

I worked with the Cleaning Services supervisors to produce a multiple choice test covering key points from all four training sessions. The purpose of administering this test was, in part, to trial computer-assisted testing as a method of evaluation for a group of candidates with very varied language and literacy skills. The test was produced with relative ease on the *Choose the Best* CALL program which allows questions to be fed in thus:

Question	How do you move the brush when cleaning a toilet?
Right answer	Round and round
Distractor	Up and down
Distractor	Very fast
Distractor	Very slowly

Participants were organised to attend a half-hour interview on their own in which they could do the computer test and give their views on the training. Given the total novelty of the testing procedure for a large number of the candidates it was considered a high priority that the experience be challenging and interesting but in no way threatening or humiliating for anyone. Help, in the form of clarificaton of questions, was freely available to anyone who seemed to need it.

People from a non-English speaking background took longer over the test (in some cases up to half an hour) but unlike their English speaking background workmates, made no errors due to careless or impulsive choices because they read and processed all the options carefully before choosing their answers. All participants scored 80 per cent or more, which provided positive evidence of their understanding of cleaning concepts and knowledge.

In commenting on the value of the course, participants noted their increased confidence as a result of greater knowledge and understanding of their work, and their ability to learn:

> You feel anxious when someone is watching you if you are just guessing what to do. When you know then you can relax a bit.

> I realise being a cleaner is professional. I'm a skilled cleaner. I know what I'm doing.

> It was very interesting. I was happy to know more. I know more and I feel better.

> I didn't expect it. I learnt too much. I got a certificate and everything.
> I never had for fifteen years and I never thought about it.

By far the majority of learners were enthusiastic about the computer segment of the course despite the severe resource constraints:

> I never sat in front of a computer before. It was very interesting. We need more, we need to go ahead.

> I love it. I wish I could do more. If one day I have to do something I don't feel like a dummy.

Many participants found the language support indispensable in that it clarified terms that were unknown and provided the opportunity to revisit and absorb the mainstream training:

> Without language teaching it would be very hard. Sometimes you don't understand if you don't have the language. Still I don't feel 100 per cent confident.

Participants who were native speakers of English commented on insights gained into the difficulty of handling a job in a second language and how both idioms and colloquialisms and the formal language often used in workplace documents can present barriers to colleagues with less facility in English:

> I think it is good for people who are native speakers to listen to the others so you can see things from their perspective. It helps you to relate.

Many people in both groups gained in self-esteem – the English background participants because they came to realise that they had an expertise in language which they could pass on to their bilingual co-workers and the non-English speaking background participants because their need for language support had been acknowledged as a legitimate component of training. Communication within the department was improved by all participants working together in the interactive context of the language learning activities:

> I learnt many things. It helped a lot. It was beautiful. All the staff are more interactive now. Everybody's talking. We feel more confident.

> It is good to be working and co-operating together because we don't usually get to do that.

The trainers themselves were impressed with the enthusiasm for learning that has been demonstrated by almost everyone, and the way in which the necessary knowledge and skills were explored and reinforced in an interactive way.

As teacher of the language component my first reaction was relief at pulling off such an ostensibly problematic venture. I also found myself fascinated by the unexpected outcomes that turned up week by week. One man who hardly said anything and nobody believed could read or write turned out to be able to connect the sentence halves and hence must have been able to read quite proficiently. A man who could not write or speak clearly because of cerebral palsy could handle the mouse on the computer and participate as well as anyone else. Various people have turned out to be remarkably sympathetic and patient teachers of others. Everybody is getting adventurous on the computers and congratulating themselves when they solve their own difficulties by luck (or occasionally judgment).

I still feel that there is a place for straight language teaching, and as mentioned above, have convened a small class to address the needs of the non-writers. Others in the group have also obvious needs for slow paced language teaching that will be followed up. Nevertheless, I am satisfied that the classes have had positive outcomes for everyone who has attended them, including those with little English. The learning environment has been demystified and connected with fun things like a television quiz show. Some of the terror has been removed from computers (which are in fact being introduced in the hospital to monitor waste disposal). People have been familiarised with the somewhat formal and Latinate language of the cleaning training manual and everyone now knows not to do what Cassie, in her various delinquent moments did!

And as for me – I have learned an awful lot about cleaning!

NOTES

1. See Sefton, R., Waterhouse, P. and Deakin, R. (eds) 1994: 25. Assessment criteria and methods are discussed in greater detail in Chapter 11.
2. See Mawer and Field 1995: 23.
3. See, for example, Mikulecky, L., 1989, Wickert, R., 1989.
4. Mawer, G. 1994. *Language, Literacy and Numeracy at Merck Sharp and Dohme (Australia) Pty Ltd: Evaluation Report of an Integrated Approach.* TAFE NSW and Merck Sharp & Dohme.
5. See, for example, Atkin, J.A. 1991. Harden, and Atkin, J.A. 1994. *Thinking: Critical for Learning,* in Edwards, J. (ed.) *Thinking: International Interdisciplinary Perspectives,* Hawker Bronlow Education: Victoria.
6. Some of these programs were designed by a teaching colleague, B. Laidlaw.
7. Also designed by B. Laidlaw.

NINE

Learning at work

In their book dealing with organisational learning, Field and Ford (1995) point out that learning is happening all the time in the workplace, although of course, the type, quality and benefits of learning can vary greatly – some individuals are better at it than others and some environments are more conducive than others. 'Training' typically refers to structured, predetermined learning arrangements, and as such, it is only a narrow subset of the learning potential of everyday work. Such learning may be planned or unplanned; and some of the most valuable learning can result from activities that do not have learning as the primary aim (1995: 11, 95).

As we saw in Chapters 2 and 3, the current interest in organisational learning is focused on developing ways of converging learning and doing, so that the workplace not only, in Peddler, Bourgoyne and Boydell's words (1991) facilitates the learning of all its members but also continuously transforms itself as a result of that learning. This type of 'double loop' or 'critically reflective' learning involves moving towards established goals and at the same time questioning and reviewing the goals themselves.[1] The notion has a great deal in common with adult education principles which encourage learners to apply and critically reflect on their learning and their environment. It goes further, however, in linking the products and processes of learning firmly to everyday activities as well as system-wide processes of change.

Apart from the inspirational rhetoric of organisational learning, there are also strong pragmatic pressures for the increasing integration of working and learning: employee numbers have often been dramatically reduced, and the remaining core workforce is undertaking more diverse functions and responsibilities. As the following comments show, in the restructured, efficient workplace, the costs and practicalities of acquiring skills through formal training alone can often be prohibitive:

Training fits in at the 'fat'. We're now very lean, we've cut down on numbers, and there is no 'fat'. (Manager, manufacturing)

If you have people working in small cells made up of a carpenter, labourer and a concreter, you can't afford to be without one of them for any length of time. The whole team suffers. (Building subcontractor)

There is a lot of pressure on to meet deadlines. The men are already working 58 hours a week, where's the time for training? (Project Coordinator)

In many organisations formal training programmes are not viable due to structural factors such as shift work, multi-site working arrangements or small numbers. Even where training opportunities are offered, many employees are reluctant to take part because of lack of language and literacy skills or self-confidence. As a building subcontractor put it:

Most of my men are hands on types that were never comfortable with pen and paper. A lot of them are happy enough to work along side someone else, and learn from him that way, but they have a real block about sitting in a classroom situation.

With the greatly increasing pace and scope of changes in the workplace, a variety of modes of learning are developing to cope with the need to develop new knowledge and skills 'on the run'. Some of these modes of learning are extensions of traditional 'buddy' or 'sit by Nelly' approaches such as one-to-one, peer tutoring and mentoring, where learning is contextualised and immediately applied. Others are encouraging more autonomous learning through the use of technologies such as computers and interactive multimedia near work stations. Learning centres, for example, are becoming a part of many workplaces where employees can access independent learning materials, or computer-based packages.

As a reflection of these developments, more and more providers of vocational education and training are being asked to develop 'flexible' products and services that minimise disruption to work routines and increase the links between learning and working. In Australia, for example, 'flexible delivery' is one of the national goals of vocational education, with several state and national research projects currently exploring the links between informal and formal training methods, and experimenting with different types of flexible delivery arrangements.

There are many similarities between these developments and self-directed approaches to adult language teaching advocated in the late 1970s and 1980s (British Council, 1978, Holec, 1981). Experiences with these approaches indicate that there are a number of assumptions behind the individualistic emphasis of flexible delivery and self-directed learning that may not be widely applicable. A common assumption, for example, is that learners will produce better outcomes if they take responsibility for their own learning and are allowed to work at their own pace. For many learners new to formal learning, or those with family responsibilities for example, such assumptions about the availability of time and resources for private study may well be invalid. So are assumptions about learners' ability to analyse their own needs, select appropriate learning objectives, methods and independently monitor their progress.

Many flexible delivery methods often inadvertently pose hurdles for learners because of their increased reliance on print, or unfamiliar technology such as computers. The individual focus of such methods also means that learners can feel isolated and find the links to their work situation even more tenuous. 'Cultural changes' which are often a valuable by-product of group learning processes are very difficult to achieve through individual distance modes. An Australian vocational school's experience in delivering workplace courses is fairly typical:

> We've tried distance modes and computer based ways of learning, and they haven't worked. Maybe later on, after the learning culture has become part of the workplace, but initially people need to feel valued and encouraged, and you don't get that from a computer.

As this comment indicates, the 'learning culture of the workplace' to a great extent determines what learning is possible. The way that work is organised, for example, prevailing attitudes to curiosity, questioning and experimenting, the way information is (or is not) shared can enormously affect individuals' interest and ability to learn or apply new knowledge and skills. Similarly, if there are no obvious benefits or reward systems for developing new ideas or skills, employees are unlikely to be motivated. Xerox's experience with workplace change over three decades is typical. In documenting the changes in the company, Kearns and Nadler (1992) identify as key ingredients to success the structures, processes and environments that not only encourage learning, but also empower people to translate that learning into action.

Yet, in many ways, educators have very little expertise and influence over contextual factors such as work organisation, management styles or reward systems. Even in the area of skill development, there may be a number of political or practical reasons preventing educators from using potential opportunities to foster reflective learning. Standard operating procedures or training manuals, for example, may have been developed centrally, or by an external specialist, with little involvement from the eventual users. Despite the rhetoric of teamwork, it is not uncommon for supervisors and specialist staff to resist attempts by 'lower- skilled' employees to apply new skills, or have access to 'privileged information'.

These challenges are compounded by the fact that educators tend generally to be involved with a workplace for a relatively short period of time. So, if informal learning mechanisms are to become established and survive long term, educators have to work creatively and strategically to develop networks or communities of learning earlier rather than later in the life of a workplace project.

In this chapter, we explore some of the practical ways that educators have attempted to use the learning potential of everyday work to support, supplement or, in some cases, replace formal learning arrangements. Some of these have been quite ambitious and imaginative, others have been modest, incremental adaptations to more traditional courses. In all cases, however, their main aims were to make clear links between what happens in formal education activities and at work, to raise the profile of learning and language and to help learners develop strategies for independent and collaborative learning that would long outlive the educator's stay in the organisation.

ENQUIRY-BASED LEARNING

Using learners' experiences and immediate environment as the context for learning is a well accepted principle in adult education. Brookfield (1986), for example, points out that the most significant personal learning is the kind which results from learners reflecting on their experiences and from trying to make sense of one's life by exploring the meanings others have assigned to similar experiences. He also stresses the need for learners to redefine the context within which they are working, as a way of helping them identify and develop the skills necessary to function in that context. Kolb's (1984) experiential learning model involves a four-stage cycle moving from experiencing to observing to conceptualising to experimenting and back to experiencing. In this way, learners use their immediate context to broaden their skills, as well as increasing competence and confidence in their analytical and reflective abilities. Educators from a social action orientation such as Freire (1972) similarly advocate enquiry-based, 'problem-posing' learning as a way of promoting critical thinking, dialogue, reflection, and ultimately guide action to improve social conditions.

Attempts with increasing worker participation have also focused on the value of 'every day learning' at work in improving quality, productivity and working relationships. Reviewing research from Sweden, Japan and Canada, Rubenson and Schütze (1993) conclude that worker participation is greatly enhanced when

- employees use their own experiences at work as a starting-point for learning
- their contributions result in concrete changes and are dealt with by management
- collective, but systematic discussion adds to increase individuals' own world view and experience
- collective analysis results in common positions and increased commitment to proposed actions.[2]

The types of enquiry that learners engage in can vary widely according to the purposes and the contexts of learning, but even learners with very basic competence in language and literacy can be actively engaged in exploring different aspects of workplace discourse and processes.

In a glassware factory,[3] for example, a workplace education project was conducted by two educators working with employees across five different rosters and three rotating shifts. Most of the participants in the programme were older workers with basic language and literacy skills in English, and limited formal education.

As a way of practising the alphabet, learners were asked to develop their own workplace dictionary by finding common words to do with their work. Words such as *gob* (a drop of hot glass), *out of stock* and *position* were discussed and categorised. Learners were also encouraged to approach other personnel for common work words, so as a result, the dictionary included terms such as *laceration* and *abrasion* (from the nurse), *penalty* and *leave loading* (from the pay-master) and *impact test*, *brain-storm* and *motivation* (from the quality manager). These words generated a great deal of discussion among learners as to the need for specific workplace terminology, the differences between spoken and written language, as well as the inevitable comparisons between the findings of the different groups compiling their work dictionaries. The aggregated list of words was translated by groups of learners into the main first languages and finally published as a dictionary of 'Glassware Work Words'.

In this process of this search for words, learners did a great deal more than just expand their vocabulary or learn the alphabet. They became much more aware of the function of particular words in different contexts, of some of the differences between spoken and written discourse and the similarities and differences between their first language and English. The exercise also provided them with the opportunity – or excuse – to interact with fellow employees and managers in a different capacity and to develop their research and analytical skills.

Enquiry-based learning need not have a narrow linguistic focus. Often, employees do not have a global understanding of their workplace, its processes or their potential role in that process. It is often the case, for example, that learners do not have 'a big picture' understanding of the different stages involved in the production process, or the role of different sections. Asking learners to develop a simple flow-chart of different stages in the work cycle, or an organisational chart, for example, can be a useful way of encouraging them to develop a more critical reflective perspective of their workplace and their place in it. In one particular workplace, for example, the charts developed by learners were displayed on bulletin boards, and the idea taken up by management and employees in the later development of quality monitoring documentation.

In a group learning situation, learners can greatly benefit from sharing information about various aspects of their work. In a manufacturing company, for example, the group worked together to develop a flow chart of the work process. They then went on a 'site tour', with learners explaining to the educator and their fellow workers what their job entailed, and pointing out the relationships between the preceding and subsequent stages in the process. Interestingly, for the majority of the group, it was the first time they had visited other sections in the workplace, or considered the possibility of working in different areas. As a result, when the manager addressed the group later in the course, they were much more actively involved in discussing not only aspects of work, but also their own training and career paths possibilities in the organisation.

Project or problem-based learning activities can be another way of using learners' immediate context to develop a range of communicative and learning skills. These can range from simple activities, such as requesting information about their leave entitlements, finding out about the role of different work committees to investigating a common work-problem and proposing suggestions to address it. In a number of workplaces, groups of learners have been actively involved in developing or reviewing work documentation relating to different processes, or developing learning resources to be used by fellow employees, e.g. operating procedures, flowcharts, simple videos. The results of such projects are usually much more effective and user-friendly resources, and often valuable proposals for improving the quality and efficiency of what is produced.

Projects in both the vehicle manufacturing and food industries[4] in Australia have experimented with different ways of incorporating a problem-based approach into integrated vocational training which addressed the development of communication skills at the same time as competence in more technical areas. In a number of food industry companies, for example, a combination of group, one-to-one and project-based learning arrangements were trialled as a way of dealing with the difficulties of learning time release. The vehicle industry projects on the other hand were more structured and required learners to undertake 'practical study projects'. These provided learners with the opportunity to research particular areas of interest relevant to their work and formally present their findings to the group at the end of the course. In doing so, learners gained valuable research, communicative and analytical skills, as well as developing technical competence and greater knowledge of their workplace. Both workplace management and learners were 'pleased and surprised' at the quality of the research projects, and the 'spin-off effects' in terms of enthusiasm for learning, improvements to work processes and participation.

MAKING WIDER LINKS WITHIN THE WORKPLACE

Part of developing communities and networks of learning involves encouraging learners to make stronger links with their fellow employees and managers, and to promoting different avenues for communication and interchange.

These informal opportunities of learning can be quite imaginative. For example, in a building and construction site in Victoria,[5] the educators decided to exploit the potential of an existing communication channel that was used by employees several times a day. The lift was used regularly to transport people and materials, and many minutes were spent travelling between floors and waiting for the lift to arrive. They regularly displayed posters, language/literacy activities, puzzles and short articles in and around the lift, and received an enthusiastic response. The lift operator soon became an informal teacher who provided feedback on how material was received and, before long, employees

themselves were submitting material for display, and the idea successfully adopted at other building sites.

According to the educators involved, 'lift learning' was effective in
many ways: it was a great way of becoming known on site, more
employees were likely to respond to the offer of training, and it provided a useful opportunity for learning 'on the move'.

In the glassware company mentioned earlier a fortnightly newsletter,
put together by the two educators, served a similar function. It helped
to raise the profile of the courses, provided a forum for learners to
practise their literacy skills, and maintained a sense of continuity across
the different shifts and learner groupings. Apart from short puzzles
and amusing anecdotes, learners wrote (sometimes anonymously) about
different aspects of their work or interesting life experiences. The newsletter was also used as a means of communicating enquiries and suggestions to management, and their subsequent responses. The following
two short articles relate to employees' thoughts about the old machinery
in the plant:

Machine Problems

I'd like to write a small story of my life in this company. I'm
having a hard time. There is too much pressure on me all the time
because the machine I work on is a hard one to operate. The
machine is very old and it gives me too much trouble most of the
time. I don't think the company wants to spend a lot of money on
it. It's like the old car that I have and I don't want to spend much
money on it either. So I have to close now, thank you for listening.

Feeling sad for a moment

On Thursday, I had to go to English lessons. When I walked in
the factory I saw my friends and the fitters working on the 16
tank taking out the glass from the furnace. I stopped and thought
for a moment. And I said to myself: I worked on that machine for
many years. We had good times and bad times all those years. And
now they are going to disappear for ever. I wish it did not happen.

Encouraging the development of wider links can be structured in as
a legitimate part of formal learning activities. At Aus Tin, a work experience component was built into the early language and literacy courses

as a way of familiarising course participants with different sections of the workplace, and providing them with an opportunity to practise their newly developed communication skills. The timing of the work experience coincided with the educator's leave and a seasonal slow down in production, thus minimising disruption to established working and learning arrangements. For half a day per week for six weeks, learners worked in a different section of the plant where they had indicated interest e.g. despatch, administration. These practical opportunities for multiskilling were strategic, both in legitimising the course as an integral part of the company's aim to equip people for new jobs, and in allowing for more informal interaction between different people and sections in the plant.

MENTORING AND PEER TUTORING

Using other work personnel as peer support and mentors in the workplace can be a very useful way of extending and consolidating both skills and learning networks. In the areas of technical skills, mentoring is being increasingly promoted as a simple and effective way of imparting knowledge and skills, as well as supporting learners.

However, mentoring and peer tutoring arrangements need to be well thought out if they are to be effective. Experiences with technical skills, for example, indicate that mentoring approaches can lead to an oversimplification or misinterpretation of content if there are inadequate mechanisms in place to ensure quality and consistency. The training and support of mentors is essential if consistent standards are to be maintained.

Interpersonal and cultural factors also need to be considered. Employees may strongly resent being paired with workmates they do not get on with particularly well, because of personality or status differences. In a manufacturing company, for example, older employees (mainly of Asian background) felt it inappropriate to be coached by younger ones, or by fellow workers from the same occupational classification level. The resistance to mentoring arrangements was so strong that they had to be abandoned, and plans to introduce teamwork had to be postponed as a result of the ill-feelings generated.

Where mentoring arrangements have worked effectively, educators have been actively involved with workplace personnel in explaining how such arrangements would work, identifying appropriate mentors and providing them with training and ongoing support in the form of resources, advice and ongoing feedback.

Structural support is often also necessary, so that mentoring is not simply an added burden to an employee's usually already heavy workload. One way of minimising interpersonal tensions has been for learners to choose or be actively involved in choosing their own mentor.

More commonly, mentoring approaches have been used to support formal learning activities. In a large mail-sorting centre, for example, there was little interaction between employees of different nationalities, mainly South East Asian and Southern Europeans. The resulting 'enclaves' meant learners had little opportunity to practise their English, and the 'us and them' mentality affected management attempts to increase employee participation.

At the beginning of a language course, the educator introduced the concept of a helper: employees were encouraged to find a workmate who would be willing to spend a few minutes on a regular basis to help them practise their English. She provided a written explanation of what was involved, and later visited the prospective 'helpers' at their work stations to discuss any concerns. The centre manager supported this initiative through the weekly newsletter and by individually encouraging staff members to participate.

Every week, the educator would suggest some follow-up work for learners to do with their helpers e.g. particular work idioms. By the end of the course, most learners had developed a good, friendly relationship with their helpers, which in some cases became long-term friendships. From both a learners and helpers' point of view, the benefits were worthwhile. The following two comments were typical:

> Before, I feel embarrassed, but now I ask him to tell me when I say something wrong, and I'm getting better. Because we work together, so he sees what I say and write. He also explains to me what other people say at meetings, so now I follow much better.

> It allowed me to talk to him in a way that I did not feel able to before. Before, I'd feel self-conscious of correcting him, in case he got embarrassed, or thought I was stuck up. But now, I know he wants to know, and we have lots of fun talking about why some words and expressions are the way they are. It's opened my eyes a lot about how illogical English is. I'm glad I didn't have to learn it as an adult!

As a result of the increasing interaction over a period of months, employees were more willing to work in different teams, participate in work discussions and social activities.

A more formalised approach was adopted by another educator, working with a group of learners across a number of work sections and shifts. As she had little opportunity to interact regularly with the learners and their supervisors at their work stations, she developed a more systematic way of creating opportunities for learners to practise what they were learning during the course. With the participants' agreement, she enlisted the support of nominated personnel (such as workmates, supervisors, canteen attendant) to provide feedback on their ability to undertake a particular communicative task. The following task, for example, served to reinforce a unit of work on ways of reporting problems and making suggestions.

English Class Practical Task Two

Reporting a problem and making a suggestion

Dear,_____

Thank you very much for agreeing to help the English class participants practise their English with you. I have asked them to come and report a problem (hopefully not a real one!) e.g. 'There are no springs fitted on any of the adjustment screws'.

Could you then say 'Why do you think this is happening? and they must give you a suggestion "I think . . ."'

You can a) accept this suggestion 'Mmm, you may be right'.
　　　　or b) push the discussion further by disagreeing 'But surely not' or 'It can't be right'.

They must defend their suggestion. When they do so, please back down 'You may have a point there . . .' etc., At the end of the practical test, could you please fill in the attached sheet.

Many thanks.

Reporting a problem and making a suggestion

Name_____

has completed the above communication task.

He/she:

1. Reported a problem clearly   Yes   No

2. Suggested a way of dealing with the problem   Yes   No

3. (Optional) Defended his/her suggestion
   when challenged   Yes   No

Comments and suggestions for improvement

_____

_____

INDIVIDUAL LEARNING ARRANGEMENTS

In a number of large workplaces, 'open learning' or 'training resource' centres have developed as a response to divergent learning needs and working conditions, such as rotating shifts and multisite working arrangements. These often offer employees an opportunity to learn at their own pace and access learning to support technical training.

In an automotive components manufacturing plant in South Australia, for example,[6] when a survey indicated that 40 per cent of the workforce were interested in improving their communication skills, a self-paced learning unit was suggested as a way of complementing the language courses already on offer. A production subcommittee was formed to manage the centre, and it was decided to locate it next to the canteen for ease of access. The centre operated at lunchtime and at the change of different shifts. Employees were first introduced to the centre in groups on a roster basis, where they were encouraged to familiarise themselves with the resources available. These included English language materials, audio cassettes, videos and computer-based resources. Learners could, in consultation with the educator, develop an individualised learning program and borrow resources for use at home.

Such complementary learning arrangements can also be established in smaller workplaces, without elaborate infrastructure. At Aus Tin, for example, a Distance Learning Programme and an Independent Learning Programme were introduced as ways of supporting learners who had completed a language course, and a small number on the nightshift who had been unable to attend. Distance learning was very popular with 'course graduates' who had begun to develop independent learning skills and were ready to take responsibility for their learning. They had also had positive experiences in classes and their confidence in their own abilities had built up. A simple system was set up: after initial discussions with the educator, learning goals were developed and resources were selected from a range of generic and work-specific materials, according to learners' interests and needs. These were left in a clearly marked envelope in a pigeon-hole near the entrance to the factory floor. They were collected, taken home, completed, then returned to another pigeon-hole for her to collect and mark. Participants could take as long as they needed, and could discuss problems face to face or by phone if necessary.

Attempts to introduce formal and individualised learning arrangements were not so successful in another area of the plant – the Printery. In the following case study, Lee Fletcher describes how she and the training manager worked to address the skill development needs of printery employees on the production line.

CASE STUDY. LANGUAGE SUPPORT ON THE LINE

The Printery department at Aus Tin had a history of 'old style' management and industrial relations. Employees from this department were subject to a different industrial award and were represented by a more conservative union than the rest of the production employees at Aus Tin. There had been little change either in employees or work practices over recent years, and these factors accentuated their separateness. Printery management and employees, for example, had declined to be involved in preliminary skills analysis and the communication skills audit undertaken in the rest of the plant, or the subsequent workplace communication courses.

Other attempts at skill development or changes to work organisation met with resistance and suspicion. An Independent Learning Programme was introduced to the department at the same time as other sections of the organisation but had very limited success. The hourly session could only be offered outside work hours, and the need for increased work-related literacy was not evident to participants as their jobs had not significantly changed. A further drawback was the teasing from some workmates ('You must give the teacher a headache . . .' 'Going to University, are we?') which led to a number of participants dropping out.

It was clear that a different approach was needed to address the department's skill development needs and, in particular, employees' communication skills. The following year at the Printery saw a change in management, pressures to seek Quality Standard accreditation and more flexible, team-based work practices. After some discussion with training personnel and the language and literacy educator, it was decided that the educator should be involved as part of a small group in documenting work procedures and encouraging informal ways of developing their technical and communicative skills.

The group consisted of two experienced operators, one of whom was trained as a trainer, and the educator. They consulted closely with employees and management as they worked to develop job descriptions, standard operating procedures, and process control forms for use on the line. Because of the lack of acceptance of language courses and the low level of English of many of the employees, the approach was to design on-line materials so that the need for writing skills was virtually eliminated and reading skills didn't need to be very advanced.

These materials (e.g. standard operating procedures, process control forms, charts, lists) were developed in such a way that they were useful both as learning aids and for quality accreditation purposes. The standard operating procedures, for example, were documented in the form of a flow chart, with an accompanying task breakdown for each machine process. Similarly, the process control forms were carefully designed and trialled to be as user-friendly as possible, and a short information booklet was also developed on Quality Accreditation and what it meant to the Printery.

Employees were introduced to the changes in procedures through a short workshop 'off-the-line', which was co-presented by the educator and one of the other team members. The structure of this workshop is outlined below.

INTRODUCTION

Outline content of the session, covering:

- the need for process control improvements,
- the new process control forms, – their structure, the abbreviations used, how to fill them in,
- the new tests all employees will have to carry out, using the forms.

Explain that further support will be given on the line to ensure that all employees can fill in the forms accurately.

1. Overview of Quality Control improvements
- why we need them
- when we need them to start
- how we are going to implement new procedures

2. Introduce new process control forms

Explain that forms are in draft form. All comments and suggestions for improving the forms will be taken up at the end of the trial period.

NB. Both Operator and assistant **must** be able to do the checks.
- Look at the layout of the form.
- Read the instructions together.
- Go through the abbreviations.
- Show an example of a completed form.

The new forms were explained and new quality tests and procedures demonstrated. This was not a problem apart from the usual resistance to anything new, especially if it was thought to add more to the workload.

In the on-line learning support which followed, the educator worked with employees on the job, monitoring their accuracy in reading and following the instructions. She visited the area on a daily basis, checking that the forms were being filled in correctly, helping with any difficult vocabulary or abbreviations and answering any questions. She also put lists of vocabulary on the machine, e.g. faults to be looked for, to develop skills in word recognition and spelling. This approach was taken until the forms were understood and completed correctly. Similarly, the introduction and demonstration of the new tests was carried out on the line by experienced operators.

The on-line training materials were designed and documented by the group, through a trialling and feedback process. The group developed the following rationale at the beginning of the training materials:

RATIONALE FOR COATING TRAINING MATERIALS

The Coating Training materials have been specifically developed to meet the needs of the Printery. They are competency based. Over 90 per cent of printery employees come from a non-English speaking background. It is essential that they all have access to training.

With this in mind, the training materials are designed

- for on-line training
- in relatively short sessions
- with a large practical component
- to include support from a Mentor/Coater Operator
- in Plain English
- with minimal writing skills required (in the Review activities)

The Coating training materials include:

TRAINER'S NOTES

These contain comprehensive notes, with
- suggested questions and answers
- headings to remind the trainer of the sequence of activities
- a Trainer's Checklist to ensure that all information has been covered

TRAINEE'S NOTES

These contain:
- standard operating procedures (flow chart and task break down)
- safe work practices
- Quality control checks and procedures
- diagrams
- specification sheets
- troubleshooting guide
- review activities

WORKPLACE COMPETENCIES

These have been developed for each area of competence and are cross referenced to the training materials developed.

COMPETENCE ASSESSMENT

Assessment takes place
- prior to training, to determine training needs
- after training and a period of practice and consolidation to determine competence as required in the workplace

A Reference book containing examples of visual faults and information on causes and solutions was also created to support the training materials.

The worksheets illustrate an example of an activity developed to support employees' learning about the starting procedures for the feeder and coater machines.

FEEDER PARTS AND FUNCTIONS

YOU NEED TO BE ABLE TO:	Name the parts on the feeder and describe the functions of each part.

Match the machine part on the left with the machine function on the right. The first one is done for you.

PILE HEIGHT SWITCH

MAGNETS

ELEVATOR CHAINS

CLUTCH HANDLE

STILLAGE GUIDES

VACUUM SUCKERS

DOG CHAINS

DROP FEED ROLLS

DOUBLE SHEET THROW-OUT

APRON/FRONT PLATE

hoist the stillage into position

raises the stillage as sheets are fed through to the feed table

send sheets forward

assist in separation of sheets

contacts the leading edge of the stillage

checks sheet thickness against operator settings

raises/lowers stillage hoist

pick up individual sheets

prevent top sheets slipping out of alignment

REVIEW OF FEEDER

YOU NEED TO BE ABLE TO: start the coater and feeder in the correct sequence.

Number the starting procedures in the correct order.

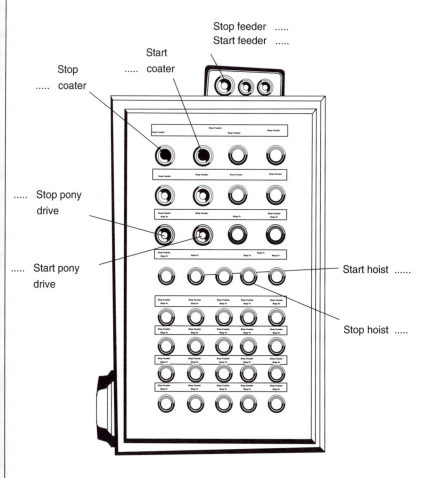

To make adjustments during a run, list the stopping procedure.

1.   ....

2.   ....

In contrast to earlier skill development attempts (including communication courses and independent learning programmes) this more informal approach was successful because it was perceived by employees to be transparently relevant to their work. Another factor was that, by not being withdrawn from the line, literacy difficulties were not highlighted, nor was production disrupted.

NOTES

1. See Argyris C., and Schön, D. A., 1978; Field and Ford, 1995.
2. Rubenson K., and Schütze H. 1993.
3. Kerr, J. and McCall, J., 1990. Literacy for Restructuring: Teaching Reading and Writing in a Glass Factory. Interchange No. 16 October pp. 21–24, NSW Adult Migrant Education Service.
4. See National Food Industry Training Council 1993, Sefton, R., Waterhouse P., and Deakin R. (eds) 1994.
5. Patterson, A. and Lucas M., DEET 1994: 7.
6. Allen, K. 1993.

TEN

Working with trainers

WHO ARE THE TRAINERS?

In the past, training roles have traditionally been part of the personnel department, with training functions focused on specific aspects such as induction and occupational health and safety. With the increasing focus on skills development in recent years, the number of personnel with training responsibilities in the workplace has dramatically increased.[1] Separate training departments, for example, have come into being, with new full- or part-time positions created. These range from training coordinators and managers – who have a responsibility for developing training plans, systems and overseeing training programmes across the organisation – to full-time technical trainers. Learning organisations are increasingly integrating 'learning coaches' and 'learning facilitators' into workplace teams and developing learning centres on site. Workplace trainers are extensively used in a full- or part-time capacity, and tend typically to be supervisors or experienced operational employees.

The increasing importance of training has also been recognised in employees' job descriptions. When industrial awards in Australia were restructured, for example, many occupational skill classification descriptions included – often for the first time ever – on the job training as part of the routine work requirements. In the metals industry, for example, the supervisor classification was redefined as supervisor/coordinator/trainer, while the first three skill classifications of employees specified part of the requirements as 'assisting in the provision of on the job training in conjunction with trades persons and trainers' (MTIA, 1990: 33–35).

A national competency standards body was established in Australia in 1991 to develop and review national standards for workplace trainers and assessors. These standards which form the basis for training programmes recognise two categories of trainers:

Category 1 applies to those for whom the training function is not a major part of their job. These people may provide on the job structured training infrequently or even regularly within a structured training context. Training is provided on a one-to-one basis or to small groups of trainees. Category 1 trainers are likely to be drawn from the ranks of skilled operators, team leaders and supervisors and technical experts.

Category 2 applies to those people for whom training is a large part of their job, or the full job function within a structured training context. They may provide training on a one-to-one, small group or large group basis. They have considerable responsibility for programme development and documentation, assessing trainees and recording training outcomes. (Workplace Trainers, 1992: *viii*)

Despite the increasing number of formal courses available, on the job training is the oldest and remains the most common means of developing skills in the workplace. In 1993, for example, in Australia, 86 per cent of people employed undertook some form of training. Of these, the great majority, 82 per cent, undertook on-the-job training, compared with 36 per cent who attended an in-house course (Australian Bureau of Statistics, 1994 b: 1).

In many ways then, workplace trainers play a vital role in developing employees' skills and translating the rhetoric of workplace reform and organisational learning into day-to-day realities. To a great extent, their own communicative competence, and the appropriateness of the materials and methods they use, determine the quality and scope of learning that does occur at work. This chapter explores some of the strategies that educators can use to develop the communication and presentation skills of on the job and full-time technical trainers, as they deal with their changing roles.

PRESSURES FACED BY TRAINERS

While most workplaces acknowledge the need for skill development, in practice, it is still common for skill development activities such as training to be regarded as a peripheral intrusion into core business. As a result, trainers often find themselves in awkward situations in that they are given the responsibility of 'championing' new ways of working, without the necessary skills or authority to do so. They may, for example, have to contend with cynical attitudes of 'old guard' management, and workers unconvinced of the benefits of new systems, such as skill-based pay or self-managing teams. Commonly, the practicalities of obtaining time for themselves and their trainees to develop and apply new skills are difficult to negotiate, as they interfere with day-to-day work pressures. Development and delivering training programmes is usually resource-intensive, and the immediate costs are often much more evident than the potential benefits.

Trainers are typically required to implement training programmes with which they have had little involvement. Many programmes, for example, are nationally accredited and have therefore been centrally developed with the use of external rather than in-house expertise, with little trialling or validation by the ultimate users. Gaps between the assumptions of the programme designer and workplace practice are often only obvious at the implementation point. Some of the mismatches occur at the level of content, while others relate to the methodologies used.

Assumptions about the types and levels of technologies used, for example, are quite common. Similarly, the training programme may stress particular aspects of the work, and specify procedures that should be followed, such as the frequency of quality checks or particular safety precautions. However, pragmatic considerations and business pressures on the ground often mean that such procedures are overlooked, or short-cuts are developed. Such discrepancies are often difficult to resolve without trainers losing either their credibility or authority.

As with industry standards, the language and format of many training programmes are often designed more to comply with the accreditation requirements of government and training bureaucracies, rather than provide trainers with a user-friendly resource. The terminology of competency-based training with its associated *units, modules* and *performance criteria* is often far from transparent. Similarly, translating every day work activities into authoritative learning outcomes can often make them daunting and unrecognisable to trainers and trainees alike. In a typical work unit for base-level employees on 'Interacting with Customers' for example, learning outcomes include the following requirements:

- Internal and external customers are identified;
- Customer enquiries are clarified and attended to courteously;
- Basic liaison functions are performed accurately;
- Customers are directed to samples of enterprise products in accordance with workplace procedures;
- Records are completed as required in accordance with established workplace procedures.

Using passive (*are identified, clarified, attended*) and abstract, jargon terms such as *internal and external customers, liaison, in accordance with established workplace procedures* does more to obfuscate than guide the learning required. A common complaint by trainers using training schedules is that they are unable to relate to such an atomistic 'formalisation' of routine daily activities, and consequently feel insecure about their ability to train others in areas they may have ironically felt quite competent about before they were described in 'competency terms'.

Trainers are usually selected for their technical skills, or experience, but their ability to communicate this expertise may not be as well developed. The methodologies of many training programmes are often unfamiliar to trainers, or assume a great deal in terms of trainers' facilitation and presentation skills. The increasing focus on concepts such as teamwork, quality, and understanding the 'why' as well as the 'what' of work requires trainers often to train others very differently from how they themselves were trained, and – until recently – operated.

Training programmes that provide 'underlying theoretical knowledge' of processes, for example, can easily become overwhelming and boring to employees without achieving the intended outcomes. At the other end of the continuum, activities such as ice-breakers, when used with groups unfamiliar with formal training and its particular set of cultural assumptions, can often work to trivialise the importance of training rather than relaxing participants and creating a friendly atmosphere. Similarly, experiential exercises or case studies are often useful in illustrating particular points, but can easily become negative diversions if trainers' facilitation and debriefing skills are not highly developed.

In a particular training programme on quality concepts, for example, one of the exercises required the trainer to blindfold a trainee, and ask him/her to walk a straight line. The intention of the exercise was to illustrate the usefulness of process checks in providing systematic feedback on quality during the production process. While such an exercise was effective in a group situation with an external trainer, the team leader, a middle-aged Italian male, felt very awkward about carrying out the same exercise in a small group, with only three female operators. Apart from the cultural/gender sensitivities, he also felt it would be detrimental to their subsequent relationships, as he had not been in the habit of 'playing games' with his team members on the shop floor. Interestingly, despite his obvious status within the workplace, this team leader did not feel sufficiently confident with his new training role to modify the exercise. Instead, his unease resulted in procrastination and vague criticisms of 'airy-fairy' training modules.

One of the greatest pressures on workplace trainers is the lack of adequate time to plan and prepare. Training is often responsive to immediate workplace needs, and trainers themselves tend to be employees with pressing operational responsibilities and deadlines. More often than not, training is an added responsibility to existing workloads. This has significant implications for planning, and structuring learning opportunities to meet employee needs. 'Just in time' training may be responsive to the workplace, but it is not so responsive in terms of providing quality learning. In many cases, little time is allowed for preparation, as the following comments by a part-time trainer in the manufacturing sector exemplify:

> I was taken off work today to look at developing a program for line efficiencies. I got two hours to put overheads together for this talk tomorrow. I said to the manager how do you expect these people to understand tolerances and cartesian graphs? He said to me 'we will just have to wave our hands a lot'. If we had time we'd think of some examples of showing them what we meant, of getting them to do an exercise but that's the realities of it, there just isn't time.

As this comment shows, trainers often find themselves ill-equipped to deal with any learners with special needs, particularly if training is undertaken in group situations. Dealing with learners at different stages of technical understanding and language and literacy competence is challenging enough for a qualified, experienced, educator, let alone workplace trainers who have themselves received minimal training. The skills and resources to adapt and adjust to suit different needs are quite considerable, especially given operational constraints. The following frustrations expressed by a trainer, for example, are typical:

> A lot of teams want to do the courses as a team and it's only halfway during the first session that you realise that you've got two people out of a group of ten that can't write their names down. The choices are invidious, exclude the two people and have them miss out on the team building value of the training, as well as the money value until they build up the language and literacy skills, drop the course standards, and get them through any which way, or spend a lot of your own time going through the course with them again and again.

LIMITATIONS OF TRADITIONAL TRAINING FOR TRAINERS

Typical 'Train the Trainer' courses consist of a two or three day workshop – often over sequential days – dealing with different methods of instruction. In a lecture-type format, participants are shown ways of analysing a task, developing learning outcomes and a logical training sequence. The content and format of the programme usually assume a highly educated 'native' level of oral and written language proficiency and a considerable degree of theoretical understanding of industry restructuring, training and assessment issues. While claiming to be competency-based, such courses usually do not contain any practical component or provide opportunities for participants to practise and gain feedback on their training and presentation skills.

One of the other significant limitations of such programmes is their implicit assumptions regarding the nature of the training context itself. In the same way that much vocational training addresses the 'task skill' aspects of competence at the expense of aspects such as task-management or contingency management skills, train the trainer courses usually focus on a behaviourist instructional model of learning that is totally inadequate for today's workplace. The complex industrial realities of the workplace environment are often ignored or assumed to be unproblematic.

Yet with the scope and pace of changes being implemented at work, skill development almost inevitably becomes entangled with a number of other issues such as work design, attitudinal problems resulting from past practices or power games to do with territory and skills hoarding. Even seemingly innocuous activities such as 'identifying training needs' can unleash a great deal of resentment and suspicion from employees if not handled thoughtfully. These issues invariably affect the extent to which trainers are able to foster employees' learning, yet they are often not recognised, let alone addressed.

Train the trainer programmes are usually focused on 'demonstrate-imitate' models of training, which are inadequate in developing the competence necessary to cope with changing work requirements. Ways of encouraging employees to find and evaluate different information, work collaboratively to solve problems or be more reflective and analytical towards their work, for example, are often not explored. Nor are ways of integrating learning and practising new skills as part of everyday work. Yet such practices need to be fostered and encouraged if skill development is to be an ongoing process.

The new target groups for vocational training are employees who have usually had limited formal education and are uncomfortable with classroom 'chalk and talk' training. Their levels of confidence, English language and literacy and study skills often lag significantly behind their technical skills. Yet traditional 'Train the Trainer' programmes do not equip trainers to deal with these diverse learning needs. Action learning methodologies, ways of building trainees' confidence and competence in formal learning, for example, are usually not addressed. Nor are strategies to ensure the content and format of training are consistent with trainees' competence in language and literacy.

Bilingual employees are very valuable resources in the workplace, and their effective communication skills are often used informally in interpreting and training other workmates. For many workplaces, using bilingual trainers is an effective way to ensure skill development across language and cultural barriers. Yet many bilingual employees are often reluctant to put themselves forward as trainers because of their own lack of confidence with English, formal learning situations or the abstracted, print-based nature of training programmes.

Vince's experience is a typical one. A former Polish shipyard welder, he was employed to carry out minor maintenance welding with a construction company. After completing a workplace English language course, Vince was asked to join a team to develop a skills module. During this process, it was discovered that he was a craftsman welder, so he was asked to run a welding course. He was quite reluctant to do this because of his perceived lack of confidence in English. According to the project manager, Vince was very worried that people wouldn't understand his accent, but was 'talked into' becoming a trainer, with very positive results. He speaks several European languages, which he often used in training others.[2] The success of these early experiences with training led to Vince being appointed as a full-time learning coach, where he is able to encourage many other bilingual employees to develop their own skills.

SETTING UP COLLABORATIVE PARTNERSHIPS

Apart from their key role in developing employees' skills, workplace trainers often have a good understanding of their organisation's culture, formal and informal networks. They also tend to be involved in structures such as training and consultative committees, and activities such as module development, and assessment. Supporting the skill development of such strategically placed personnel is likely, therefore, to lead to long-term improvements in the quality of learning for all employees and the development of more effective user-friendly learning systems and strategies.

This support can take place at a number of levels, depending on the particular context educators find themselves in. For example, if a training infrastructure already exists in the organisation, and trainers have already been conducting training programmes, the support an educator may be able to provide would be at an informal, advisory level. Whereas if no training infrastructure exists, educators may be able to assist with the initial training and development of trainers. As in any collaborative relationship, the quality of such partnerships depends on the parties' abilities to respect each other's area of expertise and clearly negotiate roles and responsibilities. Some trainers, for example, feel self-conscious about their training methodologies or may perceive educators as a threat to their territory or expertise. As with workplace managers, the effectiveness of collaboration will, to some extent, depend on the degree to which educators can be seen as a valuable resource to achieving common objectives.

Informal support

Educators in the workplace often work closely with trainers in a team-teaching or support role to address employees' language and literacy development needs as part of their vocational skill development. It is common, for example, for educators to observe training sessions to gather information about the communication skill requirements of the course. Similarly, trainers are often invited to language and literacy courses to address the group on a specific aspect of work, or provide feedback on course content and the progress of course participants.

Provided trainers are sufficiently comfortable with receiving feedback on their training practice, such observations can become informal skill-development opportunities. They can also be a valuable way for educators to learn more about the skill requirements and expectations of the workplace.

In one particular workplace, for example, the educator was able to participate in a technical course, both to gain an understanding of the communication requirements of the course, and provide feedback to the trainer on ways that the programme could be made more accessible and effective for participants. While a number of these suggestions related specifically to language, literacy and cross-cultural issues, many related to the application of adult education principles and teaching methodology.

The course was conducted over an eight hour shift, which may have been logistically practical from an administrative perspective, but proved quite taxing on participants' concentration spans. The educator suggested that trainees be given more frequent, but shorter breaks to make allowances for the fact they were not used to sitting for long periods of time. She also suggested the adaptation of a number of learning activities to a problem-solving and group work approach. These increased participants' involvement, added variety as well as providing a model for participants to follow in subsequent exercises. By allowing time for pair or small group work, participants could immediately apply what they were learning and difficulties in understanding could be addressed as they arose. Small group work also allowed for greater interaction and collaboration between the participants themselves, hence increasing their enjoyment and involvement in learning.

The educator was also able to provide some specific feedback on language and literacy factors that impeded participants' understanding. As a way of building rapport, for example, the trainer used a number of idioms e.g. *knackered, up the spout, Buckley's chance,* which were often unclear to some participants. He was also inconsistent in his use of terminology, sometimes using the technical name, an abbreviation, and a lay term, without making it explicit that they all referred to the same item.

The educator suggested to the trainer that he be more explicit about his use of technical terms and concepts, and use the board in a systematic way to reinforce unfamiliar terminology and illustrate concepts. She also gave him some positive feedback on particular strategies he used to reinforce concepts, such as using actual work samples and relating anecdotes to illustrate points. These helped participants to make the connections between theory and practice, draw on their own experience and also reduced the amount of new information being introduced in one session.

In a similar way, the educator and trainer worked together to modify some of the written course material to increase their clarity and consistency. The use of labelled diagrams, for example, consistent layout and the addition of a glossary of terms were useful in overcoming a number of difficulties. The range of assessment tasks was also increased to include practical activities that were less demanding in terms of language skills and examination techniques.

Formal skill development of trainers

In workplaces which are beginning to appoint workplace trainers, educators can be more explicitly involved in developing the skills such employees will need to fulfil their new responsibilities.

Beyond a 'demonstrate-imitate', narrow model of instruction, such skill development could address some of the challenges associated with their new roles. These include:

- discussing some of the wider industrial implications of skill development in the workplace – ways of identifying training needs, organising necessary resources to allow for training to happen, relating training to problems at work, providing opportunities for practice, for skills gained to be used.
- exploring different ways of defining competence and learning styles and methodologies that may be appropriate to 'hands on' learners and new workplace practices.
- developing an awareness of language, literacy and crosscultural factors associated with formal training and devising strategies for dealing with them.
- improving their communication skills and strategies to ensure they are communicating effectively to the diverse needs of the workforce.
- increasing trainers' confidence with the terminology of competency-based training and their ability to relate abstract concepts and terms to their own working situation.
- providing an opportunity for feedback on their training so they are able to make what improvements may be necessary.
- ways of developing learning resources that can support skill development on line.
- ways of assessing skills gained.
- reviewing training/learning resources to ensure their suitability and accessibility by intended users.

Rather than a two day block workshop, structuring a course over a substantial period of time allows participants to apply and consolidate their learning. The following case studies outline the collaborative design and delivery of integrated 'Train the Trainer' courses in two different settings. The first was aimed at 'category 1' trainers, for whom the training function is not a major part of their job. The second was designed for a group of bilingual employees who were reluctant to take on training roles in their workplace, despite their evident skills and experience. The aim of this course was to increase their confidence in their own ability, their familiarity with competency-based terminology and their formal presentation and communication skills. The third case study deals with 'category 2', full-time trainers in the vehicle industry where a longer course allowed for a more intensive focus on language and cultural issues.

CASE STUDY 1. TRAINING TRAINERS AT AUS TIN

As part of the development of the training modules at Aus Tin, a 'Train the Trainer' Course was developed jointly by the educator and the training manager to address the needs of newly appointed trainers. These trainers were drawn from the ranks of team leaders and experienced technical personnel. The course was designed to begin shortly prior to the implementation of the first technical training modules, and be held on a weekly or fortnightly basis concurrently with the technical training. The rationale for this was to provide ongoing support to the trainers while they were themselves conducting training and provide a formal feedback mechanism on the effectiveness/suitability of the completed training modules.

Both workplace educators were actively involved to varying extents, in the design, delivery and evaluation of the trainers' course. Specific sessions conducted by the educators included the following:

- What is competency based training? This session introduced the trainers to the main principles and terminology of competency based training and explored ways of defining and developing competence.
- What makes a good training session? Criteria for effective training were developed by the group, based on their experiences as trainees. These later formed the basis for a self-assessment checklist the trainers used to reflect on their own training sessions.
- Training a multicultural workforce. This session focused on how some language, literacy and crosscultural factors can reduce the effectiveness of the training and developed strategies for dealing with them (see illustration for extract of handout used during this session).
- Presentation skills for trainers. Strategies for presenting information and obtaining trainee feedback were discussed, with particular reference to the profile of trainees in the workplace.

A significant component of the training course included the observation of trainers' sessions followed up by feedback from the educator structured along the criteria which had been jointly developed (an extract from one such evaluation is provided on page 211). This feedback was a useful opportunity to discuss presentation and training techniques such as ways of eliciting information from trainees by asking open questions. Invariably, specific language and literacy points, such as the use of the passive, were also discussed. The content and presentation of the training materials were reviewed during these

STRATEGIES FOR PRESENTING INFORMATION AND GETTING FEEDBACK IN A TRAINING SESSION

1. Try to establish a relaxed atmosphere from the beginning.

   - Explain what the session will cover, how it is relevant to the trainees, what you expect of them by the end of the session.
   - Make it clear that it is OK to ask questions if something is not clear, that you're happy to go over things.

2. Break the information into logical, digestible chunks.

3. Use clear, simple English and explain difficult terms:

   - give instructions in the right order e.g. *Make sure you've waited 2 minutes before you take the can out*

   ⟶ _____

   Don't pick up the can unless it is cool enough to touch, will you?

   ⟶ _____

   (watch out for problem words like *unless, provided that, although*)
   - check understanding of jargon e.g. *corrosion, metal exposure, aperture* and idiomatic expressions e.g. *the buck stops here, all gone down the drain*
   - explain abbreviations e.g. *QTY. INV.*

4. Involve the trainees, find out what they already know and build on the knowledge they have.

5. If you are giving a lot of information, explain which parts you expect them to remember and which is just background information.

6. Look for signs of non-understanding e.g. a look of puzzlement, a fixed smile, a frown.

   - Repeat or paraphrase the information e.g.:
   How do we monitor quality?
   ⟶ *How do we check that we're making good cans?*

   Aus Tin is pledged to provide the best quality and customer service possible.

   ⟶ _____

Extract from Handout to 'Train the Trainer' Course

sessions, both to improve their effectiveness and to develop specific bridging or supplementary materials for learners' use.

PRESENTATION

Covers key points:
- in small chunks   1 2 3 ④ 5
- in logical sequence   1 2 3 ④ 5   *sequence was more along trainees' needs, which was great to see.*

Responds to trainee's needs by:
- explaining difficult and
  unfamiliar terms   1 2 3 ④ 5   *generally v. good, but need to check basic terms eg.*
- using the whiteboard   1 2 3 4 ⑤   *'gang'*
- giving concrete examples, etc. 1 2 3 4 ⑤   *whiteboard great improvt.*
  excellent use of concrete examples, recent experiences on the line etc...

Asks clear questions:
- to find out what trainees
  already know   1 2 ③ 4 5   *- Could elicit more at beginning or when*
- to find out whether they
  understand course content 1 2 3 ④ 5   *reviewing material - good use of open questions.*

Keeps to a reasonable time
frame:
- to support progress of
  learning   1 2 3 ④ 5 ⎤ *Evenly paced +*
- to keep session on track   1 2 3 ④ 5 ⎬ *well balanced*
- to avoid learner fatigue   1 2 3 ④ 5 ⎦

Varies voice, tone and volume 1 2 ③ 4 5   *Could be a bit louder ∗ clearer mainly due to background noise factor*

Gives clear instructions about
session activities and if
necessary helps trainee to get
started   1 2 3 ④ 5

Extract from Trainers' Evaluation Form

From the educators' perspective, the observation sessions were valuable in a number of respects. They provided an opportunity to discuss language and cultural issues and provide feedback on a one-to-one basis, as well as evaluating the appropriateness of the training materials developed. In addition to identifying the need for further literacy support materials for the technical modules, the educator was able to gauge at first hand particular trainees' ability to cope with the training. In some instances, for example, extra tutoring was provided for the trainees.

The 'Train the trainer' course was useful not only in developing trainers' skills, but was also used as a forum to review the effectiveness of the training programme. The trainers felt that as well as learning new skills, they were actively engaged in improving the training materials. Both training personnel and the educators were working to a common objective, which was to improve employees' skill levels and the quality of the work produced.

CASE STUDY 2. SUPPORTING BILINGUAL TRAINERS

As mentioned earlier, a number of bilingual employees use their language and cultural skills to great advantage in the workplace, but are reluctant to become official trainers. Apart from their self-consciousness about their language and literacy levels, or accents, they often feel over-whelmed by the abstraction and complexity of 'Train the Trainer' courses. Yet such employees are uniquely placed in a culturally diverse workplace, in facilitating skill development and ensuring that the training programmes implemented are accessible to the majority of employees.

In a steel construction company with a high proportion of employees from non-English speaking backgrounds, an educator developed a course in conjunction with the training manager for a number of bilingual experienced employees to prepare them for a formal training role. This course was designed to support a two day 'Train the Trainer' workshop that all prospective trainers attended.[3]

The course had a number of interrelated aims. The first was to develop participants' ability to access and actively participate in the formal training sessions they would inevitably be involved in as part of their new training role. Another was to acquire a greater competence in training. Apart from becoming familiar with the principles and terminology of competency-based training, participants developed skills in gathering and analysing information, checking understanding and participating in discussions. They became more confident in using strategies such as skimming, scanning and inferencing when faced with difficult material. They also became much more aware of the differences between the fluid, spoken language of shop-floor interactions, and the more abstracted, lexically dense forms used in training manuals and competency statements. Their increased ability to 'code-switch' between the different forms helped a great deal in de-mystifying formal training systems and programmes. Because of their bilingual and bicultural skills, they were in a unique position to recognise potential difficulties for their prospective trainees, and to consciously explain terms or adapt particular training methods and materials.

During the course, participants were also able to discuss some of the associated tensions and challenges of trainers' roles with workplace managers and have their particular language and cultural contributions formally recognised through these discussions. By practising their formal presentation and training skills in a non-threatening environment, these prospective trainees felt much more comfortable about their role as trainers, and more enthusiastic about the potential of skill-based, rather than time-based, advancement opportunities. As informal workplace leaders, their enthusiasm helped to allay many of their fellow employees' concerns about changes to work organisation and skill development in the company.

CASE STUDY 3. DEVELOPING THE SKILLS OF FULL-TIME TRAINERS IN THE VEHICLE INDUSTRY

This case study example is drawn from a project undertaken at the Ford Motor Company with Vehicle Industry Certificate trainers.[4] Virgona reports that the company had provided English language and literacy courses for its employees as a way of supporting their ultimate participation in vocational training (Vehicle Industry Certificate courses). However, there was little interaction between language and literacy educators and vocational trainers: 'while trainers regarded teachers as remote professionals, teachers regarded trainers as primarily workplace experts' (1994: 30).

A programme was proposed which would bring the two groups together and set up opportunities for skill transfer. Following a process of needs analysis, a series of eight workshops was developed – six for trainers focusing on language and literacy issues and two for educators focusing on workplace specific material. Educators and trainers were also paired and asked to team-teach and observe each other's training sessions.

The workshop sessions for trainers addressed the following issues:

- Recognising and responding to difference – through the use of case study examples of typical worker/learners, trainers were encouraged to think about individual needs and ways of addressing them.
- Adult learning principles – and ways of applying them in training.
- Presentation skills – ways of adapting difficult material, techniques for clarifying understanding.
- Developing literacy skills – analysing different texts written by workers with poor literacy to identify needs and develop strategies to assist them.
- Simplifying texts – plain English strategies and ways of making cultural assumptions clear.

The workshop sessions for educators focused on work specific processes and terminology and a practical demonstration session.

Despite practical organisational problems – shift arrangements, conflicting training and leave schedules – the course was found to be valuable by both trainers and educators. The course evaluation indicated, for example, that trainers had increased their understanding of how people develop competence in language and literacy, ways of identifying needs and supporting skill development in these areas. As well as coping better with participants' varied pace of learning, the trainers reported that they had developed strategies for presenting material in different ways and adapting content and assessment tasks to increase their suitability for learners.

Educators, on the other hand, had gained increased knowledge of shop-floor processes, the content of vocational modules and ways of incorporating those into their teaching.

Both educators and trainers gained a greater appreciation of each other's skills, and were able to collaborate to improve learning for Ford employees. The module tests, for example, were a source of frustration for all concerned in that they seemed to assess the recall of materials rather than participants' competence. The educators and trainers cooperated to redesign the assessment tasks so that they better reflected the module objectives. Suggested assessment tasks included using graphic illustrations to identify safe and unsafe work practices, and short case studies to explore contributing factors to workplace accidents. One of the tasks involved a short workplace project, where learners interviewed fellow workers to find out about the role and function of the Occupational Health and Safety committee and how they worked to resolve safety issues.

NOTES

1. See, for example, Philips and Shaw, 1989 for an overview of developments in the United Kingdom from the 1960s to the late 1980s.
2. Based on DEET, Training for Productivity, September 1994 p. 6, Field and Mawer, 1993.
3. The course was conducted by S. Russell, and the syllabus designed for the course is described in greater detail in Mawer (1993: 92–100).
4. For a more detailed account of the project, see Virgona, C. 1994.

ELEVEN

Influencing assessment structures and practices in the workplace

Assessment is one of the most difficult aspects of skills development and recognition, and is currently the subject of much research and debate at both national and international levels. It is evident that increasingly, competency-based assessment in the workplace is for high stakes. With the restructuring of industrial agreements, and the introduction of skill-based pay in many workplaces, the assessment of competence in now placed in an industrial rather than a purely educational or training context. The purposes of assessment are no longer just to determine learning needs or how well the learner has developed competence as a result of a training programme. Assessment in a workplace context takes place for a number of reasons:

- to identify the competencies an employee already has so they can be formally recognised. This is sometimes referred to as the recognition of current competence (RCC). In the case of a person applying to gain entry into a formal course, this is referred to as the recognition of prior learning (RPL), or the accreditation of prior learning (APL).
- to help identify the learning needs of employees so they can be addressed (diagnostic assessment).
- to monitor employees' progress through training (formative assessment).
- to determine whether a person has achieved particular competencies as a result of a training program (summative assessment).

Much depends on the outcome of assessments – in terms of pay increase, skill reclassification, job promotion, or even whether someone retains their job. Assessments are often conducted through indirect methods – such as written tests or interviews – so that almost inevitably, competence in these communicative modes becomes closely intertwined with competence in the particular skill or knowledge in question. For individuals who are disadvantaged in terms of communicative resources, or familiarity with particular assessment methods used, these assessment situations are then, in critical linguistic terms, *critical communicative sites*.

Given these high stakes, how can language and literacy educators influence what happens in workplace assessments? In this chapter, we look briefly at some of the problematic aspects of workplace assessments. We then explore some of the direct and indirect ways that educators can contribute to the development of effective and fair assessment practices in the workplace.

ASSESSMENT – PRINCIPLES AND PRACTICES

There is general agreement – both at national policy and local workplace level – about the need for fair and valid assessments. In both England and Australia, for example, national principles and guidelines have been developed to enhance the flexibility, validity, reliability and fairness of assessment.[1] In practice, however, the translation of these principles has been less straightforward.

Competency assessment is a process of collecting evidence about what learners can do, rather than an exam. It would make sense therefore to draw on different sources for evidence of competence, especially that which already exists from ongoing work activity, or past achievements. Yet, in practice, assessment is typically treated as an objective process of testing what someone can do against a set of rationally determined standards, through specified criteria and methods. The resulting focus is on consistency, standardisation and objectivity, rather than differential indicators that allow for the diversity of individuals and situations involved.

Practical considerations, such as cost, and the industrial pressures for assessment often mean that notions of equity continue to have merit in theory, but are often of little significance in terms of influencing implementation. A national review of assessment practices in Australia, for example, observed that:

> Without exception the industrial factors have played the dominant role
> in assessment systems initiated by enterprises and industries. They have
> provided a far greater impetus than that provided by good intentions to
> develop the skills of the existing workforce. (Toop *et al.*, 1994: 18)

As with other workplace changes, the complexity of assessment systems usually means that those with less communicative resources or influence within an enterprise are not involved in the development stages. Similarly, the selection of employees to act as workplace assessors generally reflect existing power relationships. Training programmes for assessors also tend to gloss over the specific ways that language, culture and gender can influence assessment processes and outcomes.

As a result, rather than offering employees an opportunity to have their skills formally recognised, such approaches can work to institutionalise bias and discrimination against individuals who do not fit the mythical standard. An evaluation of a skills assessment system for the Australian hospitality industry, for example, indicated that workers from non-English speaking backgrounds groups had not made use of the scheme, partly because of their lack of awareness of its existence, and partly because of the English literacy skills required to apply (Protrain, 1993).

Assessment criteria and methods

For employees who do make use of assessment systems, a common complaint relates to inappropriate methods which bear little relationship to the competencies being assessed.[2]

There is evidence that the criteria used by educators, workplace assessors, and other workplace personnel can vary considerably. Educators for example, often appear to assess for classroom-based, theoretical learning, while workplace personnel assess for performance and outcomes. Early experiences with vocational training in the Australian automotive industry for example showed how employees can be redefined as incompetent in the classroom even though their performance on the job is satisfactory (Sefton, 1993: 41).

This can lead to tensions among education providers and workplace personnel, with the validity of the assessment results being questioned. In the national Australian study of assessment just cited, for example, the authors observed that:

> A sort of guerilla warfare is taking place, with industry unconvinced about the educational providers expertise in workplace practices, processes and standards. For its part many education providers doubt the consistency and fairness of decisions made by workplace supervisors and assessors. (Toop, 1994: 19)

This lack of credibility can result in double assessments occurring for different purposes. At the completion of a course, for example, some workplaces will accept the trainer's assessment of achievement, while others will insist on assessing employees on the job to ensure that the skills learnt are able to be applied. The emphasis on the application of skills to work performance is partly driven by productivity, and partly by skill-based pay systems.

Inappropriate assessment tasks are frequently cited as a prime factor in learners' difficulties with vocational education and training programmes. This is supported by substantial research pointing to the significant effect that test methods and formats can produce on the performance of those being assessed.[3] All too frequently learners have been assessed by being asked to write about a particular procedure, for example, rather than actually demonstrating it in context. As a cost-effective way of assessing a large number of employees, many companies are using computer-generated quizzes on 'knowledge' or 'theory' aspects of the work, such as the causes of product defects. This frequently assesses reading and writing skills, familiarity with questioning techniques (such as *true or false; delete whichever is inapplicable*), and terminology (*performance criteria, evidence guide*) rather than the competencies required to complete the task.

In an assessment in a metals plant, for example, most of the employees attending a training course were unable to correctly answer the following questions:[4]

1. Before starting any electric power tool, what must be worn by the operator?
2. If you find a power tool to be broken after doing an inspection what should you do with it?
3. If a work area is wet or damp, why must we not use electric power tools in that area?

The educator observing the training session suggested changing the questions to:

1. What should you wear when you use electric power tools?
2. What do you do if a power tool is broken or faulty?
3. Why is it dangerous to use electric power tools in wet or damp areas?

These simple changes in the wording of quiz questions enabled trainees to successfully complete a test they had previously failed. The problematic aspects related to the use of linguistic features such as the passive, conditional and double negative rather than the trainees' competence in dealing with electrical tools. Multiple choice questions can be especially difficult, as the subtle differences in the options often require considerable cognitive and linguistic skills in order to understand the answers offered and then select the most appropriate one.

Verbal assessments are often less demanding for learners in terms of literacy skills. For example, a recent report on vocational training in the Australian food industry observed that learners who opted to be assessed verbally achieved higher results than those opting for written assessment. This was despite the fact that those undertaking a written assessment had a higher level of proficiency in spoken and written English. (NFITC 1993, p. 19).

However, even when an assessment is conducted verbally, and on-the-job, it can put unrealistic demands on employees' communicative ability and on their familiarity with oral exam techniques. The following incident, related by a metal industry union official, illustrates how even more informal assessment methods can be inadvertently discriminatory:

> In one workplace, a TAFE teacher was assessing a NESB worker on a particular aspect of pneumatics. He said to him: 'Say this isn't working. Can you tell me why, and can you go through the steps for fixing it?'

> The worker knew how to fix it but he didn't have the terminology to talk about it. He couldn't do it. Later on, the leading hand and his workmates talked to the teacher and, as a result, he was passed as competent. But if they hadn't spoken up for him, the worker would have been assessed as incompetent.

While standardised criteria offer a consistent framework for skills assessment, they can place unnecessary restrictions on the individuals being assessed if they are too specific. In many situations, for example, there is more than one effective way of achieving the same outcome, such as ways of identifying a customer's requirements or troubleshooting a problem. Similarly, culturally specific criteria, such as 'contribute as a team member' can easily discriminate against those who do not fit the assumed stereotype, while at the same time undervaluing complementary perspectives or competencies that reflect different views of the world.

Assessment criteria can also often overestimate the theoretical knowledge needed to perform particular work – especially if they have been developed by more senior employees or technical experts, with little trialling by the employees concerned to validate the requirements. Because conceptual, theoretical knowledge is able to be measured more easily through indirect methods, assessment criteria can easily become lists of knowledge questions, rather than tasks evaluating how and where this knowledge is applied.

Many of the difficulties with assessment relate to the misconception of the assessment process as a test, rather than a process of collecting evidence relating to an individual's skills. The test approach results in increased pressure and anxiety for those being assessed due to, for example, unfamiliar test formats, time restrictions to perform a task, or not being allowed to use a reference manual.

The following extract from a safety module for machine operators clearly illustrates how inappropriate assessment criteria and methods can appear to provide an objective and comprehensive measure of an individual's competence:

> Given a selection of 10 good and bad work practices, the trainee will be able to, without error or hesitation:
> - identify all the unsafe practices
> - correctly describe all appropriate safe practices
> - give an oral description of all the possible consequences of the continued use of the unsafe practices. (Mawer 1992(a): 16)

Such an assessment presents a number of unnecessary hurdles, such as the need to give detailed oral descriptions of 'all the possible consequences', and despite its apparent objectivity gives the assessor a great deal of discretion in determining whether the trainee has actually demonstrated competence. More importantly perhaps, it does little to assess the employees' application of safety practices in their daily, routine work situation.

In many workplaces, an assessment of English skills is undertaken to determine skill development needs, and to select trainees who may be ready to undertake vocational training programmes. Large-scale language audits have been undertaken across different Australian industries, such as automotive, tourism, building and construction.[5] While such assessments may be useful as a needs analysis tool, there are a number of educational and ethical concerns about their indiscriminate use in an industrial context. These include:

- the low validity of general language and literacy assessment instruments in predicting individuals' overall ability to perform work-related tasks – factors such as technical competence, experience, confidence, compensatory strategies are not taken into account in such assessments.
- the industrial implications of assessments – such as for example, the confidentiality of results, the possible exclusion of particular employees from training, the implications of assessments for promotion and job security.

- the tendency for the audit to assume a deficit model – in focusing on employees' individual problems rather than strengths, the onus is put onto the individual to take remedial action. Usually, only those at lower classification levels are audited. Weaknesses in systemic practices such as workplace management and communication styles and the form and content of training programmes are often left untouched.
- the costly nature of such assessments – given limited resources, large-scale audits can easily result in a professionally detailed description of the problems, with little follow up due to lack of training funds.[6]

In workplaces where job security is guaranteed and systematic training pathways developed, the assessment of language and literacy skills poses fewer ethical dilemmas for education and training providers.[7] Industry-wide assessments, for example, have been undertaken to gauge the extent of language and literacy needs, so that these factors are taken into account when developing vocational programmes.

EDUCATORS' CONTRIBUTIONS TO WORKPLACE ASSESSMENT PRACTICES

Depending on the particular local and industrial context, there are a number of ways that educators can contribute to the development of effective and fair assessment practices in the workplace. Some of these ways could be through direct involvement in the design of the assessment system. This could involve assisting in the development of assessment criteria and methods, preparing an information leaflet for employees or providing advice on language and cultural issues in relation to the assessment process. Other, more direct roles could include assisting with the skill development of workplace assessors or helping employees gain confidence with different methods as they prepare for their assessments.

Developing appropriate assessment criteria and methods

There is considerable evidence, both in research and practice, about some of the essential components of a quality, valid and reliable assessment system. We know, for example, that no single method is able to assess effectively the different elements of competence, or provide sufficient information for a valid assessment. We also know that the performance of the individual being assessed can be significantly affected by the assessment methods and formats used, and that assessors often vary significantly in rating human performance.[8]

Addressing these issues can be resource-intensive, and, as experience in the UK and Australia has shown, the tension is finding ways of balancing the demands of cost-effectiveness against quality and fairness requirements.[9] Rather than adding value, the development of assessment procedures and records can easily become excessively bureaucratic, costly and self-perpetuating. As Toop *et al.* point out, if an assessment system is to be effective in the workplace, it must primarily pass the 'feasibility' test:

> There are features or design options which might be seen as more educationally sound and others which may seem more questionable. If however an assessment system is to be used wholeheartedly by industries and enterprises, then its features must stand the test of sound workplace requirements and imperatives. Unless the assessment system can meet the workplace test, it will be ignored or corrupted. (1994: 24)

How can educators contribute to developing feasible assessment processes that are consistent with those essential for work performance, and appropriate for their intended users? One obvious way is by collaborating with other workplace personnel in developing assessment criteria and methods. This multidisciplinary, collaborative process may be initially resource-intensive, but it is likely to be more workable and cost effective in the long term. As in the development of industry standards, such a process greatly enhances the quality of the ultimate product because of the diverse perspectives that the different parties (e.g. technical personnel, trainers, educator(s), experienced operators) bring with them. The criteria developed are more likely to be relevant to work performance if they are validated by such a group. It helps to ensure, for example, that the assessment criteria are clearly expressed in user-friendly terms and that the assessment instruments designed are practical and within the language and literacy expectations of the target group. Similarly, critical or high-stake assessment contexts can be identified, and decisions or recommendations made about necessary safeguards such as the use of assessor panels. Finally, a collaborative process greatly enhances the credibility and useability of the assessment strategy in the workplace.

Experience both in the UK and in Australia indicates that a combination of methods will be needed to collect sufficient evidence of competence.[10] In a diverse workplace, this is crucial not only to ensure that the evidence gathered is comprehensive, but also to accommodate the different individual circumstances of those being assessed. A collaborative approach to developing assessment methods is valuable in identifying suitable cost-effective methods that 'add value', rather than create an intrusion to employees' everyday work.

If assessment is a process of collecting evidence about what learners can do, rather than an exam, it makes sense to integrate it with daily work activities. 'Naturally occurring evidence' from ongoing work performance can, for example, be used as the basis for assessment and supplemented by additional types of evidence already available, such as past achievements. Assessment tasks during the course of a training programme – formative assessment – are useful in helping learners become more familiar with assessment methods and gain confidence in self-assessment. A number of these tasks can be integrated as part of other learning activities. They include:

- group and peer assessment tasks
- self assessments
- small projects
- portfolios

Workplace personnel can, for example, be involved in providing feedback on learner progress as part of a structured skill development process. These include peer-tutors, supervisors of work placements, and team leaders. Such feedback can be included as part of the learners' portfolio.

Any 'evidence gaps' can then be filled by developing assessment tasks to establish elements of competence not covered e.g. verbal questions, simulations. These tasks will often relate to the less visible aspects of competence, such as a person's understanding of concepts or their ability to weigh up different factors to respond to particular situations.

Holistic assessment tasks that relate closely to the work context are often able to assess a number of competencies at the same time, including 'softer' competencies such as problem solving or teamwork. These tend to be more valid than itemised lists of disjointed assessment criteria, are able to be integrated as part of individuals' activities, and usually provide more meaningful outcomes. Learning contracts or project work, for example, provide an opportunity for employees to demonstrate competence in a number of areas at the same time as well as address an issue of concern in their work area.

Providing a choice of assessment methodologies can greatly enhance the validity of assessment decisions, as it allows learners to choose the method they feel most comfortable with to demonstrate their competence. Some learners may prefer to be assessed orally, or by more direct methods such as observation or work samples. As long as the different assessment methods are equated for difficulty, this also allows for local needs and conditions to be accommodated.

The assessment approach in training programs in the Australian automotive industry for example,[11] was collaboratively developed to ensure it was holistic, contextualised and performance-based. It included conferencing, investigative reports, class presentations, oral assessment using genuine components and documents, practical problem solving, demonstrations, group work, interpretation of documents and preparation of flow charts, models and tables.

Assessment processes were negotiated with the various stake holders. Written assessment was kept to a minimum, as it was generally considered the least appropriate form of assessment. Project officers were particularly concerned to avoid rote learnt responses, the use of yes/no responses, double negatives and multiple choice questions which place significant and unnecessary demands on trainees' linguistic ability rather than workplace competence.

Assisting employees to use assessment systems

For employees, adequate preparation for assessment is crucial. Apart from understanding the purpose of the assessment, they also need to be familiar with both the criteria and methods by which their competence will be assessed. They also need opportunities to practice with the particular assessment methods and terminology.

Educators can often play a crucial role in familiarising employees with different assessment methods through language courses. Such courses usually encourage learners to reflect on their strengths, learning needs and monitor their progress against a set of criteria. Through such a process of self-assessment, and exposure to different types of assessment tasks, learners become able to reflect on their own performance, and gain confidence in dealing with more formal assessment contexts. In some workplaces, for example, educators have assisted employees in preparing their portfolios for competency assessment, or their case for appeal following an unsatisfactory assessment decision.

A number of language courses are specifically designed to enable learners to deal with the language requirements of vocational assessment contexts. In some situations such as licensing test requirements for the operation of industrial equipment (e.g. forklifts), or large-scale examinations, written tests are mandatory. In such preparatory courses, learners become familiar with different questioning techniques e.g. multiple choice questions, short answers, true/false questions and they gain confidence with these particular assessment methods.

Supporting assessors

Given that assessment is basically a process of collecting evidence, and making a judgement, workplace assessors play a crucial role in determining the quality of the process and its outcomes. Like workplace trainers, assessors are gaining increasing recognition for the key role they play in implementing change at the workplace level.[12]

Apart from being highly skilled in the aspects of competence they wish to assess, workplace assessors are required to have completed some assessor training programme, and be endorsed by the relevant industrial parties. Assessors are usually selected by management, typically from lower middle management ranks. Even in workplaces where some assessors may be elected by their peers, the overwhelming complexity of most assessor training manuals usually favour the most confident and higher educated employees, rather than those who may be more representative of the employees' culture, language and gender mix. Bilingual assessors, for example, would be in an ideal position to deal with the possible confounding of linguistic and vocational competence, but are rarely encouraged to nominate as workplace assessors.

Assessors are expected to be familiar with the principles underlying valid and fair assessments. They also need to be able to adapt these assessment principles to a range of situations and learners to enhance the quality of the outcomes. Yet most assessor training programmes do not address issues of bias (cultural and linguistic), except at the general, 'should also consider' level. Such superficial treatment of these issues usually means that assessors are not well equipped to cope with any employees or situations that are outside narrow 'textbook' parameters.

As with programmes for workplace trainers, assessor training programmes are usually 'once off' efforts. Yet, research and experience show the need for on-going moderation and review processes to ensure reliability and consistency of assessment tasks, and of assessment decisions by different assessors.

Supporting the training of workplace assessors can take place at a number of levels, both formal and informal. At an informal level, for example, educators can do a great deal to encourage the involvement of competent bilingual employees in assessor training, and if necessary provide them with language and literacy support. Educators can also play a valuable role once assessment systems are set up, in helping to review assessment practices and moderation procedures. It is often after the initial implementation stage that difficulties with validity, reliability or indirect discrimination become apparent.

At a more formal level, language and cultural issues need to be taken into account in assessor training programmes if they are to develop the necessary skills to carry out valid assessments. This needs to be both at the awareness-raising level, in terms of sensitising assessors to some of the issues faced by many employees, as well as providing practical strategies to enhance the quality and validity of assessment outcomes.

The following two examples outline some of the ways in which such skill-development could take place.

1. AWARENESS-RAISING EXERCISE

This example outlines a training activity which aimed to raise the awareness of workplace management and training personnel who were responsible for setting up assessment systems. The purpose of the activity was to highlight the ways in which occupational competence, language/literacy competence and facility with examination methodologies could become confused in typical assessment tasks.

Participants were told they would be trained in operating a piece of equipment and then assessed on their competence in doing so. To help them gain some insights into the difficulties encountered by some of their employees, this training was conducted in a foreign language, but one which had many similarities to English–French.

The training followed a fairly routine sequence: first the task was demonstrated, with the presenter identifying the different parts, their functions and paying special attention to safety aspects.

Participants were given a handout with the names of the different parts of the machine, a set of written operating instructions (*mode d'emploi*) and hints on how to keep the equipment in good condition (*conseils d'entretien*). The trainer read through these, stressing and elaborating on some of the more important points. They were then given an opportunity to practise the operation of the machine, individually and in small groups, until they were able to correctly operate it. She checked with the trainees if they could operate the machine, by asking if there were any questions. The response was general, friendly silence.

Participants were then asked to undertake a multiple choice test on different aspects of the task such as identifying the correct sequence of steps to operate the machine and necessary safety precautions. Not surprisingly, while participants were able, with some assistance, to carry out the task, they were unable to satisfactorily complete the test. Despite making 'intelligent guesses' at the point of the questions and the likely response, many of their answers were incorrect because of their inability to decode the foreign language – for example, *il faut* as meaning one must, or the use of the infinitive in a sequence of instructions. The subtle difference in meaning between different options in the multiple-choice questions also caused difficulties – such as the use of *et* (and) and *ou* (or) as conjunctive links in different options.

The debrief of the exercise examined the extent to which the assessment criteria and task were valid, fair and reliable. Much of the discussion focused on the similarity between the participants' reactions to the training and assessment exercise, and that of their employees in the workplace. Many commented on its effectiveness in helping them to appreciate some of the issues faced by employees with limited literacy or language skills. One participant, for example, said he was able to understand some employees' apparently contradictory behaviour, where they were able to perform a task in context and seemingly follow written instructions, but unable to pass a computer-generated quiz.

Despite their cost-effectiveness, and apparent objectivity, it was evident that such indirect testing of competence was not a valid or reliable method. This exercise was followed up by the group developing specific strategies to assist them in designing appropriate assessment criteria and methods.

2. INTEGRATED TRAINING FOR WORKPLACE ASSESSORS

In a food processing plant, the development of the assessor training course was jointly undertaken by workplace training personnel, an education and training consultant and a language and literacy educator. The course encouraged participants to view assessment as a process of collecting evidence regarding someone's competence rather than a once off exam. It encouraged them to develop assessment tasks that closely reflected the work requirements, the principles of validity, reliability and minimised bias due to factors such as language, literacy or personality.

In developing these tasks, participants explored ways of ensuring they were workable and cost effective strategies which caused minimum disruption to day-to-day activities.

Through the use of case study examples, participants discussed ways of minimising bias and preparing candidates so they had a fair opportunity to demonstrate their competence and have their skills recognised.

The following extract from the training programme shows how issues of language and literacy were integrated into the course.

Common pitfalls in competency assessment

Often, the quality of assessment tends to fall down in one of three areas:

- the wording of competency statements or assessment questions
- the preparation for the assessment
- handling feedback (especially if candidate is not up to standard)

Common Pitfalls in Wording

In preparing for the assessment, you will need to check the competency statements and assessment methods to make sure they meet with the quality principles discussed earlier. In particular, check for these common pitfalls:
[Note: Each of these examples has actually been used in industry.]

Pitfall 1: Overly high expectations

The competency statements developed need to relate closely to the requirements of the different skill levels in the skills-matrix. e.g. the knowledge needed to competently perform the task.

The performance criteria also need to reflect realistic work practices, rather than an ideal situation. They should not, for example, be too demanding in terms of time limits or levels of accuracy.

In what ways are the following examples unrealistic?

Given a selection of ten good and bad work practices, the trainee will be able to, without error or hesitation:

- identify all the unsafe practices
- correctly describe all appropriate safe practices
- give an oral description of all the possible consequences of the continued use of the unsafe practices.

Pitfall 2: Vague performance criteria, focused on inputs instead of outcomes.

Check that the competency statements describe the work in enough detail to capture those aspects of competence below the surface, e.g. the knowledge of where the process fits into the bigger picture, occupational health and safety requirements, teamwork.

In specifying the standard of work required, it should be clear what standard people need to aim for to demonstrate competence

Compare: • Check transmitter
with: • Check transmitter for leaks or damage
Compare: • Knowledge of various alarm categories
with: • Identify alarm categories and appropriate
              response required

Pitfall 3: Complex/unclear language

Thinking about assessment as a process of collecting evidence does not mean we need to use 'legalese' language to describe competence! Australia has one of the most culturally diverse workforces in the world, so it is essential that the terms used are understandable to all concerned. To many employees, the concepts behind competency-based training and assessment are difficult enough, without adding obscure language. Here are some real work examples of how unclear language has complicated the process of assessing competence.

Confusing order of phrases, use of passives
Compare: If you find a power tool to be broken after doing
            an inspection what should you do with it?
with: What do you do if a power tool is broken or
            faulty?
Compare: If the solution is not at room temperature, what
            measures could be taken to compensate for this?
with: What do you do if the solution is not at room
            temperature?

Use of Negatives
Compare: If the work area is wet or damp, why must we
            not use electric power tools in that area?
with: Why is it dangerous to use electric power tools in
            wet or damp areas?

Making simple procedures sound complicated
1. Check four components per bag for visual defects at the packing station and take appropriate action to report deviation from acceptable quality to a responsible person
2. Sort torn, split, dirty and/or unacceptable packaging materials to correct production standards.

Pitfall 4: Trick questions/questions unrelated to workplace competence

Calculate the total weight of an 80 kg. man in the scoop of a forklift. (Answer: none because you are not allowed to carry any people in the scoop.)

NOTES

1. See, for example, VEETAC Working Party on the Implementation of Competency Based Training (1992). NCVQ (1988) Access and Equal Opportunities in Relation to National Vocational Qualifications, London.
2. See Mawer and Field, 1995: 72–80.
3. See, for example, Bachman, 1990, McNamara, 1990, Brindley, 1989: 94.
4. Mawer, 1992(a): 24.
5. See, for example, Mawer, 1991 (building and construction; metals; steel); Serle and Gates, 1993 (tourism and hospitality), Sefton and O'Hara, 1992 (vehicle manufacturing).
6. See, for example, Mawer, 1991, Hull, 1993 for more detailed discussion of some of these concerns.
7. In Australia, Victoria AMES (1992) and the NSW Workplace Language, Literacy and Numeracy Skills Taskforce (1994) have developed ethical guidelines in relation to this type of assessment.
8. See, for example, Burke, 1989, NCVQ, 1993, NTB, 1993, Hagar, Athanasou and Gonczi, 1994, Brindley, 1994, Bachman, 1990, McNamara, 1989, Mawer, 1991, Thomson, 1993.
9. See, for example, Bloch, B. 1994. Costing UK Testing, Australian Training Review 1994, no 9. Adelaide: National Centre for Vocational Education and Training.
10. See, for example, L Mitchell, in Burke 1989.
11. Sefton et al., 1994: 307.
12. In Australia, for example, national standards for assessors were developed in 1993, and reviewed in 1995 to give more prominence to system design and monitoring functions, and address concerns in relation to bias and discrimination.

TWELVE

Working with teams

Team-based approaches to work design have been widely adopted as a way of improving efficiency, quality and providing increased flexibility in workplaces. Recent surveys of companies in the USA, for example, show that over 50 per cent of companies have adopted self-managing teams, while British companies regard team-based work as central to bringing about changes in organisations.[1] In many quality management methodologies such as *Just In Time*, *8D* or *Grosby*[2] the concept of regular team meetings is integral to the effectiveness of the process. The purpose of these meetings is for members to identify problems, cooperatively arrive at solutions and aim for continuous improvement.

However, while teams may be more popular in workplaces, the transformation of discrete tasks performed by strictly supervised individuals to more fluid, dynamic, self-managing teams remains often more an aim than a reality. The 'vision' and expectations of teams vary from workplace to workplace, and from team to team, depending on the goals of the organisation, the particular culture of the team and the workplace and the commitment of those in positions of influence.

At one end of the continuum, teamwork may have been 'decreed' by senior management, mainly as a cost-saving measure. Rather than being individually assigned to one task, employees are expected to multiskill, rotate across a number of tasks, and have a broader understanding and responsibility for the quality of the service or product. The less prestigious tasks such as housekeeping are often the first ones to be shared among team members, rather than more specialised responsibilities such as quality control or stock control. While labels of supervisors may have changed to team leader or coordinator, the ultimate responsibility and decision making remains with them. Further up the organisational hierarchy, traditional management styles remain unchanged.

At the other end of the continuum are teams where supervisors have been removed, with the new position of leader or coach shared periodically among the team members. The team is an independent business unit within the larger organisation, and makes a wide range of decisions about what and how work is done. Management structures within the organisation have been flattened, with responsibilities devolved to teams. Bonuses and profit-sharing schemes are often used as incentives to reward such teams.

The effectiveness of teamwork is often a reflection of the preparation and training undertaken, power relationships, reward systems, personalities and time. Even in more progressive workplaces, there is usually some scepticism or resentment from those who stand to lose out as a result of the changes. This group may include employees with previously high-status specialist functions, or simply those who had managed to carve out a comfortable, predictable niche of work territory. Such resentments are often expressed through a reluctance to share specialist knowledge or skills, and a tendency to point out quickly that the new system is to blame for the inevitable mistakes that occur.

As the following comment from a foundry superintendent in the vehicle industry indicates, a long-term perspective and senior management support are crucial if team-based approaches are to be more than tokenistic:

> What we're sort of saying to the supervisors is: let the guys make the decision, and the supervisor sort of looks at you and says, but he won't get it right – [and you need to say] – So what? He needs to learn. So there's a bit of culture change . . . the supervisors again are a little frightened. Luckily at the moment we have some new supervisors, they're coping with it a lot better. . . some of the older ones are finding it more difficult. (Sefton et al., 1994: 126)

FROM COP TO TEAM COACH – THE CHANGING ROLE OF SUPERVISORS

While the traditional type of leadership – or 'knucklemen' supervision – was characterised by the ability to control and issue directions from a distance, effective team leadership depends more on the leader's capacity to create a team spirit and motivate individuals to achieve common goals and cope with changes 'on the spot'.

As the above quote from the vehicle industry illustrates, for many supervisors, the transition from 'cop' to motivational 'coach' is a difficult process that requires them to give up roles they have become accustomed to and acquire new ones they may feel uncomfortable about.

Some of these traditional activities include giving out detailed instructions, controlling the different stages of the process, and monitoring employees' performance. The new role, on the other hand, puts much more emphasis on information sharing, facilitating, delegating and helping others develop new skills. To be effective in this new role, team leaders need to understand different members' strengths and training needs and adopt different communication styles that are much more consultative. Developing a supportive environment where people can work cooperatively to achieve jointly set goals involves enabling, facilitation skills that were not previously required.

Developing common goals and a team spirit inevitably involves negotiating different perspectives and priorities, and the effectiveness of teams will depend on how constructively such difference is handled. New suggestions 'from the floor', for example, can easily be perceived as – and may in fact be – challenges to power or particular expertise. As Field and Ford point out, the challenging characteristic of teamwork in the new environment is not so much how to avoid conflict, but how people can learn to 'rock the boat and work collaboratively at the same time' (1995: 68).

At a time when supervisory- and middle-management positions are disappearing, many team leaders feel justifiably threatened by the directions towards flatter collaborative structures, as they often represent an erosion of hard-won power and privileges. Before they can take on the new leadership roles – or wider functions such as working more closely with customers and suppliers – it is often necessary for them to re-examine their own expectations of work, as illustrated by the following reflections from a section supervisor:

> At first I was really a bit suspicious about all these changes. I thought they're trying to get me to help them tell them all I know, then get rid of my job! Then the more I think about it, I can see some new possibilities opening up that might be more interesting in sales and marketing, training people, things like that, and I figure well I might gain a lot by the changes too. And if the worst comes to the worst, I'll go out with a lot more skills than I had last year.

FROM NUMBERS TO TEAM MEMBERS

Traditionally, many employees have become accustomed to adopting a passive, accepting stance to their work, and have been discouraged from exercising any initiative. In larger workplaces, for example, it was not uncommon for employees to work in isolation from their work-mates, and be referred to by their number rather than their name. Amalio's reaction to the introduction of team-based approaches is typical of many. An experienced operator, he exclaimed in a rather exasperated way: 'What I need to talk for? I'm here to work!'.

The move towards teamwork almost by definition puts a high premium on the need of employees such as Amalio to have effective communication and negotiation skills. It exposes such employees to the need to renegotiate basic roles and responsibilities. These skills often include complex communicative requirements because of increased documentation, the need to interact with more workmates, customers or different types of technology. As the following comment by an employee in a food processing plant indicates, many have difficulty in developing such skills:

> Maybe some people too scared to say they don't know, a little bit worried. They know they can do this job but don't want to move to another job to make themselves look stupid.

> Before there was no need for computers, now I have to put log in, keep account, stock take, receive everything, fix up problems, do QC [Quality Control]. Of course I was very worried at first. Then I try couple of times, I make mistake, but then, is not too bad after a time. If I do it all the time I never forget, but this rotating business is hard because you forget when you go back.

Job rotation and multiskilling may offer variety and interest to the work being undertaken, but the allocation of these different tasks can often become a source of conflict and resentment. So can different stand-ards and approaches to the performance of these tasks. Because of the discursive nature of teamwork, those who are more confident negoti-ators, or who can 'talk the walk' – rather than just doing the work – tend to be at an advantage. The following observations by Jo, a Lebanese forklift driver in his late forties, are typical of the confusion and ambi-valence many employees experience towards teamwork:

> I think a lot of this teamwork is wrong, you should have one boss responsible to say, you do this, or not. We have teams, yes but some people only work in teams when everything is all right. When work gets hard, they leave me to do cleaning and they say I'm off to do training or some meeting. I thought teamwork means you help each other, but it doesn't always work like that with everybody, you know.

Such employees also often resent the loss of familiarity and predictability. Particularly where leadership is rotated among the team, they also resent the sense that collectively, 'no one is responsible for anything', but each of them is sure to be blamed if things go wrong.

LEARNING TO WORK AS A TEAM

Team-based approaches to work are usually introduced to workplaces as part of an integrated quality management strategy. Such training programmes are often conducted by external consultants who may be specialists in the particular quality strategy and its particular notions of teamwork, but are almost invariably unfamiliar with the specific characteristics of the workforce, or their previous experiences of negotiation and collaboration. Consequently, significant problems can occur because of mismatches between the assumptions of trainers and employees' experiences and expectations.

Team skills programmes often target a 'vertical slice' of the organisation, as a way of beginning to break down traditional hierarchical relationships, or work sections as a way of building an *esprit de corps*. Yet invariably, team members are at different stages of competence in their technical, communicative and collaborative skills. For many employees, team-skills training may be their first experience of formal learning in their working life. The wide diversity of competence in language and literacy, for example, can greatly frustrate team-building efforts, as the following comment from a trainer in a manufacturing plant indicates:

> It may be halfway through the first session that you realise that you've got two people out of a group of ten that can't write their names down. The choices are invidious: exclude the two people and have them miss out on the team-building value of the training until they build up their language and literacy skills; drop the course standards, and get them through any which way; or spend a lot of your own time going through the course with them again and again.

Quite apart from the significant language and literacy skill requirements of such courses, mismatches can also occur in terms of concepts and methods used. In their study of training for teams in a US computer component manufacturer, Gee, Hull, and Lankshear (1996: 99), for example, point out the 'transmissive' nature of a curriculum which ironically aimed to encourage workers to think for themselves and show initiative. Not surprisingly, parrot learning of teamwork principles or problem-solving techniques often fail to transform compliant workers into enthusiastic team players.

More participatory team skill courses often aim to achieve 'paradigm shifts' in employees' attitudes and behaviours by engaging them in experiential simulation games and adventure learning activities. More often than not, these can leave participants perplexed as to how these activities relate to their day-to-day tasks, if not resentful for being made to look foolish.

Rather than addressing issues of diversity arising from team members' different life experiences, socioeconomic and cultural backgrounds, team skill courses tend to present a particular model of what is an effective team leader and member. Particular techniques for solving problems or dealing with conflict, for example, are presented which stress being 'up front' and explicit about concerns, without taking into account the different values and resources that individuals bring to the situation.

Such culturally biased models can effectively alienate those who do not fit the mould, while at the same time neglecting to develop the team's skills in fully recognising and utilising the resources of its members. Given the diversity of the workplace and marketplace, team leaders and members alike need to develop competence in effectively dealing with a wide range of values, attitudes and behaviour.

Learning to work as a team is a gradual process, yet much of the training offered to teams consists of a short course, with no follow up in supporting teams to apply the principles, skills and techniques developed. Ongoing support is necessary for all those involved in teamwork as they adjust to their changing roles. Team leaders and employees in specialist positions particularly can find the transition to more participative and 'chaotic' practices threatening. The inability of teams to systematically reflect and learn from their early teamwork experiences can derail participative work practices and create cynicism among employees. In times of pressure, it is often easier simply to revert to traditional ways of doing work and resolving differences. Miscommunication, mutual stereotyping and blaming are often lasting legacies of such aborted attempts.

In one particular workplace, employees were enthusiastic about the prospect of a team, and actively took on the team principles in the training course: they pointed out areas where savings could be made, were much more vocal in reporting defects in manufacturing and started to implement minor changes. However, middle management reacted defensively to the suggestions made, and seemed to perceive them as criticisms of past practices. As a result, they actively resisted sharing information or resources such as computers with the rest of the team. Six months after teams had been established, conflict was rife, and a categorical decision was taken to revert to the old hierarchical supervisory structure. Employees felt angry and frustrated by this move:

> Management need to learn too, not only us. Trust is very important, if they want work to change. It is no good us learning to do new things if then we can't put them into practice, for example [we learn] computer skills but there is only one broken computer in the section or trying to learn about teamwork and we find our self-managed team has gone back to the old way of working under a supervisor. What's the point of us thinking of better ways of doing things if managers get upset because they didn't think of it first? Why should we bother. Better I save my brain for home!

TEAM MEETINGS AS A CRITICAL COMMUNICATIVE SITE

The regular team meetings are a focal site of communication for teams, as they provide the opportunity to share information, discuss issues, generate solutions to problems, identify and address skill development needs and determine roles and responsibilities.

The complex discourse demands of such meetings favour those with more communicative resources at their disposal, or those already in positions of power through access to information. Apart from the communicative competencies required to effectively lead and participate in such meetings, there are a number of other equally important factors which influence the extent to which individuals are able, or willing, to participate.

First, one needs to be familiar with the general conventions of meeting procedures such as the role of the chair, or ways of proposing changes as well as the specific conventions relating to the particular methodology adopted in the workplace and its characteristic tools e.g. brainstorming, fishbone analysis (cause and effect analysis), *pareto* charts.

Secondly, there are the conceptual, analytical, language, literacy and numeracy skills required to interpret statistical information in the form of graphs, flow charts, scatter diagrams and control charts. Then there are the skills involved in extracting meaning from the composite genre of technical jargon, satire and idiomatic expressions that typifies the discourse of such meetings. Apart from the accessibility of the spoken and written language of the meeting, there are the assertiveness and communicative skills required to interrupt such discourse to ask a question or offer an opinion. Ways of expressing disagreement, for example, can range from very indirect and tentative ('I was wondering if there might be a point in . . .') to violent outbursts ('over my dead body!') depending on the issues at stake and past experiences of (un)successful negotiations at work.

The particular way the meetings are conducted can also greatly enhance or reduce participants' ability to contribute. The chairperson, for example, plays a vital role in setting the tone for the meeting by encouraging participation, regulating turntaking, and ensuring that topic changes are clearly signalled and issues identified. The use of compensatory mechanisms such as multilingual expertise, illustrations or visual aids can also greatly influence individuals' ability to follow and take part.

Finally, there are the sociocultural aspects of the particular workplace, perceived power relationships and individuals' cultural values such as modesty, the need to preserve harmony and show respect to people in positions of authority that significantly affect the degree to which individuals participate.

TOWARDS MORE EFFECTIVE TEAMWORK

Most workplace language and literacy courses address 'teamwork competencies' as an implicit or explicit part of the curriculum. They address effective listening strategies and general communicative competencies such as presenting information, expressing a point of view or making a suggestion. Because of the interactive nature of such courses, participants often develop teamwork strategies while working together as a group on a particular learning contract or discussing workplace issues.

Frequently, comments on the outcomes of such courses relate to the increase in confidence by course participants, and their resulting ability to contribute actively to team discussions, make suggestions and express opinions.

The degree to which developing teamwork skills can be explicitly addressed depends on the particular understandings of teamwork prevalent within the workplace and the skill development opportunities available to teams. In some workplaces where teamwork was being systematically introduced, for example, the language and literacy teacher has worked closely with the team skills trainer to modify, adapt or co-present the programme.

When a 'team briefing' process was introduced at Aus Tin, for example, an external consultant conducted a course for line and senior management on the aims and methodology of the process. The teacher participated in the course, and provided feedback for the presenter on ways of increasing the effectiveness of the process. She also covered aspects of the course in the communication skills course so that production employees were better informed and able to participate in the team briefings and ensuing discussions.

In other workplaces, bridging programmes are developed to prepare employees for 'vertical slicing' team modules, or to specifically address some of the language, literacy, numeracy and crosscultural competencies required for operating as part of a team. Examples of these include meeting procedures, interpreting charts and graphs, presenting information to groups and crosscultural aspects of dealing with problems and expressing disagreement.

The following case study example describes part of a jointly developed training programme for team leaders to support them in the transition to more participative work practices. In the second case study example, Bee Jong Ong discusses a training session for teams held in collaboration with another language and literacy teacher for a workplace where self-managing teams were being introduced.

CASE STUDY 1. TRAINING FOR TEAM LEADERS

Suncrisp, a medium-sized food processing plant, introduced the concept of teams and appointed team leaders (mainly ex-supervisors) to lead different section teams. A number of communication skills courses were started in the company to develop employees' skills in dealing with the new work requirements, and these included participation in the fortnightly section team meetings held to discuss production and quality issues.

All teams had received some initial team skills training from an external consultant, but it was decided to follow this up with a short course for the new team leaders for six three-hour sessions on a fortnightly basis. The aim of this course was to support the team leaders in the transition to the new roles, and provide them with an opportunity to 'troubleshoot', learn from each other's experiences, as well as develop strategies for dealing with the linguistic and cultural diversity of their team members. The course was jointly developed and presented by the training manager and the educator. Case studies used in the training sessions, for example, reflected the cultural diversity of the workplace and the role that language and cultural factors influence perception and communication styles e.g. accepted ways of raising difficulties, resolving conflict.

The first two sessions focused on the leaders' perceptions of teamwork and their changing roles. Their experience and preference for different leadership styles were discussed, including perceptions due to different cultural values held by the various participants. Expectations of older workers, and workers from particular Asian countries, for example, were discussed. So were the implications of adopting new roles such as delegating responsibility.

Participants discussed how to break down 'us and them' perceptions, concrete ways of communicating some of the changed expectations, and encouraging employees to take on new roles and responsibilities. One of the team leaders, for example, suggested issuing each team member with a set of measurement tools so they could monitor the quality of the product, without needing to refer 'higher up'. Another was encouraging the team members to work out their own rotation roster and break times. Another was showing some of the team members how to use the computer for production planning.

Structure of session three

The aim of the third session focused on developing team leaders' skills in running the regular fortnightly team meetings and increasing members' input and participation. It was jointly conducted by the educator and the training manager.

The session dealt with:

- the purpose and structure of team meetings
- some common barriers to participation
- communication competencies required by team members to participate actively in team meetings
- analysing part of a meeting to draw out the factors that enhanced participation
- developing specific strategies for increasing participation

Purpose and structure of team meetings

The first part of the training session began with a general discussion about how the regular fortnightly meetings had been going, with the session presenter drawing up a list of positives and negatives (e.g.

good suggestions made, hard to get people talking in the group about issues you know are problems, hard to keep people focused on subject discussed).

The presenter then led a discussion on the purpose of the meetings, and the leaders' expectations of what would be achieved by getting the team members together.

Another list was drawn up which included factors such as:

• share information about production, quality
• come up with suggestions for improvements
• give people a chance to talk about the new system of working
• find out and solve problems before they get too big
• develop a team spirit
• share information about what's happening in the company

The presenter then asked the group to think about the extent to which these expectations were shared by all members. Had they been clearly communicated to members? If so, how? Were they reflected in the way the meetings were run? During the rest of the session, the group referred back to the list to illustrate points being made, and especially during the last segment when specific strategies were being drawn up.

Common barriers to participation in meetings

This part of the session was spent discussing some of the factors that prevent people from participating in different kinds of meetings. Participants were asked to suggest reasons for being passive or active in meetings they themselves has attended at work, or in other situations e.g. sporting committees, community activities. These were listed on the board:

Factors that discouraged me from participating:

• lack of involvement, interest in subject
• didn't know enough about the subject
• didn't understand all that was being discussed
• cynicism – felt decision had already been made
• didn't want meeting to go over time
• didn't want to be asked to do more work as a result of making a suggestion
• felt shy/didn't want to show off

Factors that encouraged me to participate:

- felt strongly about the issue
- meeting was well run, effective chairperson
- people didn't attack/ridicule each other
- feeling that opinions were welcomed
- being asked for opinion
- being given the facts so had a chance to prepare

Participants were asked to think about whether any of these factors could be relevant to their own teams, particularly with team members who were not confident in English, or not used to formal meetings.

They were shown typical comments made by employees (from different workplaces) who identified a range of factors affecting their participation in meetings. The group discussed the extent to which these factors reflected the employees' individual personality or background, or the workplace or social culture they were part of.

Some experiences of meetings across cultures

We don't understand the jokes. We feel often outside the group, not sure if we should laugh or not. Australians joke a lot in meetings and use upside down humour – saying the opposite of what they mean –, you know, like 'That was really smart Bob' when they mean he did something stupid.

Meetings are a waste of time. We make suggestions but nothing is ever done about them.

I always agree, it's easier that way, but I don't understand everything . . . if they ask me why I agree, I can't answer – I just try to hide under the table.

Sometimes, I want to ask them to explain something again, but I think I'm the only one with this problem. People don't want to waste time – so is easier to say nothing.

I just get my words ready to say something and they're talking about a different subject!

> It is very important to prepare what we have to say and be sure of our facts. We never contradict someone older or a manager in a public situation. That would be dishonouring to them.
>
> I didn't understand all this business about motions and amendments, and I didn't know what we were voting for in the end.
>
> If the boss invited me by name, I would give my opinion. I would say: 'Dear manager: I think that I have an idea that can improve our company. Please permit me to express my opinion'.
>
> When I started working here, I was told: you just keep the line going, we'll tell you if there's any problems. I got used to all that stuff not being my business.

To illustrate some of the difficulties experienced by 'outsiders' to the particular workplace culture or Australian English, the presenter had noted down some of the expressions used by group participants during the earlier part of the session. These included idioms such as 'Blind Freddie could see it! Pull the other one!' specific cultural references e.g. 'I found my name on a Brownies' bottle yard roster', and workplace references e.g. 'Like the day we started on 681'. She also pointed out some of the sudden topic changes, humorous asides and references to other people and events that had occurred during earlier segments. The group discussed how these were useful in relieving tension and developing a team spirit, but could have a counter-productive effect if all members in the group did not share the same facility in language, cultural background or work 'histories'.

The presenter related to the group some general comments from participants in the communication skills courses about the concentration needed to keep up with the pace of discussion, and how they often tuned out after a short time if it was too fast and 'fluid'. They had also commented that the free-for-all informality of the meetings made it harder for them to 'fight for a go'.

She also briefly outlined for them some of the 'competencies' that had been identified as necessary for individuals to effectively participate in meetings:[3]

1. The ability to pick out information from rapid and often colloquial speech, full of idiom, humour and jargon.
2. The communication skills and the confidence to interrupt, to ask a question, offer an opinion, agree, disagree, etc.

3. The ability to read written agendas, minutes, etc.
4. The conceptual, analytical, literacy and numeracy skills to interpret flow charts, scatter diagrams, graphs, etc.
5. Knowledge of meeting conventions, roles, meeting procedures and characteristic tools e.g. brainstorm, fishbone analysis.
6. Awareness of socio-cultural factors which are reflected in meetings. Knowledge of what is appropriate and what is not.

Analysis of an effective meeting

The group was then shown a short, authentic video[4] excerpt of a team meeting by a section manager of another manufacturing company who had been the leader of his team for about two years. There was strong commitment in the company for teamwork, with the plant manager usually attending section meetings. Two hours were set aside for regular fortnightly meetings and decisions made were endorsed by management.

The purpose of the meeting was primarily to discuss issues relating to quality, cost and schedule (what was produced, how much it cost, and whether it was delivered on time).

The meeting was held in a quiet room with a medium-size round table. It was attended by the plant manager, section manager, sales manager, engineer, five operators and two tradesmen. Five team members were non-native speakers of English. The section manager acted as chair. Minutes from the previous meeting provided the agenda for the current one and the group worked through these items. Minutes were written in note form, with basic facts and figures given, action arising and the person responsible for follow-up specified.

Participants were asked to note some of the strategies used by the team leader that encouraged participation. Viewing the video was followed by a group discussion of strategies used, and the participants' comments were written up on the board. The presenter had transcribed particular parts of the video, so the group was able to examine in detail some of the more effective strategies used.

Summary of observations

- The predictable structure seemed to assist participation as people knew what was going on.
- The chair person adapted his language – relatively slow pace, lots of short pauses. Good body language: he maintained constant eye

contact, waited for nods around table before continuing. If not receiving positive feedback, rephrased sentence, e.g. *deteriorates, gets worse.*

> 'We've made the radius a bit smaller, so it doesn't have that big radius it had before, and we want to know what you think about that. Alf seemed to think it was better, I don't know, how do you feel it's going? Has it improved things or not? Do you notice any difference? Is it better or just the same?'

- He clearly introduced topics and oriented people to what was going to be discussed e.g. 'Who's been shown how to work x?' Only two responded so he changed to: 'Who knows how to use x?' and went round the table: 'Minh, have you been trained to use the x?'
- He brought samples of faulty products so could demonstrate as well as discuss faults. He used simple diagrams when necessary to illustrate a point or used gestures to good effect e.g. 'Instead of being round, it's like this' (and draws an oval with his hands).
- He uses examples and illustrations to explain points:

> These things should be picked up early on the line, not once it's been through five or six areas. If you wait for Afif to pick it up at the final inspection, when it's cold, it cost us $3.50. But if Bob's picking it up before the heat treat, or Hassan before it's binned, and throws it out, we've only lost 80c or $1.00 So we need to be looking out for quality all the time, not adding value to rubbish, then throwing it out at the end.

- He invited people to join in by acknowledging their expertise 'You work on the A line, Hassan, what do you think?' When the operator seemed to find it difficult to express himself, the team leader said 'I'll let you think about it for a minute', moved on to someone else, meanwhile Hassan consulted with a fellow worker from the same language group and was able to report back his comments a few minutes later, with his work mate adding one or two comments when Hassan seemed stuck. There was respect and tolerance for members struggling to express themselves in English
- The general tone of the meeting was problem and task centred rather than dominated by personalities. There was no blame attributed: 'We've all got to look out for, ... it 's important that we tell each other ..., we need to work out where this goes wrong so it can get fixed straightaway rather than waiting till it gets cold'.
- At the end of the meeting the chair person asked if there were any comments, or questions. He went around naming people and gave them an opportunity to raise any issues. This was a regular part of the meeting and two members seemed to have prepared for this particular timeslot to have their say.

As a concluding activity, the group participants returned to the lists drawn up at the beginning of the session, and worked in small groups to develop specific strategies for assisting their team members to participate more actively in the meetings. The group suggestions were collated and discussed at the end of the session, and particular points noted for discussion at future sessions e.g. different ways of writing up minutes.

HINTS FOR ENCOURAGING PARTICIPATION IN TEAM MEETINGS

- Ask for suggestions for agenda before meeting and give each member a copy before the meeting so people can be prepared.
- Meet somewhere quiet, around a table or semi-circle.
- Make sure the purpose and rules for meeting are understood and agreed to by everyone, e.g. share information, discuss and decide by consensus.
- Explain specific meeting rules or tools used e.g. fishbone analysis, consensus.
- Group leaders and managers should set the tone for consultation and participation e.g. respect all opinions, explain the value of group's input, make it clear interested in what they've got to say, not how they say it,
- Discourage interruptions or sarcastic comments (talk to trouble makers outside meeting too).
- Use a predictable structure e.g. working through the agenda, or the previous meeting's minutes.
- Use clear language and explain difficult terms e.g. intermittent, give examples of abstract concepts, bring in samples (e.g. of faulty products) illustrations (pamphlets, graphs).
- Chairperson needs to make sure everyone has an opportunity to have a say – not just the loud ones.
- Use positive feedback and reflective listening strategies to encourage discussion and clarify issues.
- Give some notice and allow time for people to collect their thoughts (and words) before asking for their opinion.
- Break up into pairs or small groups to discuss specific issues and report back – maybe break into language groups.
- Write up minutes in Plain English, showing follow up actions, and person responsible.
- Make sure actions are followed up, so meetings don't become a waste of time and effort.

CASE STUDY 2. WORKING WITH TEAMS TO EXPLORE PERCEPTIONS OF ROLES AND EXPECTATIONS/ ASSUMPTIONS OF EFFECTIVE TEAMWORK

Working in a team environment was one of a number of new work practices introduced in a large manufacturing company. A full-time teacher was contracted to assist operators, particularly those of non-English speaking background, develop language and literacy skills to cope with these new changes to the workplace. Teams were to work on a rotation system with each operator acting as team leader for a period of three months. Operators were expected to participate fully and contribute to the successful operation of their team.

Despite working closely with operators to develop language skills for participating in meetings – particularly strategies for giving opinions and making suggestions – participative team practices were not working effectively. Some operators were also reluctant to take on the leadership role. Operators who were from diverse language and cultural backgrounds had very different and often conflicting expectations and perceptions of the role of a leader. Comments like the following reflected these attitudes:

> She should stay at home and look after her family instead of trying to be the boss.

> My job is not to talk about problems but to do what the boss says.

> I'm not strong enough to be the leader. I can't give directions.

The teacher recommended that, in conjunction with a crosscultural trainer, a session be offered to all operators to assist them in looking at some critical issues related to teamwork and participative work practices in a culturally diverse workplace. It was felt that this training would also provide management and operators with an opportunity to:

- reflect on their own values and expectations as well as develop a deeper understanding of those of their workmates of different backgrounds;
- explore how these values and expectations either facilitate or interfere with the successful implementation of the new work practices;
- develop strategies to encourage a more effective team environment with greater participation and contribution from individuals.

The workshop was developed and conducted in conjunction with the crosscultural trainer, and was held initially with management personnel, and then with groups of twelve to fifteen employees over a number of months. The following is a description of one such work-shop held with a group of operators who were also expected to take on leadership positions on a rotation basis.

An activity developed for these sessions involved the operators work-ing in small groups of three or four and brainstorming what they thought were the qualities of a good team member and those of a good team leader.

The workshop presenters had to intervene on a number of occasions to facilitate the brainstorming in some groups where people became preoccupied with arguing over their conflicting views. In some groups, for example, some people strongly felt that 'good' leaders should clearly give directives to be obeyed, whereas others felt equally strongly that they should be more democratic.

The workshop presenters emphasised that it was not a question of any quality being right or wrong but rather one of finding out different perceptions on these issues. They also made a conscious effort to invite more reticent participants to give their views, for example, by joining some of these in the group discussions. Some expressed themselves very cautiously while a few still chose to remain quiet.

As a whole group, participants then shared their findings on the whiteboard. Then people were asked to sort out these qualities on dif-ferent sheets of butcher's paper under the following headings:

- Qualities of a good team leader   – Traditional Team
                                     – Participative 1990s Team
- Qualities of a good team member – Traditional Team
                                     – Participative 1990s Team

The group came up with the following responses:

Qualities of a good team leader

Traditional   – the leader should make decisions on who does what and when
                     – the leader should be one to judge situations and solve problems
                     – the leader should make decisions and give directions
                     – the leader should have a lot of power

Participative 1990s – the leader should ask team members for their suggestions for improvement
                     – the leader should listen to different ideas from team members

- the leader should do the job, not just supervise
- the leader should know the skills and knowledge of members and help individual members to use their talents

Qualities of a good team member

Traditional
- a team member should quietly support and follow the leader
- a team member should not have any responsibilities apart from doing his/her job
- a team member should not be expected to make decisions

Participative 1990s
- a team member should give ideas
- a team member should be able to vote for his/her own leader
- a team member should take responsibility for his/her job
- a team member should be directly involved in workplace issues e.g. quality and safety

A number of people expressed their amazement at the many differences that existed within the small group and went on to seek clarification from those who had views which were very different from theirs. There was very active discussion for the next thirty minutes or so, with people gaining new insights about their workmates. Those who believed that the leader should lead and give directives to the team members expressed their difficulty in showing any respect for a leader who was always asking for ideas from them. They also said that they were not comfortable taking on the leadership role for three months and then returning to being a team member again. This made it more difficult for them to relate to the other members. Others, however, argued that they saw the leader as just one of them and, as such, it was good that every one of them was given the opportunity to take on the role.

Through the English course, some of the quieter operators had discussed with the teacher how they found themselves under additional stress during team meetings, when everyone was expected to speak. They mentioned that they were aware of the need to speak but it was extremely difficult for people like them 'who are not used to it'. These issues were discussed in general terms in the workshop. The cross-cultural trainer related her own difficulties with speaking up at her workplace meetings, particularly when she first joined the organisation shortly after her arrival in Australia. Participants were genuinely surprised and almost glad that someone who was a teacher also experienced similar difficulties.

The group was then shown some comments collected from employees of other workplaces which were also introducing participative team practices. They included comments such as:

> I would always agree with my boss. In my country you are expected to do that.

> You have to participate but you usually think what the majority like.

> In my country to compromise is weak, a sell out of values.

Many participants seemed reassured to see that employees of other organisations also shared their views. The group was then shown a diagrammatic representation developed by the presenters of the two different perceptions of the team.

THE TEAM

The Traditional Team

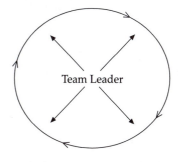

- Supervisor directs
- Team members follow
- minimal interactions with fellow team members

The Restructured Team

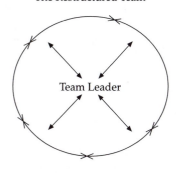

- Supervisor facilitates
- Team members fully participating & contributing
- extensive interaction with fellow team members

Source: B.J. Ong and M. Semple 1994

This was followed up by a brief discussion of collectivist and individualist values based on the work of Brislin, Triandis and Hui (1988).

Individualism and Collectivism
(Based on the work of Triandis, Brislin and Hui, 1988)

Individualist	Collectivist
• individual is smallest unit of survival	• group is smallest unit of survival
• primary attention to own needs	• primary attention to group needs
• self is autonomous	• self is part of the group
• positive attitudes towards horizontal relationships	• positive attitudes towards vertical relationships

Individual differences exist within all cultures and are affected by:

• personality traits
• age
• gender
• education
• social class
• degree of urbanisation
• life experience

The collectivist team member who valued group harmony, humility and respect for the leader would see his/her role as quietly supporting the leader by following directions given, and not disrupting the harmony of the team by expressing his/her own views, questioning and disagreeing with the leader or another member. On the other hand, the individualist team member who saw him/herself as an independent individual who was entitled to his/her own views, would be comfortable being a fully participating and contributing member of the team – even if those views were different from those of the rest of the team.

The presenters were careful to point out that there should be a continuum and not a divide between the two sets of values and that individuals could move anywhere along this continuum depending on a number of factors – age, education, life experience, degree of urbanisation, etc.

Participants were able to relate to this framework by identifying their guiding values and became more aware of those influencing their workmates. Some operators who were from the same background as one of the presenters were interested to know where she would locate herself and if she had thought about how much she had moved along the continuum, as she migrated and experienced different ways of life and work.

Some of them expressed a sense of relief that they did not need to feel inadequate or pressured any more when they experienced difficulty speaking up at meetings or being actively involved in the new participative work practices. It was liberating for them because they realised that their reluctance to participate no longer reflected their abilities but rather the values which they had grown up with. They felt that the session was an important first step in understanding the many uncomfortable and stressful moments at work and also some of the misunderstandings they experienced with their workmates.

The session finished with the operators developing some simple strategies which they intended to apply to their different situations:

- Operators who are not ready to be leaders could be given more time to prepare themselves for the role.
- Operators who are quiet may have good ideas, so leaders need to invite them to give their ideas.
- Operators could write down their suggestions and give them to the leader before team meetings and be prepared to talk about them.

The workshop evaluation indicated that all participants found the workshop was important in enabling people to work through these issues. There were strong recommendations that such training should be extended to all employees and management in the company. Through her continuing work in the company, the teacher was able to follow up some of the points discussed in the workshop with communication course participants and other work personnel.

NOTES

1. Osterman, 1994, Storey, 1993.
2. See, for example, Aguayo, 1990, Dawson, P. and Palmer, G. 1995, and Scherkenbach, W., 1986.
3. Mawer, G., 1993. *Communication Skills Framework for the Metals and Engineering Industry.* National Centre for English Language Teaching and Research, Sydney.

4. Commercially produced videos of team meetings have also featured in the Special Broadcasting Service/National Centre for English Language Teaching and Research *English at Work* series (1992–5) and *In a Nutshell – Cross Cultural Communication at Work: A Training Package* (1995), produced by the Office of Multicultural Affairs and Open Channel Productions, Fitzroy, Victoria.

THIRTEEN

Improving customer relations

Customer focus is becoming one of the hallmarks of progressive, innovative workplaces, with customer responsiveness being closely linked
with all aspects of operations, from the design of products and services, to production, delivery and marketing. This focus is also evident
in the organisational change literature, quality management strategies,
company mission statements as well as new education and training
initiatives. Writers such as Tom Peters (1987), for example, advocate
that managers 'focus with a passion on customers needs' if they are to
achieve a 'quality revolution'. In a similar vein, the British City and
Guilds educational newsletter emphasises a customer-driven approach
to the form and content of their services:

> Customer service is about exceeding customer expectations rather than just
> meeting them. It is about solving problems and not avoiding responsibility,
> about treating people with integrity and courtesy. Customer service means
> more than just a smile or saying have a nice day; it represents an ongoing
> commitment through which continuous improvement becomes a real and
> practical proposition. (1994: 4)

Moreover, customers are not only external consumers of goods and
services. An integral part of quality management strategies involves
regarding different sections within one's workplace as 'internal customers' who also need to have their expectations met if not exceeded
– expectations of quality, on time and at the right price.

The pressures for an increasingly customer-focused orientation are
due to a number of factors. First, there is the obvious recognition that
an organisation's survival is dependent on its ability to fulfil its customers' needs. Tariff deregulation and increasing global competition
has reduced the power of monopolies, and increased both the range
and quality of products and services available to consumers. Even
in government or public utility organisations, the increased moves to

privatise and corporatise these sectors have meant that their continued survival can no longer be assumed. In a competitive market, the rights and expectations of increasingly sophisticated customers have great influence. The adoption of quality standards by many workplaces and strategies such as 'Just in Time', for example, has often been in direct response to customer insistence rather than internal pressures.

Mass production and mass markets are giving way to niche marketing and 'tailor made' goods and services, which almost by definition need to be responsive to the needs of discerning customers. Entry to new overseas markets is also often as dependent on establishing positive customer relations as it is on price. Consequently, researching customer needs and inviting feedback are no longer just token, peripheral activities. Customer service departments, for example, are now a standard part of workplaces, with hotlines and surveys providing valuable feedback mechanisms. Similarly, interaction with customers has become an accepted part of all employees' roles, rather than just specialised sections such as marketing personnel. As part of 'downsizing', many organisations have abolished customer contact positions such as purchasing officers and devolved these responsibilities to operational teams.

So what are the implications of these trends for the communicative practices of a workplace? One of the more immediate implications is the need for more interactional skills for employees at all levels as they attempt to understand and respond to the needs of their internal and external customers. With the greater sophistication and expectations of consumers, standards of service have accordingly been set at increasingly higher levels, in terms of both the quality and the breadth of service provided. These increased expectations are often reflected in role descriptions and competency standards for different jobs.

In an attempt to be more responsive to increasingly diverse customers, workplaces also need to more effectively manage the diversity of their own personnel. Many workplaces, for example, are seeking to reflect the demographic characteristics of the customer base across the different levels of the organisation. As well as providing customers with access to a range of language resources, such moves help to promote customer responsiveness at all levels of operations by factoring in a wider range of perspectives. Rather than being perceived as a potential source of miscommunication and tension, workforce diversity is becoming a key contributing factor to success in the marketplace – provided it is effectively managed.

This diversity is particularly valuable in seeking overseas markets and joint ventures. Reports such as the *Australian Manager of the Twenty-*

first Century, a government-commissioned study on the growing import-ance of the Asian market, point out the need for managers to learn how to manage personal and business relationships with Asian customers, partners and investors, and to acquire a high level of know-how about Asian business norms (The Boston Consulting Group, 1994: 20).

Some of these changes – such as regular customer surveys – are peripheral ones, whereas others require more dramatic shifts in atti-tudes and practices – at both individual organisational levels. Treating different others 'with integrity and courtesy' and seeking to 'meet and exceed' a diversity of expectations requires more than just tolerance to cultural, linguistic, class and gender differences. It also requires skills in intercultural communication and situational adaptability. Managing 'productive diversity' invariably challenges traditional power bases and practices as workplaces seek to become more inclusive and reflect the diversity of their customers.

In this chapter, we look at some of the ways that educators can contribute to these changes.

IMPROVING EMPLOYEES' INTERACTIONAL SKILLS

Relating to others, dealing with complaints, and using appropriate polite-ness strategies are often standard learning objectives in communication courses. In many situations, the increased need for customer contact is one of the main reasons for workplaces requesting the services of language educators. In the case of Chiswell Hospital (discussed in Chapter 6), the 'Customer Focus' initiative meant that cleaners needed to interact more with clients as well as complete workplace tasks. Hos-pital assistants who could only say 'You move please' needed to learn the more indirect 'Could you possibly move' and so on. Various incidents had also highlighted the need for greater understanding of hospital notices and medical practices, as cleaners' roles expanded. A cleaner had only just been prevented from responding to a patient's request for a glass of water because she had been unable to decode the 'Nil By Mouth' sign over the bed.

Educators have traditionally paid less attention, however, to improv-ing the communicative competence of English-speaking background employees in relating to their diverse customers. Yet notions of respond-ing courteously and appropriately to an increasing range of customer contact situations are becoming an accepted part of competency stand-ards, role descriptions and mission statements.

In the following case study, we look at a short training programme developed by Catherine O'Grady and Jan Porter for the public contact staff of a culturally diverse local council. This request was initiated by the Equal Employment Opportunity officer following a communication skills course for bilingual council employees.

CASE STUDY 1. CROSSCULTURAL TRAINING FOR PUBLIC CONTACT STAFF

A request was made by the Equal Employment Opportunity officer of a metropolitan council to conduct a crosscultural training programme for public contact staff. These included counter officers, health and building surveyors, building inspectors and rates clerks.

At the initial planning meeting with council personnel, it became evident that some members of staff would be strongly resistant to such training, as they felt that the problems were with particular migrants groups who were deemed to be aggressive, or unwilling to adapt to their new life in Australia. Typical reactions included comments such as:

Why do we have to change? They're the migrants.

Why should the council pay for such training?

They don't want to understand. They speak English OK, then say they don't understand.

Following the planning meeting, it was decided that the training target public contact personnel from the Planning, Health and Building and Rates departments and emphasise the practical benefits of improving crosscultural communication skills. The workshop would acknowledge the difficult reality of service provision across cultures and survey workshop participants individually to ensure that their views and experiences were taken into account.

A survey was distributed to prospective participants to gather individual perceptions about crosscultural difficulties encountered in dealing with clients of non-English background. It asked them, for example, to briefly describe an incident where tension or misunderstanding arose during their interactions with the public due to language or cultural differences. To supplement these surveys, telephone interviews were conducted with a sample of participants. The EEO officer nominated four participants considered to represent a range of views and attitudes.

These interviews proved most useful in gaining detailed information necessary for developing effective and accurate case studies.

Analysis of the data

In analysing data emerging from the planning meeting, surveys and telephone interviews, the workshop presenters identified three specific categories of difficulty interfering with effective crosscultural communication during service encounters:

1. Incidents of non-understanding

Many difficulties cited arose because of the limited language skills of clients. Service staff seemed unaware of strategies for making their own language more accessible. Further, lack of sympathy for the difficulties of second language speakers was founded in unrealistic perceptions of the language learning process.

While the council employed bilingual personnel, Asian languages were not represented. Access to interpreters was limited and bilingual information was yet to be developed.

The workshop needed, therefore, to raise awareness to the difficulty of acquiring another language as well as to facilitate the development of useful strategies for minimising non-understanding.

2. Incidents of misunderstanding

Data also indicated tensions between council officers and clients despite apparent fluency in English. Words, phrases and behaviours which signal a certain meaning and intent in one language and culture can carry unintended meaning and emotional force in another. Such pragmatic differences were causing misunderstanding, ill feeling and misjudgement.

The workshop needed therefore to provide insight into the nature of cross-cultural misunderstanding and to assist participants to recognise and deal appropriately with pragmalinguistic differences.

3. Clashes in outlook and values

The research brought to light strong feelings of disapproval towards some immigrant clients who may not share the majority culture's attitudes towards such matters as responsibility for public property, the environment and constraints on the use of private land. In response to the question 'What would you like to gain from attending this workshop?'

for example, one participant wrote: 'Ways of avoiding contact with non-English speaking members of the public'. The workshop needed to deal with racist attitudes and assist participants to assert council regulations while avoiding moral judgement. It also needed to address frustration arising out of different perceptions about how decisions are made and what constitutes appropriate persuasive behaviour.

These different areas of cross-cultural communication breakdown provided a framework for the workshop, based on Jenny Thomas' levels of crosscultural difficulty (1983) and research in intercultural discourse.[1] Participants would analyse incidents and case studies from their experience to build knowledge of the nature of crosscultural miscommunication. From the knowledge gained, skills would be developed for recognising, identifying and dealing effectively with crosscultural difficulties.

The workshop

Drawing upon insights and data gained during the research stage, two two-hour workshops were developed and conducted for two groups of public contact personnel. These included rates clerks and supervisors, ordinance officers, town planners and building inspectors.

The workshop aims were outlined as follows:

- to provide the opportunity to share difficulties that may arise in providing service to a multicultural clientele;
- to explore language and cultural factors which may contribute to miscommunication;
- to develop skills and strategies for improving communication with clients from different language and cultural backgrounds.

In the introductory part of the session, the presenters explicitly acknowledged the difficulties encountered by participants in providing often complex and unwelcome information and advice to people who have limited English or different perceptions of their role and how the system works. They presented participants with a summary of their survey responses which included comments such as:

An immigrant complained of rubbish on railway land. He would not listen to the fact that council has no powers with Crown land.

It's difficult to explain to elderly migrants that changes in pension regulations affect changes to rebates. They sometimes don't want to understand. We're not telling them what they want to hear.

It happens often at the front counter and on the phone that people's accents are hard to understand and they also have difficulties understanding me.

Sometimes people are aggressive, emotional, on the attack. It's hard not to get on the offensive straight off.

The laws are complex and not in plain English.

In some cultures, money might be involved. People from different backgrounds have different views about how the system operates.

Following some additional comments and discussion, participants were presented with a framework for situating these responses within three different levels of crosscultural communication difficulty:

Different Levels of Difficulty in Crosscultural Communication

Non-understanding when people simply do not have enough language in common. While frustrating for both parties such difficulties are usually recognised for what they are and no judgements are made beyond the fact that people have language difficulties. People take practical steps to achieve understanding including finding interpreters.

Misunderstanding when people seemingly are speaking fluently together, yet are misreading each other's intention. The linguistic basis of misunderstanding is seldom recognised and judgements are likely to be made about the speaker's attitude and intent. Phrases, words, ways of speaking carry particular force and intention within a language and culture. Across cultures they may carry different and unintended meaning. Misunderstanding can result.

Clashes in outlook and values frequently lead to misjudgement and disapproval across cultures. Person A, for example, may view offering money to an official as bribery and morally reprehensible. Person B because of experience in a different context, may consider it a frustrating but necessary last resort when dealing with officials. Such a person may be shocked to realise that this reflects on their personal integrity.

Subsequent workshop activities explored these different aspects through role plays, videos and case studies. A summary of the main activities is outlined below.

1. Dealing with non-understanding

To provide some insights into the difficulties of communicating with little language, participants were involved in a short 'foreign language experience', where they were asked to imagine they had migrated to a Spanish speaking country and needed to install a fire alarm in their house. In Spanish, the presenter/council officer explained council policy about the installation of fire alarms, showed them the alarm and distributed written (Spanish) instructions for its installation.

In the debrief of the exercise, participants discussed the different strategies they used to make any sense of the instructions. The notion of 'top-down and bottom-up processing' (Cook, 1989) was introduced to explain how we draw upon our experience and background knowledge to predict the likely meaning of what we are about to hear or read. Our hypotheses and predictions are checked and refined against the language we hear or read in a dynamic interactive process.

In the exercise, for example, participants had drawn their knowledge of what is usually found in forms to assist them to understand unfamiliar words. They had also drawn upon those words and phrases which were similar to English, but by and large they had depended heavily on top-down processing – a common strategy for people operating in a second language.

The group then discussed some of the difficulties that could arise from over-dependence on top-down processing. Suggestions elicited from participants were written up:

They may miss details and nuances.

They may understand what you *think* is there rather than what is actually said or written.

Predictions may be informed by different procedures, e.g., form layout may be different in different cultures and this will be confusing.

Participants were also shown a short video of a customer contact interaction, where the customer's English was limited. They were asked to take note of what caused communication to break down, and to think about how these difficulties could have been minimised.

Discussion following the video involved suggestions for adjusting language as well as suggestions for improving council procedures and practices.

Strategies for avoiding non-understanding:

- Provide a context for the listener by framing what you are going to say:
  'These are the rules the council has developed about tree planting.'
- Signpost your talk: e.g. First, then after that . . .
- Mark transitions from one topic to another:
  'Now I'd like to explain where you can get your tree.'
  Use direct, explicit language.
- Chunk the information.
- Avoid hypotheticals.
- Avoid idiomatic and colloquial language.

---

2. Dealing with Misunderstanding

To introduce this segment the presenter asked participants to examine the way we use indirect forms of language, drawing on council customer interactions recorded during the initial research:

It might be an idea to move that rubbish.

If I were you, I'd get that dog registered ASAP.

Listen mate, we've got a problem with that trailer. Can you do something about it?

She explained that native speakers of English would recognise that these are not requests, but directives. They would be likely to pick up on such cues as the tone of voice, or body language, whereas someone with less English may understand the words but miss out on the intent. They may therefore believe they have a choice, and not comply with the directive.

She then presented other examples of interactions with council staff:

You must give me approval for my fence.

Give me paper for my dog.

You ask a person who approaches the Accounts section holding a rates notice if they would like to pay their rates. They reply 'Of course'.

A discussion of polite forms and politeness strategies in different languages followed, with participants relating some of their experiences.

It was pointed out that in some languages, for example, the equivalent of 'give me' is entirely appropriate, whereas forms such as 'I wonder if you could possibly . . .' sound obsequious.

Some of the strategies developed for dealing with misunderstanding were presented and discussed:

Dealing with Misunderstanding

- recognise that difficulties may be due to cultural difference
- withhold judgement
- respond rather than react
- explore further
- negotiate meaning

---

3. Clashes in outlook and values

In this segment, participants were presented with a number of case studies based on situations identified in the initial research phase. The aim was to provide participants with the opportunity to explore in small groups difficulties arising out of different values and outlook and to share and develop practical strategies for handling such situations.

Case study 1: 'We don't make the rules mate.'

A resident approached the counter in the Planning Department, handed over a plan for a brick fence and said he wanted it passed by the end of the month.

The town planner explained there would be a waiting period of six to eight weeks. Noting that the plan was for a high brick fence directly across the front of the house, he also told the man this was against council regulations.

The resident listened and then repeated his need for the plans to be passed as soon as possible. The planner again referred to the procedures and regulations. The resident continued to persist despite the town planner's repeated efforts to present the rules. Eventually a conflict developed between them.

- What's happening here?
- How would you handle the situation?

In the debrief of this case study, participants discussed different perceptions about the power of the officer to change rules. They explored culturally different views about how decisions are made and what behaviours and strategies are considered persuasive and appropriate (Johnstone, 1989). In Anglo-Australian bureaucracies, for example, decisions are guided by a set of rules and regulations laid down at some previous time, usually by a committee. The decision a council officer gives to a resident is prescribed and constrained by these regulations. Residents who know this realise that they can only go so far in attempting to persuade the officer to change the rules. He/she does not have the authority.

In some cultures and societies, however, decisions are made by individuals. It is therefore up to the client to persuade that individual of the validity of his case. In many Arabic speaking communities, for example, persuasion involves finding the right words, the most apt phrase, the most appropriate reference in order to move the official to perceive the validity of one's request. Persuasion involves persistence. If one does not succeed in persuading one official, perhaps one should approach a different person. Reference to rules and regulations may be perceived as rejection of the individual and will be resented.

So, in this case study the resident may feel dismissed and may be frustrated by his inability to use this second language persuasively. The council officer on the other hand may resent what s/he perceives as an implication that s/he should bend the rules.

Following the discussion of these and other case studies, participants explored some practical strategies for handling such potentially difficult situations.

Strategies for dealing with conflicting values

- Resist judging according to one's own values
- Acknowledge the client's frustration
- Explain the restrictions and limitations of one's role
- Explain the reasons for the council's regulations.

Evaluation

Workshop evaluation was by means of a questionnaire completed anonymously by each participant and discussion with workplace personnel such as the EEO officer. Participants' evaluation of the session was very positive, with most of them noting the value of case studies, and specific council interactions. Insights of linguistic features such as stress and indirect speech were also mentioned:

It was good to see examples as to what not to do.

The case studies were easy to relate to because they were based on real-life experiences.

When another language is spoken, it makes you see their difficulties.

It has made me see another side which perhaps I have been arrogant towards.

MAKING BETTER USE OF INTERNAL LANGUAGE AND CULTURAL RESOURCES

Another way that educators can contribute to improving customer relations is by assisting workplaces in recognising and utilising the diverse backgrounds and experiences of their employees. There is increasing recognition that the demography of the workforce is often a micro version of the demography of the target community and marketplace. The cultural and language diversity of the workforce are therefore valuable resources that are ignored to the loss of both the workplace and its employees. A study by the Ethnic Affairs Commission of NSW and Equal Opportunity Commission, for example, pointed out that:

The more the workplace reflects its intended market in terms of composition, the more likely it is to effectively meet the needs of its intended customers through understanding their needs, perspectives and be able to use networks to reach them, and therefore be competitive. (1993: 62)

One such obvious resource is the diversity of languages reflected in the workforce. Employees with bilingual skills often make use of them to great advantage in customer contact situations. However, the formal use and recognition of these skills is not widespread.

A research Australian report was undertaken, for example, into local councils' policies in relation to the use of bilingual staff (Poulos, 1993). It found that the staff's language skills were measurable, were extensively used and provided an important service to the public. It also found that the use of the language and cultural skills resulted in a reduction of misunderstandings, improved customer public relations and improved access to council services by community members.

However, the report concluded that 'the skill is one that is possessed by the employee, rather than a skill that is required of any particular position in council' and recommended that an allowance be offered to council staff using their language skills, rather than incorporating it into a competency-based system. The rationale for this decision was that the skill is one that is possessed by the employee, rather than a skill which is required of any particular position in council.

With competency standards and role descriptions becoming more flexible, and customer oriented, there are moves in some industry sectors away from a rigid, 'one size fits all' system of recognising the diversity of skills and resources individuals bring to their work. In the Australian tourism and hospitality industry, for example, some consideration is being given to flexible packaging of competency standards to allow for the recognition of bilingual resources as an integral part of certain customer contact roles.

As with bilingual trainers, bilingual employees often lack confidence in their own competence in English, and are therefore often reluctant to put themselves forward for public contact positions. Educators can play a valuable role in developing this competence and enabling them to use their language and cultural resources more effectively.

The use of these resources is not just limited to public contact situations. With the increasing diversification of markets and products, the language and cultural resources of a workplace can greatly enhance the quality of its products and services. An article in the Australian Business Review Weekly, for example, pointed out that:

> Most Australian companies ignore the ethnic market, dismissing it as fragmented, difficult and expensive to reach. As a result, they ignore a group of consumers who represent (depending on how ethnic people are defined) up to 40% of Australia's population. (Shoebridge, 1995: 50)

As a number of workplaces are discovering, ensuring a diversity of perspectives in all stages of design, production and marketing can greatly contribute to improved quality and increased market share. Shoebridge relates the experience of one of Australia's largest insurance companies, the AMP Society. Following market research revealing it was not well known or understood in the 'ethnic marketplace', the AMP has adopted a new approach to widening its customer base and better serving its culturally diverse clients. According to the Managing Director:

> We will become recognised as an organisation that listens to and deals with the ethnic population in a mature and responsible way. We want to change people's perceptions of AMP and one way to do that is to ensure our advertising reflects the new Australia. The new Australia is not white, middle-aged men sitting around talking about insurance; the new Australia is multicultural, it's working women, it's two-career families.

As well as an extensive promotional campaign in nineteen community languages, the new English advertisement features a female, Eurasian accountant giving advice to her male, Anglo client. The company has hired interpreters and is working to increase the number of bilingual agents.

It is ironic that companies often make little use of the skills and experiences of their own employees when embarking on such new initiatives. This is particularly the case in export ventures, where management are often reluctant to allow bilingual employees from lower ranks of the organisation to 'leap-frog' their way into such high-stake ventures, preferring to hire external expertise. Educators can do a great deal in alerting management to the unused skills and resources they have, as well as encouraging bilingual employees to be more actively involved in such initiatives.

This involvement can take place at a number of different levels, as illustrated by the experiences of employees of Vulcanite, an Australian manufacturer of rubber and steel composite mouldings for use in railway, construction and agricultural industries.[2] By effectively using the resources of its employees to build good customer relationships, the company was able to dramatically increase its export initiatives. According to the manager,

> We have a good cross-section of Asia working here in responsible positions, and each contributes in one way or another to our marketing in those countries.

With nine nationalities represented among its workforce of twenty-eight, Vulcanite management encouraged staff by promoting them to strategic positions – such as sales, as well as encouraging them to use their language and cultural skills in their everyday work. For example, bilingual employees labelled export components in both Cantonese and English. Bilingual manuals were included as part of the tender for overseas contracts. The manager also reported that ventures in Hong Kong, Vietnam and the Philippines were well received because employees were able to produce company brochures and other documentation in the customers' languages.

The involvement of bilingual staff in early negotiations with overseas clients was very useful in establishing a close rapport. As the manager put it,

> Having someone on staff to speak to them in their own language made all the difference. If it had been left up to me, I would have failed.

Managers do however play a key role in identifying the types of skills that are valued, and encouraging employees to use them. Whilst it is difficult to quantify, research indicates there is a considerable number of underemployed workers with overseas qualifications, languages and cultural resources who are reluctant to go public about their backgrounds for fear of appearing overqualified or presumptuous. As an operator who, in her country of origin, has been a qualified teacher, commented:

> There is no point telling them that I can do these things unless I know that the supervisor will not be upset, that I will be able to use my skills and that I'll get paid for them.

Educators can assist in this process by ensuring that competency standards, role definitions, and skills analyses are broad enough to recognise and reward the diverse resources that individuals bring to their work.

NOTES

1. See, for example, Bremer, K., Roberts, C., Vasseur, M., Simonot, M., and Broeder, P., 1996, *Achieving Understanding*. Longman: London. Chapter 13 'Improving Customer Relations'.
2. This case study is related in greater detail in Staff 'the key to export success' *Benchmark*, Issue No. 13, pp. 15–16, November 1995. Department of Industrial Relations: Canberra.

PART FOUR

FOURTEEN

Negotiating new ways of working

The case studies described in earlier chapters have explored some of the challenges faced by educators as they move beyond the relative predictability of the workplace classroom. They have illustrated a number of key factors upon which workplace communication practice is based. The first relates to how the discourses of the workplace are to be described, interpreted and explained. The second revolves around how educators define their roles and practices in the light of those discourses, the ideologies that underpin them, and the prevailing models that govern their activity and determine how their effectiveness will be judged. The other vital determining factor relates to the local organisational context – the extent to which educators are able to create an effective partnership to promote the learning and development of individuals and to improve communication, learning and management practices at work.

In this final chapter, we outline a number of implications relating to the role of the workplace educator, and the profession generally. Just as workers are confronting the practices of the restructured workplace, it is clear that educators are themselves undergoing a 'restructure'. We are being asked to do more with less, become familiar with new technologies and more focused on delivering quality 'products', 'outcomes' and services that meet our diverse clients' needs and expectations. As well as these demands for greater multiskilling, we are being faced with more problematic ideological and philosophical challenges, in terms of how our practice is to be defined, and how we, ourselves are being positioned as agents of the workplace, of the particular institution that employs or funds us and by the demands of wider national training and employment policies.

Just like our counterparts in industry, educators are having to deal with the fuzziness of boundaries in terms of hierarchies, roles and areas of specialisation. Part of the cost of the 'mainstreaming' of language and diversity issues is a new set of dilemmas that educators have not usually had to confront in past self-contained 'social justice', language courses. Some of these dilemmas relate to immediate issues of day-to-day practice, others to the longer-term future of the profession:

- What knowledge, skills and attitudes do workplace educators need to have to be effective in the present context? With the increasing emphasis on the non-teaching roles of the workplace educator (facilitator, consultant, researcher, advocate), are ESL and literacy teaching qualifications still the only relevant ones for workplace educators?
- Given the multidisciplinary 'integrated' nature of the work, where do educators draw their boundaries? Is there a danger of practitioners becoming Jacks and Jills of all trades and losing their specialised expertise?
- Is it realistic to expect an individual practitioner to develop all the necessary competencies? How can educators' work be organised to allow for support, skill-sharing and continued involvement with both the educational institution as well as the client workplace?
- In a privatised, competitive education and training market, how can educators remain committed to educational and social justice goals while maintaining their own economic viability?
- In attempting to sail some of these uncharted waters, where can educators turn for support, guidance and professional development? How is the profession to redefine itself? What are the implications for initial and ongoing training?

There has been remarkably little public debate on these issues in educational circles, with attention more closely focused on perhaps more familiar, 'turf' issues, such as the relationship between language, literacy, communication and basic education teaching, the relative merits of different linguistic traditions or competency-based approaches to education and training.

An interesting parallel can be found in the challenges currently faced by professionals in a closely related field to workplace education – the 'Human Resource Development' (HRD or HRM) area. Professor John Storey (1996),[1] for instance, traces developments over recent years in the transition from personnel to human resource management, and notes that while the organisational significance of the move has been extensively debated, the implications of this shift for teaching HRD professionals has not. If the profession has moved beyond the specialist personnel function he asks, where does it now draw its boundaries, and therefore the scope of HRD and HRM courses – organisational behaviour, management thought (scientific management, human relations, interpersonal skills), management of change, and management development? What of related functional disciplines, such as sociology, occupational psychology and strategic management? His discussion focuses on four main aspects that seem equally applicable to workplace educators:

1. Competing value systems and perspectives – Is the profession itself supposed to be concerned with an approach or a subject matter? Soft approaches stressing the people side of the profession, or the measurement of efficiency and outcomes? The pursuit of 'efficiency with justice', or business mission and goals?
2. The management and business course contexts within which HRM is taught, with their increasing focus on competencies in modularised form, skills and immediate relevance rather than theoretical understandings, reflection and the contextualisation of learning. Can such narrow-focused courses adequately prepare professionals for the complexity of their roles?
3. The interface between teaching and research, and the increasing gulf between the two. He points out, for example, that while large numbers of HR practitioners have been spending their time in managing redundancy programmes, the focus of teaching and textbooks remains firmly on recruitment and selection. In the same way, it could be argued that organisational behaviour, industrial relations or more bread and butter issues such as the preparation of tender submissions and contractual agreements are still to feature in courses for workplace educators.
4. Curriculum design, with a shift of emphasis from the history and development of the personnel function to a different set of priorities focusing on aspects such as outcomes, benchmarking, quality, customer service, re-engineering, the management of change, and overarching all, the needs of the business.

Storey argues for a more critical, reflective and strategic approach to HRM:

> The rise of HRM has impelled many tutors to engage with issues which would previously have lain outside their span of concern. At the same time, other, previously longstanding topics have been often crowded out of the contemporary curriculum . . .

> The shifting agenda stems from more fundamental change in product markets and in political agendas which expose the public sector to market

pressures. Issues of quality, innovation and cost-competitiveness have inescapably been foisted on to the people-management curriculum. Viewed in this light, HRM is merely a transmission medium for a much more powerful set of forces. Tutors may indeed choose to eschew the term if they so wish, but the underlying pressures will remain. (p. 13)

As a way of further illustrating some of the underlying and conflicting pressures faced by workplace educators, we return briefly to Aus Tin and outline how the workplace educator, Lee Fletcher, dealt with a delicate issue that was not in any way addressed in her teacher training courses – that of assisting in the process of negotiating an Enterprise Agreement.

FACILITATING ENTERPRISE AGREEMENT NEGOTIATIONS AT AUS TIN

As part of her work at Aus Tin, the educator had been invited to be an observer of the Consultative Committee,[2] so that she could be better informed on issues being raised in the company, and she could recommend appropriate training, both for the committee and the wider workforce.

Reflecting national changes in industrial relations, the company embarked on a new enterprise agreement to replace the traditional industrial award system, and a large part of the consultative process centred around the negotiation of an enterprise agreement. The negotiations took well over a year, but finally, an agreement for a particular section of the plant was ready for signing and ratification by the employees.

Aus Tin had three main reporting back mechanisms: from the consultative committee, the union representatives and team leaders in team briefing sessions. However, the effectiveness of these mechanisms was in question, because many employees still claimed they did not understand the proposals being put up and expressed feelings of vulnerability and powerlessness.

Draft copies of the proposed agreement (25–30 pages long!) were made available by management so that employees could have access to the information. To one team leader's knowledge, no one had asked to see the document. There seemed to be a lack of understanding of the process and the content of the negotiations. Though a number of employees sought verbal clarification, indicating that they did want to understand the content of the agreement, some employees were heard to say that management was going to make the decisions anyway. This was a view management and the consultative committee wanted to discourage. Employee involvement was crucial to the successful implementation of the agreement.

Enterprise agreement communication sessions

In discussions with the consultative committee, the educator was asked to design and deliver a number of information sessions for employees to attend on a voluntary basis, with particular encouragement to employees from a non-English speaking background. As well as reflecting a genuine desire for consultation, there was also a legal requirement to ensure that all involved were informed participants. Section 130 of the Industrial Relations Act, 1991 states:

> If any of the employees concerned cannot understand the language in which the agreement is written, the employer must ensure that accurate, but simply expressed, summaries of the agreement are publicly exhibited in a language understood by the employees in question.

In the committee's view, while the educator may have had little expertise in industrial relations, she was a neutral, credible person known to the workforce, and familiar with the different levels of competence in English. As well as having skills in Plain English, her active listening and clarification strategies were perceived to be valuable in facilitating effective communication.

The final part dealt with issues and concerns. These were documented on the whiteboard before the arrival of the plant manager so they remained anonymous. The plant manager addressed each issue in turn, which promoted a very productive interaction. At the conclusion of each session , the issues and concerns were typed up and given out to team leaders and union representatives for further follow-up where necessary.

The feedback from these sessions was very positive and this style of communication very useful. As well as facilitating the successful negotiation of this particular agreement, the educator was able to recommend a number of changes to the Consultative Committee which were taken into account in subsequent negotiations with different sections of the company. These included issues such as the use of more user-friendly, consistent terminology, summaries of the main elements of an agreement, training for Consultative Committee members, short feedback meetings and the use of interpreters.

MAKING THE ENTERPRISE AGREEMENT WORK

HOW CAN I CONTRIBUTE?

- **Continuous running**

  - be flexible
  - take staggered meal breaks
  - be prepared to relieve in any team

- **Reduction of spoilage**

  - know who our key customers are
  - understand and talk about quality procedures in place in particular work areas
  - make changes to procedures if necessary
  - complete documentation on quality procedures accurately
  - suggest solutions to product quality problems

- **Support your team**

  - problem solve as a group/discuss with others
  - accept responsibility for group performance
  - be co-operative/help out when necessary
  - communicate freely with other teams/share information

- **Multiskill (accept training)**

  Elect to do training to improve your job performance and to learn new skills

WHAT'S IN IT FOR THE EMPLOYEES

- pay increase

- gainsharing

- more job satisfaction

- technology improvements

THE COMPANY

- more competitive in the marketplace

- increased production

- fewer customer complaints

- less spoilage

- better quality

- new customers

This short case study illustrates some of the dilemmas and pitfalls faced by educators once they redefine the workplace as curriculum and their contribution to improving communication, learning and management practices at work. Enterprise agreements have emerged as a prime 'critical site' determining employees' pay, work, training and advancement conditions, yet the discoursal demands of consultation and negotiation are so complex and multilayered as to exclude the majority of those affected from meaningful involvement.[3]

In this particular instance, the educator had been working at the company for a sufficiently long time to have established credibility as a trustworthy, neutral facilitator. With support from both management and the unions, she was able to design a format that enhanced interaction between management and employees, while safeguarding employees' confidentiality and helping them to articulate their concerns and have them addressed. While drawing on her skills as an adult language and literacy educator, these on their own would not have been sufficient to enable her to deal with the challenges and potential risks she faced in this particular exercise, or many of the other earlier initiatives that she undertook at Aus Tin.

Engaging with the complex critical discoursal sites and interactional dynamics of the workplace requires educators in turn to exercise a delicate balancing act of responsive praxis. To return to Brookfield's phrase, it is clear that as well as being able to draw on contextual factors, more and more, the 'improvisational ability' of educators is becoming critical to their successful practice as adult educators in today's turbulent workplace:

> Without a realisation that context is crucial in affecting the possibilities and forms of practice, practitioners are likely to experience something close to despair each time a carefully planned program has to be altered because of some unforeseen eventuality... [Practitioners] should learn to value their capacity to make programs more meaningful and relevant in terms of contextually specific features. Hence improvisational ability should be recognised as crucial to successful practice. (1986: 25)

How can educators then be prepared for such fluid, responsive practice? What are some of the specific issues that educators will need to grapple with as they broaden their repertoire of competence and negotiate new ways of working? We conclude by reviewing a number of key interrelated factors that will continue to present challenges for educators, their trainers and employers. They revolve around the need to:

- critically evaluate our constructs of language and learning
- broaden our role definition and repertoire of competence
- balance considerations of social justice in a competitive education and training market
- provide meaningful professional support and development.

CRITICALLY EVALUATING OUR CONSTRUCTS OF LANGUAGE AND LEARNING

Educators are almost daily confronted by a struggle between a view of language and communication as a negotiative discursive process and that of language merely as an aggregate of grammatical or textual elements and skills. The negotiative and discursive view, premised as it is upon the enhancement of capacity and critical reflection tends to focus more on process than content. Such a view is also at odds with the incremental development of discrete elements within a modularised competency standard system.

In the same way, views of learning range from those that are totally self-directed and informal, to more teacher-directed and technology-driven approaches. Rather than just individual skill development, learning at work is increasingly seen as part of system-wide processes of organisational and cultural change. Learning which occurs in a training room is becoming only a small part of such transformational learning, with informal and incidental learning playing a crucial role in developing and applying new knowledge, skills and attitudes.

Narrow definitions of language and learning can all too easily translate into reductionist approaches or simplistic solutions to the complexity of communicative workplace demands. Yet, with the blurring of definitional and discipline boundaries, there is the danger of new constructs becoming unrealistically all-encompassing and unmanageable. One of the main dilemmas for educators, for example, is working out the extent to which they are offering their learners vocationally oriented language or accessible modules of vocational training. While helping learners obtain the forklift licence they need to keep their job, to what extent can they help learners develop broader language and learning skills so they can continue to access other vocational training independently and participate more actively in shaping their work environment? How can they account for incidental and informal learning, valuable though it might be, under a competency-based system?

Can educators facilitate organisational learning without compromising their commitment to those most vulnerable in the workplace? To what extent can learning be at the same time a competitive business tool and a means of individual empowerement for those traditionally disadvantaged? Gee, Hull, and Lankshear's (1996) study of a computer component manufacturer graphically illustrates the tensions and paradoxes of what they term 'the new capitalism in transition' – the contradictions within talk about non-authoritarian work structures and the democratization of work through a quality, team-based strategy. They conclude:

> Humanistic, democratic reforms are being enacted, not because they create more humanistic, less hierarchical conditions for workers but because they are viewed as the way to create more and/or continuing profit. (1996: 125)

Along with workers and managers, workplace educators are also needing to deal with the paradoxes of the opportunities presented by the rhetoric of organisational learning.

BROADENING OUR ROLE DEFINITION AND REPERTOIRE OF COMPETENCE

The 'multi-skilling' of the roles and functions of practitioners is a logical flow-on from the adoption of a more encompassing view of language and learning. In Hull's words, educators need to ask 'How much after all, depends on literacy itself? What else must we be concerned with, besides literacy, if we want to improve the conditions and products of work?' (1993: 44).

A recent Australian project examining 'what is a competent adult literacy and basic education teacher?' for example, found that community consultation, communication and advocacy formed an integral part of teachers' roles. It proposed that the term 'teacher' was no longer an adequate descriptor for the roles of functions of educators in increasingly diverse and complex learning/teaching contexts (Scheeres *et al.* 1993). As well as the more traditional literacy teacher, titles used for educators in different workplaces have reflected this broadening of role. Educators have been referred to as literacy project officer, learning manager, facilitator, consultant, skills development coordinator, lecturer and communication skills trainer. Each of these titles carries different implications in terms of scope and authority.

As the case studies in earlier chapters have illustrated, facilitation, negotiation and mentoring are becoming essential core skills. Yet adopting such mediating roles brings a whole range of new challenges and uncertain allegiances. In discussing this shift in roles, Butler and Connole (1994) succinctly describe the tensions and ambiguities that 'working in the middle' can present:

> The work of those occupying this middle ground is that of 'riding the binaries' of challenging discourses and discursive practices . . . to reframe ways of knowing, of learning, of working that acknowledge diversity

rather than homogeneity. It seeks to insert values of social justice into corporatist frameworks and practices. It seeks to open up spaces for voices from the bottom to speak.

To work in the middle is also to mediate, to translate and demystify texts . . . for workers and interested others while facilitating the communicating of ideas upwards to challenge, inform or shift policy and practices at the top. Such a stance positions the mediator as other, not belonging to the top or the bottom, always out of place and aware of the tensions involved in 'speaking on behalf' of those who are always absent, since top and bottom never meet.[4]

Such a shift is a far cry from the more radical 'missionary' stance of the critical literacy tradition. In these more mediatory and interventionary roles, educators can easily find themselves subtly co-opted as gate-keepers, or subservient agents of the company's mission statement. Gee *et al*'s (1996) study clearly illustrates how notions such as worker empowerment and teamwork can be little more than dressing for achieving a compliant workforce.

How can educators develop their awareness of the social and political contexts of their practice so they can select particular methodologies and strategies rather than others? At the level of 'teaching' methodologies, it is evident that educators need to develop their skills in utilising new contexts and technologies to facilitate learning and its application. Mentoring of trainers, distance and computer-mediated learning, modularised, project-based and informal learning are some of the more common examples emerging. Supporting key personnel such as managers, and developing the crosscultural communication skills of key personnel are also critical for success. Yet accounting for such learning in ways that do not disadvantage either educator or 'learner' can present real challenges in the brave new world of national vocational qualifications. The accreditation of language and literacy courses, for example, may be beneficial for educators in these particular disciplines, but for worker/learners, are vocational outcomes not more meaningful? In many workplaces, those vocational outcomes themselves may relate more to less tangible improvements in communication and work practices than visible qualifications held by particular individuals.

At a wider level, educators' concern with social justice is bound to lead them beyond the workplace itself, to wider 'critical sites' where broader vocational educational policy, services and products are developed. Developing collaborative relationships in such arenas as vocational education and training policy, the development of vocational standards, curriculum and assessment guidelines, the training of vocational educators and trainers, presents real professional, ideological and practical challenges, as educators negotiate competing discourses, values and interests.

BALANCING CONSIDERATIONS OF SOCIAL JUSTICE, AND COLLABORATION IN A COMPETITIVE EDUCATION AND TRAINING MARKET

In a supposedly 'business-led', privatised education and training market, educators increasingly need to define their clients, and re-package their offerings. The profession itself is becoming more discursively complex as it is restructured. For example, is the client workplace management, the individual worker, funding body or employing institution? To what extent do predetermined funding criteria – often developed by non-educators – shape the curriculum process and outcomes?

In an increasingly casualised profession, how can educators ensure we, ourselves are not marginalised because we represent marginalised people? What negotiating power can educators wield, if our funding base is precarious? How can we establish new collaborative relationships that acknowledge both differences and commonalities? To what extent can educators afford to stand by high professional ethics and not be seen as 'blue stocking welfare ladies', or as just irrelevant? Reflecting on his experiences over a number of years, an employer representative pointedly observed:

> Education providers need to review how they go about doing business. They are the only ones in the training marketplace who say 'I sold it but they didn't buy'.

> A lot of them don't seem to know how to get employers on side and to start where managers are at, in terms of addressing their concerns while at the same time giving them an educationally sound service or product.

> They need to understand that any training that happens in the workplace needs to be in line with the business goals and the rest will come. Otherwise it will be marginalised and ultimately useless.

As a number of the case studies have illustrated, as educators, we will only be as effective as our ability to successfully negotiate and link our aims and work in to key people's concerns. More and more, evaluations of workplace programmes are needing to justify their 'outcomes' in quantifiable, bottom-line terms, rather than qualitative, subjective criteria. This shift is likely to involve difficult compromises, given the usual constraints of resources, time, goodwill and divergent agendas. Such negotiations will almost inevitably require us to reflect on our own values and how we and our learners are being positioned.

In reviewing a workplace education project in the US, for example, Tannock[5] points out how in the leap from design to implementation, the programme came up short of its aim to be worker-centred and participatory. He analyses the classroom discourse of a literacy program run cooperatively by company and union at a US canning factory to show how, even in apparently 'worker-centred' efforts, local discursive choices made by instructors may close off opportunities for students/employees to freely express their opinions and ideas. There was little critical discussion of the company mission statement, for example, as compared with an analysis of union literature. Tannock argues that such choices tended to align students/employees with culturally stereotyped attitudes, behaviours and values – that were desirable to company management.

While Tannock's critique may well be valid, there are dangers in extrapolations based on such a narrowly focused discoursal analysis of the program. He does not, for example, seem to take sufficient account of some key structural factors that gave rise to the course in the first place, such as the aim and length of the programme. The course was an integrated thirty-hour 'literacy job training programme', providing certification for two different positions at the company (label line operator, and floor supervisor) and involved twenty-eight employees. Given these structural parameters, to what extent can an educator be realistically expected to actively facilitate free-ranging discussion and critical analysis of company and union discourse? What is the 'art of the possible' in such a scenario? To what extent did the educator trade critical literacy for vocational outcomes? How closely was her compromise aligned with participants' own goals and aspirations?

PROVIDING MEANINGFUL PROFESSIONAL SUPPORT AND DEVELOPMENT

Evaluations of workplace programmes regularly demonstrate how central the commitment and dynamism of the educator is to the success of programs. The following comment by workplace employees are typical:

> Mary's been the primary driving force – she bubbles with enthusiasm – we
> wouldn't be so far along the track as we are without her . . . She asks for
> our input, keeps us informed of what's happening and is agreeable to
> change – overall a top person. (Hislop, 1994: 10)

How can educators be prepared and supported in these expanding roles so that their 'bubbling enthusiasm' does not end up in burn-
out? What are the prerequisite knowledge, skills and qualifications for
today's workplace educators? How can an increasingly competency-
based approach to teacher education adequately capture educators'
responsiveness to an ever-changing learning context? To what degree
should the processes of researching, teaching, learning and collaborating at work replace content? If educators' initial training is to take more
account of the social and political by drawing on other disciplines,
what aspects of the traditional teacher-training curriculum are to be
condensed or deleted? Given the crucial role of the local context, is it
realistic for workplace educators' training to happen in isolation from
the workplace itself?

How can educators' work be organised to allow for ongoing support
and skill-development? In an increasingly privatised and casualised
education system, notions of efficiency, customer responsiveness and
flexibility can easily lead to an erosion of professional standards and
working conditions. What are some of the career paths open to educators? Apart from greater job satisfaction, what are some of the incentives for educators to develop skills in new areas? Reviews of vocational
education and training indicate a considerable degree of resistance to
change, from practitioners and administrators alike.[6] As one Australian
vocational institute director pointed out, there are often little incentives
to attract many practitioners to workplace education, apart from the
desire for a challenging, interesting job:

> The average teacher is in their forties, very happy in a safe classroom
> situation where they have total power. They may have not entrepreneurial
> or negotiation skills, and may not want to become 'totally subservient' in a
> customer focused industry context. There is no motivation and no rewards
> unless they are the sort of person who likes a challenge. If they do, they'll
> become frustrated with the system, leave us and become a consultant.
> (Mawer and Field, 1995: 71)

Given structural pressures and precarious funding, how can educational institutions themselves reflect some of the 'best practice' of learning organisations? As educators' work changes, is it realistic for them
to also expect that their own institutions espouse some of the principles

they aim to develop in their clients: team-based approaches to work, open and effective communication, opportunities for skill recognition and development? With limited, unreliable funding sources, how can educational institutions keep and offer incentives to highly skilled professionals?

Like other related professions, there is clear evidence of tensions, struggles and experimentation as educators make the transition from the workplace classroom to wider critical sites. Some workplace education institutions in Australia have adopted more flexible, team-based approaches to their work as a way of supporting and developing the skills of their educators. Others have placed individual teachers in a workplace for the duration of a programme, with fortnightly visits back to base for professional support and development. In expanding their teachers' knowledge and skills base, they have drawn on related areas such as industrial relations, human resource development, social policy and organisational behaviour.

Others have provided opportunities for the secondment of educators to different institutions for specific research and development projects. Strategic alliances with vocational, management/teacher training institutions, employer and union groups have also enabled crossfertilisation of skills. In Australia at present, a sizeable number of workplace educators are involved in policy, research, and vocational curriculum development. Several work with Industry Training Advisory Boards to develop competency standards and curriculum and encourage employers to implement training programmes for their employees. A significant number are employed as independent consultants or training managers in workplaces, trainers of vocational trainers and crosscultural communication for managers.

Despite the increasing variety of contexts such educators find themselves in, they are often engaged in a similar cycle of critical reflection as they try to navigate the multilayered discourses of the workplace and the rhetoric of vocational skill development and organisational change. With the scope of workplace education moving beyond the classroom, holding in tension the various paradoxes of the 'praxis' of individual and organisational learning, involves a delicate balancing act. At the same time, with the profession itself undergoing similar changes as its clientele, educators are having to redefine their aims, approaches and working conditions in ways that are both visionary and pragmatic. While educators often comment on the tensions and 'steep learning curves' that such new ways of working entail, they usually also note the immense satisfaction of making a real difference.

NOTES

1. Storey, J., 1996. 'From Personnel Management to HRM: the Implications for Teaching.' *Asia Pacific Journal of Human Resources, 33 (3), pp. 4–14.*
2. As outlined in Chapter 5, the Consultative Committee at Aus Tin had four management and eight employee representatives, and was set up to formulate a strategic plan for the business, and make recommendations on work organisation and skill development issues.
3. Candlin, C.N., Maley, Y. and Sutch, H. (in press). *Industrial Instability and the Discourse of Enterprise Bargaining* in Roberts, C., and Sarangi, S. (eds) *Discourse at Work: Communication in Institutional, Professional and Workplace Settings.* Mouton: the Hague and Charlesworth, S., 1996. *Stretching Flexibility – Enterprise Bargaining, Women and Changes to Working Hours.* Human Rights and Equal Opportunity Commission, Sydney.
4. Butler, E., and Connole, H. Training Reform and Gender: Reframing Training for Women Workers 1994. *Conference papers Vol. 2 Reforming post-compulsory education and training Reconciliation and reconstruction 7–9 December.* Centre for Skill Formation Research and Development, Griffith University.
5. Tannock, S. 1997.
6. Centre for Educational Research and Innovation, 1992. Australian National Training Authority 1994.

References

Ackland, R. and Williams, L. 1992 *Immigrants and the Australian Labour Market: The Experience of Three Recessions*. Canberra: BIR, AGPS.

Adult Migrant Education Services, 1991 *Language Audits in Industry*. Melbourne: Adult Migrant Education Services.

Aguayo, R. 1990 *Dr Deming – The Man Who Taught The Japanese About Quality*. London: Mercury.

Allen Consulting Group, 1994 Successful Reform: Competitive Skills for Australia and Australian Enterprises, Report to the Australian National Training Authority. Unpublished report.

Allen, K. 1993 Plain English, Please. *Australian Training Review*, No. 8. South Australia: National Centre for Vocational Educational Research.

Argyris, C. and Schön, D.A. 1978 *Organizational Learning: A Theory of Action Perspective*, San Francisco, CA: Jossey-Bass.

Atkin, J.A. 1994 Thinking: Critical for Learning. In J. Edwards (ed.) *Thinking: International Interdisciplinary Perspectives*. Victoria: Hawker Bronlow Education.

Auerbach, E.R. 1986 Competency-based ESL: One Step Forward or Two Steps Back? *TESOL Quarterly*, 20, 3.

Auerbach, E.R. and Burgess, D. 1985 The Hidden Curriculum of Survival ESL. *TESOL Quarterly*, 19, 3.

Australian Bureau of Statistics, 1994 *Training and Education Experience, Australia 1993*. Catalogue No. 6278.0. September. Canberra: AGPS.

Australian Bureau of Statistics, 1997 Catalogue No. 6203.0. February. Canberra: Australian Bureau of Statistics.

Australian National Training Authority, 1994 *Towards a Skilled Australia: A National Strategy for Vocational Education and Training*. Brisbane: ANTA.

Australian National Training Authority, 1996 *Ministerial Decisions, Australian Training* (August). Brisbane: ANTA.

Australian National Training Authority, 1996 *Participation and Attainment of Individual Client Groups within Vocational Education and Training* (May). Brisbane: ANTA.

Australian National Training Authority, 1996 *Report on National Industry Vocational Education and Training Plans* (May). Brisbane: ANTA.

Australian National Training Authority, 1997a *Stocktake of Equity Reports and Literature in Vocational Education and Training* (June). Brisbane: ANTA.

Australian National Training Authority, 1997b *Australian Training, Special Edition* (June). Brisbane: ANTA.

Australian National Training Authority, 1997c *Guidelines for Training Packaged Developers* (July). Brisbane: ANTA.

Australian Textile, Clothing and Footwear Industry Training Board, 1994 *Industry Training Plan.* Melbourne: ATCFITB.

Bachman, L. 1990 *Fundamental Considerations in Language Testing.* Oxford: Oxford University Press.

Baylis, P. 1995 *Post-Implementation Review of the Workplace English Language and Literacy Program under the Australian Language and Literacy Policy.* Canberra: Department of Employment, Education and Training.

Benson, P. and Voller, P. 1996 *Autonomy and Independence in Language Learning.* London: Longman.

Bhatia, V.J. 1983 Simplification versus Easification – The Case of Legal Texts. *Applied Linguistics,* 4, 1.

Bloch, B. 1994 Costing UK Testing. *Australian Training Review 1994, No. 9.* Adelaide: National Centre for Vocational Education and Training.

Boud, D. and Griffin, V. (eds) 1987 *Appreciating Adults Learning.* London: Routledge and Kegan Paul.

Bremer, K., Roberts, C., Vasseur, M., Simonot, M. and Broeder, P. 1996 *Achieving Understanding.* London: Longman.

Brindley, G. 1989 *Assessing Achievement in the Learner-centred Curriculum.* Sydney: National Centre for English Language Teaching and Research.

Brindley, G. 1994 Competency-based Assessment in Second Language Programs: Some Issues and Questions. *Prospect,* 9, 2. Sydney: National Centre for English Language Teaching and Research, Macquarie University.

Brislin, R., Triandis, H. and Hui, 1988 Individualism and Collectivism: Cross-Cultural Perspectives on Self-Group – Ingroup Relationships. *Journal of Personality and Social Psychology,* 34, 2.

British Council, 1978 *Individualisation in Language Learning.* ELT Documents 103. London: British Council.

Brookfield, S. 1986 *Understanding and Facilitating Adult Learning.* San Francisco, CA: Jossey-Bass.

Brookfield, S. 1989 *Developing Critical Thinkers: Challenging Adults to Explore Alternative Ways of Thinking and Acting.* San Francisco, CA: Jossey-Bass.

Brown, P. and Levinson, S. 1987 *Politeness: Some Universals in Language Usage.* Cambridge: Cambridge University Press.

Bureau of Industry Economics, 1994 *Job Growth and Decline: Recent Employment Changes in Large and Small Business.* Occasional Paper 21. Canberra: AGPS.

Burke, J.W. (ed.) 1989 *Competency-based Education and Training.* Brighton: Falmer Press.

Butler, C. 1988 Pragmatics and Systemic Linguistics. *Journal of Pragmatics*, 12.

Callus, R. 1993 *Change and Bargaining in Australian Workplaces: A Report on the 1992 Workplace Bargaining Survey*. Sydney: Australian Centre for Industrial Relations, Research and Teaching, University of Sydney.

Canale, M. 1987 Participatory Evaluation: Learners and Teachers as Co-investigators. Keynote Address to the ATESOL Summer School. Sydney, January.

Candlin, C. 1992 Easification versus Simplification. In P.H. Peters (ed.) *Australian Style into the Nineties: Proceedings of the Style Councils 1990 and 1991*.

Candlin, C. and McNamara, T. (eds) 1989 *Language, Learning and Community*. Sydney: National Centre for English Language Teaching and Research.

Candlin, C.N. and Crichton, J. In press Interdiscursive Methodology and a Question of Accountability. In N. Coupland, S. Sarangi and C.N. Candlin (eds), *Sociolinguistics and Social Theory*. London: Longman.

Candlin, C.N., Maley, Y. and Sutch, H. 1995 Industrial Instability and the Discourse of Enterprise Bargaining. In C. Roberts and S. Sarangi (eds), *Discourse at Work: Communication in Institutional, Professional and Workplace Settings*. The Hague: Mouton.

Carnevale, A., Gainer, L. and Meltzer, A. 1990 *Workplace Basics: The Essential Skills Employers Want*. San Francisco, CA: Jossey-Bass.

Centre for Educational Research and Innovation, 1992 *Adult Illiteracy and Economic Performance*. Paris: Organisation for Economic Cooperation and Development.

Centre for Workplace Communication and Culture, 1994 *Cultural Understandings as the Eighth Key Competency: Final Report*. Brisbane: Department of Employment, Education and Training.

Charlesworth, S. 1996 *Stretching Flexibility – Enterprise Bargaining, Women and Changes to Working Hours*. Sydney: Human Rights and Equal Opportunity Commission.

Cicourel, A.V. 1992 The Interpretation of Communicative Contexts: Examples from Medical Encounters. In A. Duranti and C. Goodwin (eds), *Rethinking Context: Language as an Interactive Phenomenon*. Cambridge: Cambridge University Press.

City and Guilds, 1994 *City and Guilds Broadsheet*, No. 131 (October). London: City and Guilds.

Clyne, M. and Ball, M. 1990 English as a Lingua Franca in Australia, especially in Industry. *ARAL* (Series S), 7 pp. 1–15.

Coates, S., Fitzpatrick, L., McKenna, A. and Makin, A. 1995 *National Reporting System – A Mechanism for Reporting Adult English Language, Literacy and Numeracy Indicators of Competence*. Canberra: ANTA/DEET.

Collins, J. 1988 *Migrant Hands in a Distant Land – Australia's Post War Immigration*. Sydney: Pluto Press.

Collins, M. 1991 *Adult Education as Vocation: A Critical Role for the Adult Educator,* London: Routledge.

Cook, G. 1989 *Discourse.* Oxford: Oxford University Press.

Cope, B. and Kalantzis, M. 1995 A Pedagogy of Multiliteracies: Designing Social Futures. Paper written with the other members of the New London Group and presented at the Twenty-First Australian Reading Association National Conference. Sydney, July.

Courtenay, M. and Mawer, G. 1995 *Integrating English Language, Literacy and Numeracy into Vocational Education and Training – A Framework.* Sydney: TAFE/DEET.

Cox, E. and Leonard, H. 1991 *From Ummm . . . to Aha! Recognising Women's Skills.* Canberra: Australian Government Publishing Service.

Criper, C. and Davies, A. 1988 *ELTS Validation Project Report.* Cambridge: The British Council/University of Cambridge.

Davies, I.K. 1976 *A History of the Objectives Movement in Education, Objectives in Curriculum Design.* Maidenhead: McGraw-Hill.

Dawson, P. and Palmer, G. 1995 *Quality Management – The Theory and Practice of Implementing Change.* Melbourne: Longman.

Deakin University, 1994 *A Collection of Readings Relating to Competency-based Training.* Geelong: Deakin University Press.

Department of Employment, Education and Training, 1993 Training for Part-Time and Casual Workers. Discussion paper (unpublished), Strategic Planning and Development Branch, Vocational Education and Training Division. Canberra: DEET.

Department of Employment, Education and Training, 1993 *Training for Productivity.* Canberra: DEET.

Department of Employment, Education and Training, 1994 *Training for Productivity* (September). Canberra: DEET.

Department of Employment, Education and Training, 1996 *More than Money Can Say – The Impact of ESL and Literacy Training in the Australian Workplace.* Canberra: DEET.

Department of Industrial Relations, 1995 Staff – The Key to Export Success. *Benchmark,* 13 (November), pp. 15–16. Canberra: Department of Industrial Relations.

Dispatches, 1993 *All Our Futures: Britain's Education Revolution.* London: Channel Four Television.

Downs, C. 1988 *Communication Audits.* Scott Foresman and Co. U.S.A.

Eagleson, R.D. 1990 *Writing in Plain English.* Canberra: AGPS.

Ellis, R. 1990 *Second Language Acquisition.* Oxford: Blackwell.

Ethnic Affairs Commission of NSW and Human Rights and Equal Opportunity Commission, 1993 *Retrenched Workers' Rights Project.* Sydney: Ethnic Affairs Commission.

Fairclough, N. 1989 *Language and Power.* London: Longman.

Fairclough, N. (ed.) 1992 *Critical Language Awareness.* London: Longman.

Fairclough, N. 1992 *Discourse and Social Change.* Cambridge: Polity Press.

Field, L. and Mawer, G. 1993 Learnsite – Workplace Case Studies Conducted for the Economic Development Branch Department of Employment, Education and Training. Unpublished paper.

Field, L. and Ford, B. 1995 Managing Organisational Learning. Melbourne: Longman.

Fitzpatrick, L. and Roberts, A. 1997 *Workplace Communication in National Training Packages: A Practical Guide.* Melbourne: DEETYA.

Ford, B. 1991 Integrating Technology, Work Organisation and Skill Formation: Lessons from Manufacturing for Ports. In M. Costa and M. Easson (eds), *Australian Industry: What Policy?* Sydney: Pluto Press.

Foucault, M. 1972 *The Archaeology of Knowledge.* London: Tavistock.

Freebody, P. and Luke, A. 1990 Literacies Programs: Debate and Demand in cultural content. *Prospect, Vol. 5, No. 3.*

Freire, P. 1972 *Pedagogy of the Oppressed.* Harmondsworth: Penguin.

Freire, P. and Macedo, D. 1987 *Literacy: Reading the Word and the World.* South Hadley, MA: Bergin and Garvey.

Gee, J.P., Hull, G. and Lankshear, C. 1996 *The New Work Order: Behind the Language of the New Capitalism.* Sydney: Allen and Unwin.

Godfrey, A. 1992 Update on the National Training Board. Paper presented at AIC Competency-based Training Conference, Sydney, 21 July.

Gowen, S.G. 1991 Beliefs about Literacy: Measuring Women into Silence/Hearing Women into Speech. *Discourse and Society,* 2, 4.

Gowen, S.G. 1992 *The Politics of Workplace Literacy: A Case Study.* New York: Teachers College Press.

Green, G. 1989 *Pragmatics and Natural Language Understanding.* Hillsdale, NJ: Lawrence Erlbaum Associates.

Grice, P. 1975 Logic and Conversation. In D. Davidson and G. Harman (eds), *The Logic of Grammar.* Incino, CA: Dickinson. (Reprinted in P. Cole and J. Morgan (eds). *Syntax and Semantics, Vol. 3, Speech Acts.* New York: Academic Press.

Gumperz, J. (ed.) 1982 *Language and Social Identity.* Cambridge: Cambridge University Press.

Hagar, P., Athanasou, J. and Gonczi, A. 1994 *Assessment Technical Manual.* Canberra: AGPS.

Hall, W. (ed.) 1993 *What Future for Vocational Education And Training?* Adelaide: NCVER.

Halliday, M.A.K. 1978 *Language as a Social Semiotic.* London: Edward Arnold.

Halliday, M.A.K. 1985 *An Introduction to Functional Grammar.* London: Edward Arnold.

Halliday, M.A.K. 1990 New Ways of Meaning: A Challenge to Applied Linguistics. Paper presented to the Ninth World Congress of Applied Linguistics, Thessaloniki-Halkidiki, Greece, 15–21 April.

Hammersley, M. 1992 *What's Wrong with Ethnography?* London: Routledge.

Hammersley, M. and Atkinson, P. 1983 *Ethnography: Principles in Practice*. London: Tavistock.

Hirsche, D. and Wagner, D. (eds) 1993 *What Makes Workers Learn: The Role of Incentives in Workplace Education and Training*. Philadelphia, PA/Paris: National Center on Adult Literacy/Organisation for Economic Cooperation and Development.

Hislop, J. 1994 *Evaluation of Workplace English Language and Literacy Project at John Holland Construction and Engineering*. Sydney: Foundation Studies Training Division, NSW TAFE.

Holec, H. 1981 *Autonomy and Foreign Language Learning*. London: Pergamon (for the Council of Europe).

Hull, G. 1993 Hearing Other Voices: A Critical Assessment of Popular Views on Literacy and Work. *Harvard Educational Review*, 63, 1, pp. 20–49.

Hutton, W. 1994 *The State We're In*. London: Jonathan Cape.

Hymes, D. 1974 *Foundations in Sociolinguistics: An Ethnographic Approach*. Philadelphia, PA: University of Pennsylvania Press.

Institute for International Competitiveness, 1994 Customers' Views of Australian Management: Asia-Pacific Viewpoints. Canberra: Karpin Task Force on Leadership and Management Skills.

James, D. 1997 Social Peril if Knowledge and Work Get Out of Step. *Business Review Weekly*, 4 August, pp. 68–9.

Johnstone, B. 1989 Linguistic Strategies and Cultural Styles for Persuasive Discourse. In S. Ting-Toomey and F. Korzenny (eds), *Language, Communication and Culture: Current Directions*. Newbury Park, CA: Sage.

Kalantzis, M. and Brosnan, D. 1993 *Managing Cultural Diversity*. Sydney: Centre for Workplace Communication and Culture, University of Technology.

Kearns, D. and Nadler, D. 1992. *Prophets in the Dark: How Xerox Reinvented Itself and Beat Back the Japanese*. New York: HarperCollins.

Keat, R. 1991 Consumer Sovereignty and the Integrity of Practices. In R. Keat and N. Abercrombie, *Enterprise Culture*. London: Routledge.

Kemmis, S. and McTaggart, R. 1988 *The Action Research Planner* (3rd edn). Geelong: Deakin University Press.

Kerr, J. and McCall, J. 1990. Literacy for Restructuring: Teaching Reading and Writing in a Glass Factory. *Interchange*, 16 (October), pp. 21–4.

Knowles, M. 1978 *The Modern Practice of Adult Education: From Pedagogy to Androgogy*. Cambridge: Cambridge University Press.

Kolb, D.A. 1984 *Experiential Learning*. Englewood Cliffs, NJ: Prentice-Hall.

Kress, G. and Hodge, B. 1993 *Language as Ideology*. London: Routledge.

Kristeva, J. and Moi, T. 1986 *A Kristeva Reader*. New York: Columbia University Press.

Layder, D. 1993 *New Strategies in Social Research*. Cambridge: Polity Press.

Leech, G. 1981 *Semantics: The Study of Meaning*. Harmondsworth: Penguin.

Levinson, S. 1979 Activity Types and Language. *Linguistics*, 17, pp. 365–99.

Lewis, J. 1992a Literacy Test by Engineer Puts Jobs at Risk. *Sydney Morning Herald*, 30 June.

Lewis, J. 1992b Six Sewage Workers Claim Bias over Test. *Sydney Morning Herald*, 4 July.

Luke, A. 1992 Literacy and Work in New Times. *Open Letter*, 3, 1.

Lundberg, D. 1994 *Where Are We? Reviewing the Training Reform Agenda*. Adelaide: NCVER.

McKelvey, C. and Peters, H. 1993 *APL: Equal Opportunities for All?* London: Routledge.

McNamara, T. 1989 The Challenge of Communicative Assessment: Defining the Terms. Paper presented at NAF LASSL National Assessment Consultation. Sydney, 4–6 December.

McNamara, T. 1990 Assessing the Second Language Proficiency of Health Professionals. PhD Thesis. University of Melbourne.

McNamara, T. 1994 The Assessment Implications of Competency Standards. Seminar presentation, Language and Cultural Diversity at Work: The Changing Standards of Competency Standards and Competency Assessment, Language Expo Australia, Sydney, 22 July.

Mager, R.F. 1975 *Preparing Instructional Objectives*. San Francisco: Fearon.

Manidis, M. 1993 An Investigation of the Perspectives on Language Proficiency of Teachers, Learners and Supervisors Within Workplace English Language and Literacy Classes (AMES NSW) and Teacher Practices Relating to Spoken and Written Language Development. Master of Education thesis. University of Technology, Sydney.

Marsick, V. 1988 Learning in the Workplace: The Case for Reflectivity and Critical Reflectivity. *Adult Education Quarterly*, 38, 4, pp. 187–98.

Marsick, V. and Watkins, K. 1992 *Informal and Incidental learning in the Workplace*. New York: Routledge.

Martin, J.R. 1984 Language, Register and Genre, in *Children Writing Reader*. Geelong: Deakin University Press.

Martin, J.R. 1986 Intervening in the Process of Writing Development. In *Writing to Mean: Teaching Genres Across the Curriculum*. C. Painter and Martin, J.R. (eds), Sydney: ALAA.

Martin, J.R. and Rothery, J. 1980 Writing Project Report, No. 1. *Working Papers in Linguistics*. Linguistics Department, Sydney University.

Mawer, G. 1991 *Language Audits and Industry Restructuring*. Sydney: National Centre for English Language Teaching and Research.

Mawer, G. 1992a Developing New Competencies for Workplace Education. *Prospect*, 7, 2. Sydney: National Centre for English Language Teaching and Research.

Mawer, G. 1992b Exploring the Implications of Competency-based Approaches for the Multicultural Workplace. Unpublished Masters Thesis. University of Technology, Sydney.

Mawer, G. 1993 *Communication Syllabus Framework for the Metals and Engineering Industry*. Sydney: National Centre for English Language Teaching and Research.

Mawer, G. 1994 *Language, Literacy and Numeracy at Merck Sharp and Dohme (Australia) Pty Ltd: Evaluation Report of an Integrated Approach*. Sydney: Foundation Studies Division, TAFE NSW and Merck Sharp and Dohme.

Mawer, G. and Field, L. 1995 *One Size Fits Some! Competency-based Training and Non-English Speaking Background People*. Canberra: AGPS.

Mayer, E. 1992 Key Competencies: Report of the Committee to Advise AEC and MOVEET on Employment-related Key Competencies for Post-compulsory Education and Training. Canberra: Australian Government Publishing Service.

Metal Trades Federation of Unions/Metal Trades Industry Association, 1990 *Award Restructuring Implementation Manual*. Melbourne.

Metal Trades Industry Association, 1990 *Award Restructuring – Consultation, Training and Award Flexibility*. Canberra: MTIA.

Mezirow, J. and Associates, 1990 *Fostering Critical Reflection in Adulthood*. San Francisco: Jossey-Bass.

Mikulecky, L. 1984 Preparing Students for Workplace Literacy Demands. *Journal of Reading*, December, pp. 253–257.

Mikulecky, L. 1989 Real-World Literacy Demands: How They've Changed and What Teachers Can Do. In D. Lapp et al. (eds), *Content Area Reading and Learning: Instructional Strategies*. Englewood Cliffs, NJ: Prentice-Hall.

Mikulecky, L. 1993 Workplace Literacy Programs: Organisation and Incentives. In D. Hirsche and D. Wagner (eds), *What Makes Workers Learn: The Role of Incentives in Workplace Education and Training*. Philadelphia, PA/Paris: National Center on Adult Literacy/Organisation for Economic Cooperation and Development.

Mikulecky, L. and Ehlinger, J. 1987 *Training for Job Literacy Demands: What Research Applies to Practice*. Philadelphia, PA: Institute for the Study of Adult Literacy, Pennsylvania State University.

Miles, M.B. and Huberman, A.M. 1984 *Qualitative Data Analysis*. Beverly Hills, CA: Sage.

Miltenyi, G. 1989 *English in the Workplace: A Shrewd Economic Investment*. Canberra: Office of Multicultural Affairs.

Mitchell, L. 1989 The Definition of Standards and their Assessment. In J.W. Burke (ed.), *Competency-based Education and Training*. Brighton: Falmer Press.

Morrissey, M., Dibden, M. and Mitchell, C. 1992 *Immigration and Industry Restructuring in the Illawarra*. Bureau of Immigration Research Canberra: AGPS.

National Board of Employment, Education and Training, Australian Language and Literacy Council, 1996 *Literacy at Work – Incorporating*

English Language and Literacy Competencies into Industry/Enterprise Standards. Canberra: AGPS.

National Board of Employment, Education and Training, *Progress and Prospects in Improved Skills Recognition*. Canberra: AGPS.

National Collaborative Adult English Language and Literacy Strategy, 1993. Sydney: Adult Literacy Information Office.

National Council for Vocational Qualifications, 1988 *Access and Equal Opportunities in Relation to National Vocational Qualifications*. London: National Council for Vocational Qualifications.

National Food Industry Training Council, 1993 *Fine Food: Five Training Approaches to Hygiene and Sanitation A, National Certificate in Food Processing: 1: Peer Tutoring; 2: Group Training; 3: Triform Training; 4: Team Teaching; 5: Recognition of Prior Learning*. Brisbane: NFITC.

National Training Board, 1991 *National Competency Standards: Policy and Guidelines*. Canberra: National Training Board.

National Training Board, 1992 *National Competency Standards: Policy and Guidelines* (2nd edn). Canberra: National Training Board.

New South Wales Local Government Industry Training Committee, 1992 *Interim Competency Standards and Training Tables*. Sydney: New South Wales Local Government Industry Training Committee.

NSW Community and Health Services Industry Training Board, 1994 *Direct Care Workers in Aged Care Services: National Competency Standards Development Project*, Bulletin No. 1, April. Sydney: NSW Community and Health Services Industry Training Board.

Nunan, D. 1988 *The Learner Centred Curriculum*. Cambridge: Cambridge University Press.

Nyhan, B. 1995 NTB Network (Special Conference Edition). *NTB Network*, 16, January, p. 5. Canberra: National Training Board.

O'Connor, P. 1992 Choosing Sides in Workers' Literacy, *Critical Forum*, 1, 2.

Office of Multicultural Affairs, 1995 *In a Nutshell – Cross Cultural Communication at Work: A Training Package*. Produced by the Office of Multicultural Affairs and Open Channel Productions, Fitzroy, Victoria.

Organisation For Economic Cooperation and Development, 1993 *Industry Training in Australia, Sweden and the United States*. Paris: OECD.

Organisation For Economic Cooperation and Development, 1996 *Employment Outlook*. Paris: OECD.

Osterman, P. 1994 How common is Workplace Transformation and Who Adopts it? *Industrial and Labor Relations Review*, 47, pp. 173–88.

Patterson, A. and Lucas, M. 1994 Language Learning in the Lift. *Literacy Update*, 12, July. Canberra: Department of Employment, Education and Training.

Peddler, M., Bourgoyne, J. and Boydell, J. 1991 *The Learning Company*. Maidenhead: McGraw Hill.

Peters, T. 1987 *Thriving on Chaos*. Pan: London.

Peters, T. and Waterman, R. 1992 *In Search of Excellence: Lessons from America's Best-run Companies*. New York: Harper and Row.

Phillips, K. and Shaw, P. 1989 *A Consultancy Approach for Trainers*. Aldershot: Gower.

Poulos, E. 1993 More than Just the Voice: The Recognition of Languages other than English Skills of Local Government Staff in Relation to the Skills-based Award in New South Wales. Unpublished report. Federal Municipal Employees Union.

Prince, D. and Solomon, N. 1995 *Language and Literacy in Competency Standards*. Sydney: National Language and Literacy Institute of Australia Centre for Workplace Communication and Culture.

ProTrain, 1993 *Access Evaluation*. Sydney: Tourism Training Australia.

Roberts, C., Davies, E. and Jupp, T. 1992 *Language and Discrimination Communication in Multi-ethnic Workplaces*. London: Longman.

Rogers, C. 1951 *Client-centered Therapy*. Boston, MA: Houghton Mifflin.

Rothwell, W. and Brandenburg, D. 1990 *The Workplace Literacy Primer*. Massachusets: Human Resource Development Press.

Rubenson, K. and Schütze, H. 1993 Learning at and through the Workplace: A Review of Participation and Adult Learning Theory. In D. Hirsche and D. Wagner (eds) *What Makes Workers Learn: The Role of Incentives in Workplace Education and Training*. Philadelphia, PA/Paris: National Center on Adult Literacy/OECD.

Scheeres, H., Gonczi, A., Hager, P. and Morley-Warner, T. 1993 *The Adult Basic Education Profession and Competence: Promoting Best Practice*. Canberra: Department of Employment, Education and Training.

Scherkenbach, W. 1986 *The Deming Route to Quality and Productivity*. London: Mercury.

Scollon, R. and Scollon, S. 1995 *Intercultural Communication: A Discourse Approach*. Oxford: Blackwell.

Scott, G. 1991 How Clever Are We in the Way We Train Our Workers? The Great Australian Competence Caper. *Training and Development in Australia*, 18, 2, pp. 7–12.

Scott, G. (ed.) 1992 *Defining, Developing and Assessing Higher Order Competencies in the Professions*. Sydney: UTS.

Sefton, R. 1993 An Integrated Approach to Training in the Vehicle Manufacturing Industry in Australia. *Critical Forum*, 2, 2, pp. 39–52.

Sefton, R. and O'Hara, L. 1992 *Report of the Workplace Education Project*. Melbourne: Victorian Automotive Industry Training Board.

Sefton, R., Waterhouse, P. and Deakin, R. (eds) 1994 *Breathing Life into Training – A Model of Integrated Training*. Melbourne: National Automotive Industry Training Board.

Serle, O. 1994 *Branching Out: A Report on the Forest and Forest Products Industry National Literacy and Numeracy Project*. Victoria: Forest and Forest Products Employment Skills Company Ltd.

Serle, O. and Gates, M. 1993 *At Your Service, Language, Literacy and Numeracy Project Report: Tourism and Hospitality Industry Training Board*. Workplace Skills Unit. Swinburne University of Technology, Melbourne: TAFE Division.

Shoebridge, N. 1995 The Marketers' Missing Millions. *Business Review Weekly*, 6 November, pp. 50–6.

Silverman, D. 1993 *Interpreting Qualitative Data*. London: Sage.

Simosko, S. 1992 *Get Qualifications for What You Know and Can Do*. London: Kogan Page.

Smith, L. (ed.) 1987 *Discourse Across Cultures*. Englewood Cliffs, NJ: Prentice-Hall.

Stephens, J. and Bertone, S. 1995 *Manufacturing Uncertainty: Non-English Speaking Background Women and Training*. Canberra: Australian Government Publishing Service.

Sticht, T. 1980 Testing and Assessment in Adult Basic Education and ESL Programs. San Diego, CA: Applied Behaviour and Cognitive Sciences Inc.

Sticht, T.G., Armstrong, W.B., Hickey, D.T. and Caylor, J.S. 1987 *Cast-off Youth: Policy and Training Methods from the Military Experience*. New York: Praeger.

Storey, J. 1993 The Take up of Human Resource Management by Mainstream Companies: Key Lessons from Research. *International Journal of Human Resource Management*, 4, pp. 529–53.

Sweet, R. 1989 Identifying Skills for Developing Career Paths Based on the Requirements of Industry: A Summary. Paper presented at a seminar on Developing Effective Industry Training, Sydney, 20–21 November.

Tannen, D. 1984 *Conversational Style: Analyzing Talk Among Friends*. Norwood, NJ: Ablex

Tannock, S. 1997 Positioning the Worker: Discursive Practice in a Workplace Literacy Program. *Discourse and Society*, 8, 1, pp. 85–116.

Taylor, C., Lewe, G. and Draper, J. (eds) 1991 *Basic Skills for the Workplace*. Ontario: Culture Concepts.

The Boston Consulting Group, 1994 *The Australian Manager of the Twenty-First Century*. Canberra: Industry Task Force on Leadership and Management Skills.

Thomas, J. 1983 Cross Cultural Pragmatic Failure. *Applied Linguistics*, 4, 2.

Thomson, P. 1993 Assesssment – a 'Value-Added' Approach. *National Training Board Network*, 10, June.

Tollefson, J. 1986 Functional Competencies in the US Refugee Program: Theoretical and Practical Problems. *TESOL Quarterly*, 20, 4.

Toop, L., Gibb, J. and Worsnop, P. 1994 *Assessment System Design*. Canberra: AGPS.

Tough, Allen, M. 1971 *The Adult Learning Projects: A Fresh Approach to Theory and Practice*. Toronto: Ontario Institute for Studies in Education.

Tyler, R. 1960 *Basic Principles of Curriculum and Instruction*. Chicago: University of Chicago Press.

VEETAC, 1992 Working Party on the Implementation of Competency-based Training. *Assessment of Performance under Competency-based Training, Administration of Competency-based Training*. Canberra: AGPS.

Virgona, C. 1994 *Seeking Directions: Training Industry Trainers in a Multilingual Workforce*. Sydney: National Centre for English Language Teaching and Research.

Wickert, R. 1989 *No Single Measure: A Survey of Australian Adult Literacy*. Canberra: DEET.

Williams, A. 1994 How Competent are Competencies? *TESOL in Context*, 4, 2, pp. 9–11.

Willing, Ken, 1992 *Talking It Through – Clarification and Problem-solving in Professional Work*. Sydney: National Centre for English Language Teaching and Research.

Wooden, M. 1990 *Migrant Labour Market Status*. Melbourne: BIR/AGPS.

Wooden, M. 1993 *Underemployment, Hidden Unemployment and Immigrants*. Canberra: BIR/AGPS.

Workplace Trainers Ltd, 1992 *Workplace Trainers' Competency Standards*. Sydney: Workplace Trainers.

Index